THE BIBLE:

The True and Reliable

WORD OF GOD

Or

(A General Introduction to the Bible)

Charles A. Crane

Author

Dr. Charles A. Crane, BSL, M.A. M. Div., D. Min.

2014

The Bible: The True and Reliable Word of God is available at special quantity discounts for bulk purchase for sales promotions, premiums, fund-raising, and educational needs. For details write Endurance Press, 577 N Cardigan Ave Star, ID 83669.

Visit Endurance Press' website at www.endurancepress.com

The Bible:
The True and Reliable
Word of God

PUBLISHED BY ENDURANCE PRESS
577 N Cardigan Ave
Star, ID 83669 U.S.A.

®2014 Dr. Charles A Crane
Printed in the United States of America
First Edition 2014

The Bible: The True and Reliable Word of God

Contents

SECTION THREE – THE GENUINENESS AND AUTHENTICITY OF THE SCRIPTURES

SECTION FOUR – TEXTUAL CRITICISM

   Literal Word-for-Word Translations

   Semi-Literal Thought-for-Thought Translations

   Paraphrases

   Translation Comparison Charts

SECTION FIVE – CONCLUSIONS

EXHIBITS

THE BIBLE: THE TRUE AND RELIABLE WORD OF GOD

(A General Introduction to the Bible)

Dr. Charles A. Crane, BSL, M.A., M.Div., D. Min.

Preface

A few preliminary comments will help clarify the purpose of this book. There is a serious need for a new and comprehensive work that shows the evidence proving that the Bible is a uniquely inspired book. If a book could be written about the Bible, at a popular level, and this book could be understood by the average church member, certainly it would have meaning for the serious scholar as well.

Some books that deal with parts of the subject are scholarly and may be difficult for some to read. It is the author's goal to make the subject understandable for Christians of all levels of maturity, and at the same time to be detailed and footnoted so as to satisfy the biblical scholar.

As in the past several hundred years, still today there are scholars who attack the accuracy of the Bible. Many of these teach in seminaries. A reasoned response needs to be made to reply to these attacks. Some religious groups teach as one of their basic doctrines that the Bible has suffered many changes since it was written. Their missionaries have spread this message across the earth. Today many Christians do not know what sort of proof there is to substantiate biblical accuracy. For these, and other reasons, there is a need for an up-to-date and comprehensive work on biblical inspiration and accuracy.

One of the finest books from the past on this subject was called *General Biblical Introduction*, written by H. S. Miller. At the time it was written (1937) it was possibly the only book of its kind. While many have since written about parts of this subject, Miller's book remains one of the most comprehensive.

In the years since Miller wrote, significant additional information has been discovered that was not known in his day. The result is that his work is now in need of updating. A serious effort has been made to ascertain whether it remains under U.S. Copyright protection. The initial copyright has long since expired and a search of books under present copyright does not contain this book. The publishing company does not appear to remain in existence.[1]

The author has had a keen interest in this subject since taking a class in 1956 in which Miller's textbook was used. This produced a strong interest in biblical criticism, including higher and lower textual criticism. This subject still remains a keen interest more than fifty years later. I have had the opportunity to travel widely and see, first hand, several thousand of the most important biblical texts, both Hebrew and Greek.

In our day there is again a need to restate and reaffirm the doctrines of inspiration and show the strong case for biblical accuracy. Still today there are many unbelievers and supposed Christians alike who mistrust the Bible text. Many of these people are not aware of the large volume of evidence for biblical accuracy.

Miller's book is comprehensive and very detailed. A serious effort will be made to update and cover the important material, but in a more concise, and hopefully, less tedious form, with a somewhat different format; some of his subject matter will purposely not be covered, as it may not be entirely relevant to this study.

It is with a great sense of humility and trepidation that I proceed with this work, as Miller's work is truly a classic. Only time will tell if I can cover this subject, preserving the power of his work, while updating it with the latest information.

— Charles A. Crane, BSL, M.A., M.Div., D. Min.

---

1   This work contains many quotations from H.S. Miller's book, *General Biblical Introduction*, Rev. H. S. Miller, M.A., The Word-Bearer Press, Houghton, N.Y. copyright 1937.

SECTION ONE

THE DOCTRINE OF INSPIRATION

I. THE BIBLE—AN INSPIRED BOOK—GOD SPEAKING

"...the Scripture cannot be broken." Jesus[2] —John 10:35

"Forever, O Lord, Thy word is settled in heaven." —Psalm 119:89

"The sum of Thy word is truth, and every one of Thy righteous ordinances is everlasting." —Psalm 119:160

The Bible makes many very strong statements about its inspiration. It says that God has spoken to mankind in the Old Testament by the prophets, His ancient spokesmen and writers. In the Christian era "He has spoken through His Son and by those that heard" (Hebrews 1:1−2). This message was "confirmed unto us by those who heard," who were very reliable witnesses (Hebrews 2:3−4). God spoke by the mouth of His holy prophets (Luke 1:70). "As He spoke by the mouth of His holy prophets from of old..." (Romans 1:1−2). "Paul, a bond-servant of Christ Jesus, called as an Apostle, set apart for the gospel of God, which He promised before-hand through His prophets in the holy Scriptures." The Bible is full of similar claims of inspiration. (The *New American Standard Version* is quoted throughout.)

The Bible is not God, but it is God speaking. "In the beginning was the Word, and the Word was with God, and the Word was God ... and the Word became flesh, and dwelt among us, and we beheld His glory, glory as of the only begotten from the Father, full of grace and truth" (John 1:1 & 14). God has spoken to mankind through His Son and thus Jesus could be

2   The New American Standard Version is quoted throughout.

9

called "the Word." 2 Peter 1:21 is very clear: "Men moved by the Holy Spirit spoke from God." Since the Bible is God speaking to us, it is of primary importance to know we have the words originally written. Has the Bible come down to us unchanged? This question will be a primary focus of this work.

Revelation is the communication, by God to man, of those truths concerning Himself, His plans, and His will concerning man and his salvation. The things revealed are things we could not know from intuition or from nature, but only by revelation. Divine revelation is the revelation by God to man of Himself, or of His will, over and beyond what He has made known by the light of nature, creation, or reason. Things revealed are that God is, He created the universe, He created man, He made known regarding His will and purpose, that man was made in His image, for His companionship, His glory, His pleasure, and man is His offspring (Genesis 1:1, 26, 27, 3:8; Isa. 43:7; Rev. 4:11 & Acts 17:29). The Bible claims to be a revelation from God to His intelligent creatures, revealing Himself and His plan.

Our premise is that God has given us a special supernatural revelation, a revelation of who and what God is, who and what man is, and what God has done for us. We believe this truth for the following reasons:

1. A revelation is possible. With God "all things are possible," and "nothing shall be impossible" (Mark 10:27; Luke 1:37). Surely the infinitely wise and powerful God can, if He will, reveal Himself, His plans, and His will to humanity.

2. A revelation is necessary. a) We might, from intuition or from reason, know something about sin and its penalty, yet we could know little of God's love, His provision for justification, reconciliation, salvation, and the blessings of the new life in Christ. These truths must come from revelation. b) The truths of the Trinity, the person and work of Christ and of the Holy Spir-

it, immortality, future rewards and punishment, can be known only through revelation. c) Human opinions and human reason are conflicting, contradictory, and not sufficient guides in matters of life and conduct. The opinions of men are various and often outright harmful. The law of God is the only safe and sufficient rule and can only be known by revelation. d) The heathen world is hopelessly corrupt, and is powerless to make itself better or save itself (Romans 1:21−31; 3:9−18; 1 Corinthians 6:9−11; Ephesians 2:1−3, 11, 12; 4:17−19). The best of heathen philosophers and moralists were corrupt and taught many things which are contrary to the law of God and Christian principles. e) Man's moral and spiritual nature longs for God and holiness. God has begun to supply this need in the revelation of Himself in nature (Psalm 19:1; 95:3−5 and Romans 1:20; Isaiah 40:12, 26). Shall He not complete this beginning revelation?

3. A revelation is probable. If it is possible and necessary, and if God loves His creatures, yearns for them, and longs to bring them into fellowship with Himself, then surely a revelation is preeminently probable. Philosophers of all ages have thought a divine revelation probable, and expected it.[3]

4. If a revelation is possible, necessary and probable, it is overwhelmingly credible. In fact, it would be most difficult to believe that such a revelation should not be given. The truly thoughtful person would be inclined to look for it.

5. A revelation is reasonable and it contains a long series of messages from God to man. There is nothing to stumble at in this. If humans can communicate between each

---

3   Pardington, *Outline Studies in Christian Doctrine*, page 31.

other, why should it seem unreasonable or impossible that the Creator would not be able nor want to communicate with His creation? Reason calls for a revelation.[4]

6. The revelation is certain and is found in our wonderful Bible, which claims from beginning to end to be a revelation from God. There are so many proofs that can be given of this revelation being from God: prophecy, miracles, the propagation of Christianity, the fruits of Christianity, and the satisfaction it brings to the human heart the world over are but a few of its fruits.

II. INSPIRATION, OR THE DIVINE AUTHORSHIP OF THE BIBLE

"All Scripture is inspired by God..." —2 Timothy 3:16

Inspiration, as applied to the Bible, "is the in-breathing of God into men, thus qualifying them to receive and communicate divine truth."[5] It is God working through the Holy Spirit and through people to communicate to people. It is God working through men to deliver His message, enabling them to receive and deliver divine truth without error. It makes the speakers and writers infallible. It is by this means that truth, not previously or otherwise known, is revealed to mankind. This makes the message divinely authoritative. For this reason the Bible reads like no other book. No other explanation makes sense in light of the information found in its pages.

The Bible is not only inspired, it is God inspired. The Bible is the product of an all-knowing and powerful God; the same power that created the universe is behind the Bible. The writers of the Bible were God-inspired men (2 Peter 1:21 and 2 Samuel

---

4   Girdlestone, *The Building Up of the Old Testament*, page 295.
5   H. S. Miller, *General Biblical Introduction*, pg. 17. This section seeks to update Miller's work.

23:2), in order that we might have an inspired book (2 Timothy 3:16). This inspiration extends to the whole of the Bible. The Bible, therefore, contains two types of material: revelation and already known facts.

The revelation of God extends to every part of the Bible: history, poetry, prophecy, and teaching. Revelation reveals to humans information otherwise not knowable. There are many proofs of inspiration—among them are the hundreds of prophecies. The accuracy of the Bible in regard to all matters, whether known or unknown, is another proof. That the Bible is always historically, scientifically, medically, and archaeologically accurate is strong evidence for its supernatural origin.

When we speak of prophets, we are talking of those who were God's spokesmen, a "forth teller" as well as a "foreteller." They were inspired and wrote even of things they did not understand themselves (1 Peter 1:10−12).

While talking about the information in the Bible, it might be helpful to remember that there is a difference between statements and records of statements. The Bible does record lies, though it does not lie. For example, Satan told Adam and Eve that they would not die if they ate of the fruit of the garden. This, of course, was a lie, but the historical record of what Satan said was true, even though he lied. Other examples could be given.

III. THEORIES OF INSPIRATION

Most theologians and people claiming Christianity will say they believe the Bible is inspired. It is necessary to delineate what is meant by inspired, since there are many different theories today.

1. Genius or Natural Inspiration.

This theory suggests that the Bible was written by good and faithful men who were guided by the Holy Spirit, but only in the sense in which any writer of genius or moral worth is inspired. According to this theory, every great poet is inspired, and every person who has brought a helpful message for mankind is as much a prophet of God as were the Bible writers. Milton, Shakespeare, Bunyan, and the great preachers and writers, were inspired by the Spirit of God as were Isaiah and Paul, although possibly in a lesser degree. Those whose messages touch hearts are inspired as were David and John.

There are many problems with this theory. It eliminates the supernatural and reduces the Bible writings to the level of the secular, making them human productions, to be criticized and mutilated at will. This theory does not take into account the prophecies or supernatural material found and confirmed in the Bible. Such a theory denies the supernatural and opens the door to denials of miracles and prophecy. Check the claims of Bible writers (Ex. 4:10−12; 2 Sam. 23:1; Isa. 8:11; 48:16; Jer. 1:5−10; Ezek. 2:2−7; Hos. 1:1; Joel 1:1; Amos 7:14; Acts 1:2; 1 Cor. 2:13; 1 Thess. 2:13; Eph. 3:5) with any secular writer. The Bible writers claim to be speaking or writing the very words of God.

2. Degrees of Inspiration.

Some modern theologians believe in what they call *degrees of inspiration*. The first, or highest degree, covers those portions of Scripture which were revealed to the writers, that is, those not previously known. The second, or lesser, degree secures the writers against any serious error in recording facts and doctrines already known to them. The third, or least degree, they say were composed without inspiration. This leaves it up to the reader to decide for themselves what is inspired and what is not, which means there is really no inspiration at all.

The problems with this theory are somewhat less objectionable than the first, yet it also comes far short of the Bible teaching on the subject. But who is to decide to which of the three categories each passage belongs? It makes man the judge of Scripture rather than the Scripture the judge of man.

3. Illumination or Universal Christian Inspiration.

This theory teaches that the writers of the Bible were inspired in the same sense in which Christians of all ages have been inspired; that is, the average Christian of today is as much inspired as was Moses or Paul or any other biblical writer. If this is true, then why do not the advocates of this theory write us some more Bible? It is true that every Christian may have illumination from the Holy Spirit to understand the Bible and may have religious zeal and fervor from the Spirit. But they are far distant from the level of inspiration given to the holy writers of the Scriptures. Reading the early church fathers gives a good comparison between biblical inspiration and Universal Christian Inspiration, as it is evident that the inspired text is very superior to other Christian writings in many ways.

4. Inspired Concepts.

What the advocates of this popular theory mean by this high-sounding title is *inspired thoughts*. That is, God gave thoughts to the writers, and permitted them, years afterwards in some cases, to express these thoughts in their own words as they might remember them. This also leaves lots of questions about the reliability of what was written.

This theory makes the infallible God entrust His infallible truth to fallible men who were permitted to write it as they thought best. This allows for errors even in the original manuscripts. This leaves the Bible prone to error. This theory, though good sounding, is far from what the Bible teaches about itself. This, in reality, is not inspiration at all.

5. Partial Inspiration.

This theory teaches that the Bible is inspired in spots; some parts are inspired and some not. They like to say, "The Bible contains the Word of God." These teachers cannot agree as to what portions are and what are not inspired. Some say the fundamental truths are inspired, but that the arguments and explanations, the numbers and historical facts are of human origin. But who is the infallible person to judge what is or is not inspired? Others teach that the portions of the Bible that are morally excellent are inspired and the other parts which they deem less good are not. These folk like to set up categories to set one part of Scripture above others. Luther, for example, taught that "James was a book of straw," as it did not fit the standard of what he believed about faith. Some others have said, "What teaches Christ," is inspired while other parts are of lesser inspiration and are less binding. Others limit inspiration to the prophetical portions that obviously could not have been the work of man. Others say the doctrine is inspired and other parts not.

This theory is in conflict with 2 Tim. 3:16: "... All Scripture is given by inspiration of God." This is the standard text on inspiration and is in harmony with hundreds of other verses. This theory leaves us with an awful uncertainty as to what may be inspired and what may not be. If the writers were guided only in matters of real importance, then who is to decide which portions those are? Why did not God advise us as to what portions were important and what were not so important? What biblical teaching do we have that teaches us that God guided the writers sometimes and in other times He did not? The Bible not only contains the Word of God, the Bible *is* the Word of God.

6. Occasional Inspiration.

This is similar to Partial Inspiration. It teaches that the Bible writers were inspired occasionally when writing, they were not always under the power of the Spirit, and therefore, they were often left to their own ideas and so mixed with the divine the human reasoning that the result was that errors are mixed in with the truth. This theory also leaves us wondering what is and is not from God. This lets the reader decide what parts they like and will live by and what parts they do not like and will not follow.

7. Verbal Dictation.

This theory teaches that every word of Scripture, in the original languages, was dictated by God to the writers, just as the business professional would dictate material to his assistants. It is sometimes called "Mechanical Inspiration." It is sometimes confused with Verbal Inspiration. It is clearly not the true teaching as it flies in the face of the obvious. It does not take into account the various styles of writing found throughout Scripture. It makes the writers mere machines and robs them of the human touch. It is true that some of the Bible was dictated. Verbal Dictation is too strong a teaching and not what the Bible teaches about its inspiration. The theory of Inspired Concepts is too weak, while the theory of verbal dictation is not consistent with the evidence.

IV. THE TRUE DOCTRINE OF INSPIRATION

"God, after He spoke long ago to the fathers in the prophets in many portions and in many ways, in these last days has spoken to us in His Son..." Hebrews 1:1–2

There are two parts to, or two phases of, biblical inspiration. Taken together, they express what the Bible teaches about itself, and what is clear to those who carefully examine it. Sometimes this teaching has been expressed in more than one way. Some have insisted on "inerrancy" and we have no objection to this term. Others would insist that Jesus' own statement is enough when He called the Scripture "the Truth" (John 10:35). We have no objection to this either. But there is a fuller and clearer way to express the true teaching of Inspiration. The clearest way is to say it in two ways: "The Bible is plenary (fully) inspired and verbally (words) inspired, or plenary–verbally inspired, meaning that all of the words were given by Inspiration."

The first part is Plenary Inspiration. Plenary means full or complete, entire, and extending to every part. Therefore, plenary inspiration teaches that the Bible is inspired fully and equally from beginning to end. The claim is based on 2 Timothy 3:16 and many other passages that we will examine at a later point. Many of the great theologians of the church have held to this teaching. It teaches that all parts of the Bible come from God, God qualifying humans to receive and communicate divine truth through their own personalities and experience. It states that inspiration extends to every part of the Bible.

The second part is that the Bible is Verbally Inspired. Verbal means pertaining to words. Verbal inspiration is the work of God, through the Holy Spirit, directing men not only in their choices of the subject matter but also in their choices of words so that all things are written accurately, exactly as God desired, and contain all that He desired them to contain. It is the doctrine of superintendence, or guidance; that is, God guided the writers so that the words are His within each Bible writer's style.

Plenary verbal inspiration means that every word of every book, in the original manuscripts, is given by inspiration of God, or given by God through the Spirit. This is not verbal dictation, although some parts are dictated, in the Law of Moses, for example. This doctrine applies to the original Hebrew and Greek manuscripts. For this reason the scribes were taught to not drop even one letter and thus lose the very words of God.

Plenary verbal inspiration covers the selecting and accurate recording of the subject matter of the entire Bible, whether it is by revelation, dictation, already known facts, or existing records; whether it was a divine inscription to be copied, or a divine utterance, or the saying of a saint, a sinner, or the devil. The principle categories of Bible composition, then, are these:

1. Divine inscription covers matter given directly by God. Examples are The Ten Commandments, the pattern of the temple, or the handwriting on the wall of Belshazzar's palace.

2. Divine revelation was also given in prophecy and apocalypses. This covers much of the writing of the prophets and biblical authors from Genesis to Revelation. This covers such things as were impossible for man to know such as the account of creation, the nature of God, and the hundreds of prophecies of Christ. Not all of the prophetic books are prophecy, but a prophet was not only a foreteller, but a forth-teller.

3. Divine dictation covers several parts of the Bible. Parts of the Law of Moses were given by revelation from God directly to Moses. The pattern of the Tabernacle

and its furniture are examples. There are the examples of the warnings given to Israel by the prophets. The messages given to the seven churches of Revelation are another example of divine dictation.

4. Existing records of law and history were possibly used in several parts of the Bible. It is probable that Noah carried onto the Ark records that reached back many generations, possibly even to the time of Adam and Eve. Adam knew Methuselah, Methuselah was a contemporary of Noah and could have passed on records to him. People wrote about things they knew to be true, about things they personally had experienced, as well as from existing records in their possession, God guiding and guarding them in their writing.

5. Poetry and philosophy would include worship and wisdom literature, such as the books of Job, Psalms, and Proverbs. Much of these books are comprised of beautiful lyric songs and poetry.

6. Doctrine and practice would be covered by the New Testament epistles and portions of other books.

The Bible is not only a revelation from God, but is a record of that revelation. This record is divinely and verbally inspired. If God is; if God can talk and made us so we can talk; if God is love and made us so we could love—then it is reasonable and probable to suppose He would want to communicate with us, His creation.

There was a terrible blizzard and the farmer was trying to herd the cows into the barn. His best efforts were thwarted due to the cold, wind, and blowing snow. He thought to himself, if I could become a cow and talk to these cows, I could tell them what would save them. Thus, God tried and tried to talk to us, through prophet, priest and king. Finally He became a man, in the incarnation, lived as we live, was tempted as we are tempted, and told us about the Father and showed us the way to safety from the greatest enemy, the storm of death. At the center of this all is the central fact of all of history, that Jesus lived among us, taught us, demonstrating beyond doubt that He was God, died for us and proved He had the power over death by His resurrection. He, as the living Word, has given us His written Word, the Bible.

Plenary Inspiration does not say that all parts of the Bible are equally important, but they are equally inspired. Inspiration of the writers of the Bible means that the Bible writers were inspired in their writings, not in all the rest of their lives. Inspiration applies to the original languages, Hebrew and Greek, and not to the translations made by people since. It is the work of textual critics to help us know for sure what the original texts said so we can make quality translations for our use today. A study of biblical manuscripts will be a great part of this book, showing how the biblical texts have survived and are today studied to give us an accurate text from which to translate. There can be little doubt today about what was originally written.

So the question remains, is the Bible verbally and plenarily inspired? The conservative scholar says yes, while the liberal critic denies it. Thus we have Lower and Higher criticism of the Bible. The Lower critic seeks to show the foundation for the text and the Higher critic seeks to destroy the foundation for the text. The liberal critic points to supposed problems in the text and the believing critic seeks answers for the supposed problems. Almost all supposed problems in the biblical text have been answered repeatedly. Many of the objections made by "learned" men are so ridiculous as to make one question the word "learned."[6]

6   The terms higher and lower criticism have had a progression in meaning from the 1930s until today. Both have offered contributions to understanding how we got our Bible and what it is. Higher Criticism today (more commonly called Historical Criticism) investigates the origins of the ancient text in order to understand it. It seeks to determine the original meaning. It seeks to identify the author, date, and place of

Dr. William Evans gives us an important summary of what has been said in this chapter.

"The Spirit employed the attention, the investigation, the memory, the fancy, the logic, in a word, all the faculties of the writer, and wrought through these. He guided the writer to choose what narrative and materials, speeches of others, imperial decrees, genealogies, official letters, state papers, or historical matters He found necessary for the recording of the divine message of salvation. He wrought in and with and through their spirits, so as to preserve their individuality as they communicated to others. He used the men themselves, and spoke through their individualities. The gold was His; the mold was theirs."[7]

If the question be asked whether or not inspiration affected the words, it must be answered in the affirmative. It is hardly possible that inspiration could insure the correct transmission of thought without in some way affecting the words. Yet it affected the words not directly and immediately by dictating them in the ears of the writers, but mediately, through working on their minds and producing there such vivid and clear ideas of thoughts that the writers could find words fitted to their purpose.

"We must conclude, therefore, that while from the divine side the Holy Spirit gave through men clearly and faithfully that which He wished to communicate, from the human side that communication came forth in language such as men themselves would naturally have chosen.

---

writing. Lower textual criticism today is concerned with the identifying and preserving a text that most closely reflects the original. It studies variant readings, families of manuscripts, and seeks to reproduce the exact original manuscript. Today, both higher and lower criticism are valid and used by both liberal and conservative scholars in an attempt to understand Scripture.

7   Evans, *The Book of Books*, pages 35–37.

"We may therefore safely say that we believe in plenary and verbal inspiration, that is to say, the words as well as the thoughts have been given, whether mediately or immediately under the influence of the divine Spirit. We claim that the Bible is indeed and in truth the very Word of God; that it is the Word of God in the language of men; truly divine, and at the same time truly human; that it is the revelation of God to His creatures; that infallible guidance was given to those who wrote it, so as to preserve them from error in the statement of facts; that what the writers of the Scriptures say or write under this guidance is as truly said or written by God as if their instrumentality were not used at all; that the ideas expressed therein are the very ideas the Holy Spirit intended to convey; that God is in the fullest sense responsible for every word. This is what the Bible claims for itself."[8]

V. BIBLICAL TEXTS ON INSPIRATION

The Bible refers to inspiration throughout, and the total number of references to inspiration numbers in the thousands. Yet, there are a few verses that can be called the classic texts on inspiration. The selection of just six may seem arbitrary, but these six cover the main teachings of the Bible on the subject and it is not the purpose of this chapter to cover the subject exhaustively.

The six texts we will refer to are: Hebrews 1:1−2; 2:2-4; 2 Timothy 3:16−17; 2 Peter 1:19−21; John 10:34-35; 1 Peter 1:10−11; 2 Samuel 23:1−2. (*Scriptures will be quoted from The *New American Standard Version* unless otherwise noted. Permission granted.)

---

[8]   Evans; *The Book of Books*, pages 35−37.

Hebrews 1:1−2; 2:2−4

"God, after He spoke long ago to the fathers in the prophets in many portions and in many ways, in these last days has spoken to us in His son, whom He appointed heir of all things, through whom also He made the world," and "For if the word spoken through angels proved unalterable and every transgression and disobedience received a just recompense, how shall we escape if we neglect so great a salvation? After it was at the first spoken through the Lord, it was confirmed to us by those who heard, God also bearing witness with them both by signs and wonders and by various miracles and by gifts of the Holy Spirit according to His own will."

The Bible is God speaking in many different ways. He used various methods to speak—prophets, apostles, and, finally, in these last days, His Son. The message of the Son was taken up by those witnesses that He chose as Apostles to bear the message to the whole world. These men were given the power to work signs and wonders to confirm their message and prove their message was from God.

This tremendous message covers the entire Old and New Testaments. Peter places Paul on the same level as the other Apostles in 2 Peter 3:2 & 16 when he calls Paul's writings Scripture. Luke's Gospel is the message as preached by Paul, while Mark's Gospel is the message as preached by Peter.

God has spoken to mankind in at least four different ways:

1. He has spoken by a voice from heaven. We give as an example the Ten Commandments, or Him speaking to Adam and Eve in the Garden of Eden. He spoke from heaven at the beginning, middle, and end of Jesus' ministry (Matthew 3:17; 17:5; John 12:28).

2. He spoke by "the Angel of Jehovah." This happened repeatedly in the Old Testament. For example, Genesis 16:7−13; 21:17−18; 22:11−12; Judges 2:1−2; 6:12, 14; 13:3−5 and in many other places. One of the names given to the Angel was "Wonderful."

3. He spoke by the prophets and Apostles.

4. He spoke by His Son, Jesus throughout the Gospels and Revelation.

2 Timothy 3:16−17

"All Scripture is inspired by God and profitable for teaching, for reproof, for correction, for training in righteousness; that the man of God may be adequate, equipped for every good work."

This passage refers to all Scripture, both Old and New Testaments. If it is Scripture then it is to be used as the standard for teaching and living. The subject of this text is "Scripture." Scripture is given by inspiration of God. It is to be used for doctrine, reproof, correction, and instruction in righteousness.

This passage teaches in the plainest possible language plenary verbal inspiration of the Bible. The word translated inspiration here is the Greek word *theopneustos* from *theos* (God) and *pneustos* (breathed). The Bible is God breathed. It is His divine word. The purpose of the Bible is to make Christians adequate, or mature. How much of our Bible is Scripture? All of it!

2 Peter 1:19−21

"And so we have the prophetic word made more sure, to which you do well to pay attention to a lamp shining in a dark place, until the day dawns and the morning star arises in your hearts. But know this first of all,

25

that no prophecy of Scripture is a matter of one's own interpretation, for no prophecy was ever made by an act of human will, but men moved by the Holy Spirit spoke from God."

This passage expands on the teaching of 2 Timothy 3:16–17, enlarging and emphasizing it. The three terms, "prophetic word," "prophecy of Scripture," and "prophecy" are doubtless equivalent to one another and to the word "Scripture" and are not to be limited to the portions of the Bible that are predictive.

Peter is saying that his teachings about Christ's return were Scripture and authoritative. The Word of God did not come from man's will but God's; therefore, we do not have the right to read into it what we want it to say. God said what He meant and in a way we could understand it. This Scripture came from God, not from the will of man. When we hear and receive the word, then Christ, the day star and morning star, arises in our hearts. This verse in itself should settle the matter of inspiration once and for all, even if it were all we had, but there are many others.

John 10:34–36

"Jesus answered them, 'Has it not been written in your Law, I said, YOU ARE GODS? If he called them gods, to whom the word of God came (and the Scripture cannot be broken), do you say of Him, whom the Father sanctified and sent into the world, 'You are blaspheming,' because I said, 'I am the Son of God'?"

It is not the strong argument Jesus makes for His deity that is our primary interest here, but His statement about Scripture. He quotes from Psalm 82:6 and calls it "your Law." This is not a section of the Old Testament commonly thought of as the Law. We learn that the term "Law" can sometimes be applied to the entire Old Testament.

A second lesson is that Jesus argues on a plural word, "gods" showing His high view of Scripture. He argues and wins an argument on the basis of a plural word in the Hebrew Bible. This illustrates His view of how accurate the Scriptures are.

But most important of all is his statement, "the Scriptures cannot be broken." This is the word of Jesus Himself about inspiration. Some modern theologians wish to take exception to Jesus about the nature of inspiration. The Law, or Scripture, cannot be broken. The Psalms cannot be broken.

I Peter 1:10–12

"As to this salvation, the prophets who prophesied of the grace that would come to you made careful search and inquiry, seeking to know what person or time the Spirit of Christ within them was indicating as He predicted the sufferings of Christ and the glories to follow. It was revealed to them that they were not serving themselves, but you, in these things which now have been announced to you through those who preached the gospel to you by the Holy Spirit sent from heaven—things into which angels long to look."

This passage says several important things. 1. The theme of the Old Testament prophets was salvation. 2. They wrote beforehand of the glories of Jesus, which would, of course, be prophecy. 3. Salvation would be worked out in the sufferings of Christ. 4. The Holy Spirit was the Spirit of Christ in them doing the predicting. 5. They preached the gospel to us by the Holy Spirit. 6. The prophets spoke beforehand. 7. They did not even understand what they were writing; their words were inspired of God. 8. The things they wrote were so important that angels were anxious to look into them.

This is another very strong statement of inspiration, God qualifying men to receive and communicate divine truth. This sounds very much like Plenary Verbal Inspiration.

2 Samuel 23:1−2

"Now these are the last words of David. David the son of Jesse declares, And the man who was raised on high declares, The anointed of the God of Jacob, And the sweet psalmist of Israel, 'The Spirit of the Lord spoke by me, And His word was on my tongue.'"

Here is an Old Testament statement on inspiration, a direct testimony of the man "after God's own heart." (His final words—nothing could be stronger than David's deathbed testimony.) He claims that the Holy Spirit spoke by him and God's words were on his tongue. Not his thoughts, ideas, concepts, but His words were on David's tongue. This testimony covers a good part of 2 Samuel and 1 Chronicles as well as a large part of the Psalms.

The Anvil of God's Word

Last eve I paused beside the blacksmith's door
And heard the anvil ring the vesper chime.
And looking in upon the floor,
I saw many hammers worn by beating years of time.

How many anvils have you had to wear and batter all these hammers so?
Then said he with twinkling eye,
Just one, the anvil wears out the hammers, you know.

And so I thought, the Anvil of God's Word,
For years the skeptics' blows have beat upon
And though the sound of falling blows was heard
The anvil is unharmed, the hammers gone.[9]

---

9   John D. Clifford

VI. OLD TESTAMENT INSPIRATION

The Hebrews and Christians used different ways to arrange the Old Testament books. The Jewish Scriptures begin with Genesis and conclude with 2 Chronicles. It contains the same books, but they are arranged differently. They divide their Scripture into three parts: Law, Psalms and Prophets. The Christian Old Testament begins with Genesis and ends with Malachi, and has 39 books which are divided into five parts: Law, History, Poetry, Major and Minor Prophets. In reality the Christian and Hebrew Bibles are the same books, only arranged in a different way.

Both Hebrews and Christians have believed and taught that the Old Testament is inspired of God. They have shown that each of these sections is inspired and, beyond that, that each of the separate books is inspired.

H. S. Miller lists twelve ways that the Old Testament can be shown to be inspired.[10]

1. The general texts on inspiration, covered in the previous chapter.

2. The divine origin of the writers' words, that the words are God's words, according to the testimony of the writers.

3. The work of the Holy Spirit in their writings, shown by prophecy about the future and their writings remarkable accuracy.

4. The use of the word "Scripture" in the New Testament applying to the Old Testament.

5. The words "it is written" in the New Testament.

---

10   Evans, *The Book of Books*, pages 49–62

6. Other New Testament quotations of the Old Testament.

7. The authority and testimony of the Lord Jesus Christ.

8. The authority and testimony of the New Testament writers, primarily the Apostles.

9. The terminology "Oracles of God."

10. Statements and illustrations in the Old Testament about itself.

11. The faith and testimony of the Hebrew Church.

12. The faith and testimony of the Christian Church.

We have now covered the first of these, the great texts on inspiration, in the last chapter. These texts primarily refer to the Old Testament. Together, the above categories (numbers 3−10) comprise hundreds of references in the New Testament to the inspiration of the Old Testament. In addition, the Old Testament has many hundreds of references by the writers of their inspiration. A common phrase is "The Word of the Lord came unto me." The total number of references to the inspiration of the Old Testament, by the New Testament writers, comes to about 1,000 times. Is it not reasonable to suggest that Christ, and the New Testament writers, were not fully convinced that the Old Testament was the inspired word of God? The New Testament writers believed in the plenary verbal inspiration of the Old Testament. This can be demonstrated by the words of Jesus in John 10:35: "the Scriptures cannot be broken," and by the words of Paul in 2 Timothy 3:16: "All Scripture is inspired by God and profitable for teaching, for reproof, for correction, for training in righteousness." If the Scriptures cannot be broken and are all inspired by God, then they are plenarily verbally inspired. When we question the Old Testament accounts of creation, the origin of sin, Satan, the flood, Job, Moses, or other historical or miraculous accounts, we have an issue with Jesus and the Apostles who clearly believed these accounts. We cannot accept Jesus and the Apostles for what they claimed to be and then question their word and judgment on inspiration.[11]

VII. NEW TESTAMENT INSPIRATION

We have learned that the Old Testament and New Testament both teach that the Old Testament is inspired. The New Testament is full of this teaching. However, we have no inspired record beyond the New Testament to bear testimony of its inspiration. This is not to say that there is not abundant and convincing proof of its inspiration given by the early Christian Church, the church fathers and even the heretics and enemies of the church. The New Testament is placed on the same level as the Old Testament by the apostolic church and early church leaders. The New Testament is recognized with the same inspiration as the Old.

The Teaching of the New Testament about Itself

Few question the inspiration of the Lord Jesus; He was divine and spoke the words of God. Passages such as Heb. 1:8; John 3:34; 6:63; 12:49−50; 14:24; 17:8, 14, and many others confirm that His words were inspired. His words, like the Old Testament, were imperishable. They were the words of God.

On six different occasions Jesus promised His Apostles the aid of the Holy Spirit in their utterances: Matt. 10:19−20; Luke 12:11−12; Mark 13:1−4, 11; Luke 21:14−15; John 14−16; and Acts 1:8. Jesus made it clear He was empowering them to speak authoritatively.

---

11   The information in this chapter is more fully developed in H. S. Miller's book, *General Biblical Introduction*, pages 38−63.

The Gospels were inspired—Jesus promised to bring to their remembrance all that had taken place (John 14:26). Hebrews 2:3–4 reminds us that the truth was confirmed by the apostolic witnesses. Matthew and John as Apostles certainly were inspired. Luke's Gospel was acknowledged as "Scripture" by Paul, who quoted Luke 10:7 in 1 Tim. 5:18. Paul tells us that "all Scripture is inspired of God" (2 Tim. 3:16).

The book of Acts is filled with the messages of inspired people—Peter, Stephen, and Paul, for example. In the Pauline Epistles we find repeated claims of inspiration (1 Cor. 2:13; 1 Thess. 2:13; 1 Cor. 14:37; 1 Tim. 1:1). Throughout Paul's writing there are repeated claims for his writing by inspiration from God.

Other epistles were written by James, Peter, John, and Jude. In the book of Revelation there are constant claims that John wrote by revelation from God (Rev. 1:10–11; 4:2; 14:13; 17:3; 21:10). Readers are warned to not add to or take away from the inspired record (Rev. 22:18–19).

Passages like 2 Tim. 3:16–17 refer to all Scripture, which would include New Testament Scripture as well as the Old. Soon the entire New Testament would be referred to as Scripture.

The Testimony of the Early Christian Church

The early church leaders of the second century held the same high view of the Old Testament that the Jews did; they also received the New Testament as being equally inspired of God. It had the additional testimony of Jesus and the Apostles. Some of these early writers include Clement, Bishop of Rome, a contemporary of the Apostles. Justin Martyr claimed the Gospels were written by men full of the Holy Spirit. Irenaeus said the Apostles received the Gospels by divine revelation. Theophilus claimed both Old and New Testament writings were inspired of God. Clement of Alexandria said that the Apostles wrote by the same authority as the Old Testament writers. Origen said the New Testament proceeded from the Holy Spirit. By the year 150, few, if any, Christians did not fully accept the New Testament as fully inspired of God and authoritative for the church. In the writings of Tertullian, Origen, Cyprian, and Hippolytus, the idea of the New Testament is fully accepted.

Inspiration to the Present Day

During the Dark Ages the Bible was not available to the common person, but not questioned as to its inspiration. With the coming of the Reformation, the teaching of plenary verbal inspiration of the whole Bible was fully accepted. There were only a few stray heretics and heretical sects that questioned the Bible.

Critical scholars considered the Bible a storehouse of divine and infallible information concerning doctrinal truths and moral precepts, but nothing more. It was not to them a means of grace. Much of the Bible, they said, in its literal, historical sense, would give no information concerning doctrines and moral values hence it must be interpreted in a fourfold sense: historical, allegorical, moral or figurative, and anagogical sense. For an example as to how this worked for them, Jerusalem is historically a city of Palestine, allegorically the Church, morally the believing soul, anagogically the heavenly Jerusalem. This left the Bible confusing and without understanding to most. Thus it was left to Popes and Councils to interpret what the Bible meant to the Christian. Thus the churches' interpretation of the Bible became more important than the Bible itself.

The people of the Reformation believed in the supreme power of a fully-inspired and authoritative Bible. They believed that in the Old Testament God spoke through prophets; in the New Testament He spoke though Jesus and His Apostles. They believed Scripture was God speaking to His people and gave the answers of faith and salvation to those who heard and obeyed. Calvin said, "We owe to the Scripture the same reverence which we owe to God, because it has proceeded from Him alone, and has nothing belonging to man mixed with it."

During the seventeenth century came a period of controversy that called for a clearer definition of what the Bible was. During this period students of the Word held an exalted view of Scripture and inspiration with the Holy Spirit as the author. They taught: 1. The Divine authority was shown by internal and external evidence. 2. That the Bible was perfect and sufficient, containing everything necessary for salvation. 3. Perspicuity, that is, that the Bible is self-explanatory—hard passages should be understood in the light of clearer ones. 4. Efficacy, the Scriptures were a means of grace, converting the sinful and consoling the sad.

In the following century came a period of sectarianism, intolerance, indifference, and carnality which led to the decline of the church. The church still held to the inspiration of the Word, but neglected to preach the Gospel, spending their time in argumentation over sectarian issues. This led to deism, which denied a written and inspired revelation. There was a God, but He was beyond the reach of humans, to be worshiped but not able to be well known.

France was infected by atheism and immorality. The church was carnal and in general rejected by the majority of people. The serious decline of the church helped lead to the terrible French Revolution (1789-95). Voltaire spent three years in England (1726—29) and became acquainted with, and fascinated by, the greatest and most brilliant of the English deists, Bolinbroke. It is said that "He left France a poet, literateur, and wit; he returned the declared and determined foe of Christianity." He determined to destroy it. Thus English deism poured into France, and became mixed with the inspiration of French skepticism.

In Germany things were bad enough. The churches were empty because the church leaders embraced German rationalism. This led to the breakdown of marriage, parenting, and society in general, setting up the opportunity for evil leaders like Adolph Hitler to take over. It went from abortion, to mercy killings, euthanasia of the elderly, to the holocaust of the Jews.

German rationalists were Semler, Eichhorn, Paulus, DeWette, Jean Astruc, Graf, and Wellhausen, taking us from 1725—1918. All of this set the stage for the First and Second World Wars, with Germany having a key role in both. The loss of faith broke society loose from restraint and decency.

The influence of English deism and German rationalism had their influence in America and brought with them the seeds of destruction of American Protestantism. This led to modernism.

Out of all of this came Higher Criticism, which helped foster German rationalism. These disciplines sought to destroy the Bible and made serious inroads in the intellectual world and infected the church worldwide. They questioned Bible miracles and its historical accuracy. What was their motivation? It may have been an effort to throw off the moral restraints that come with the belief that the Bible is God's inspired Word.

All the while the conservative fundamentalist Christians continued to believe the Bible to be the inspired word of God. This led to many conflicts and research to support both positions. The fundamentalists produced many very fine scholars, some of whom were superior in learning and comprehension to the rationalists. These were born-again Christians and were men like Hengstenberg, Keil, Zahn, Moller, Winckler, Sayce, James Orr, Pusey, Green, Bissell, Machen, Keyser, and men of great learning and devotion to the word of God.

In the midst of all of this the lower critic (those seeking to support biblical inspiration) of Scripture has carefully been at work examining the Bible from every aspect to demonstrate the foundation that it is built upon. This work has examined the supposed contradictions, mistakes, and manuscript evidence to support the long-held view that the Bible is the inerrant and infallible word of God that is plenarily and verbally inspired by the Holy Spirit. We will examine a good measure of the information that has been brought to light by this extensive effort in a later chapter.

Where We Stand Today

The battle lines still remain. The conservative lower critic welcomes investigation, knowing that additional light on the

Scriptures will validate it further. We do not oppose biblical criticism, only when it is done by those who are predisposed to refute the Bible at all costs: the rationalists, naturalists, agnostics, freethinkers, and skeptics. These are predisposed to show the Bible false at all costs. As one modern speaker, Dinesh D'Souza says, "The unbelievers' objections to Scripture are more moral than intellectual."[12] When the goal is to disprove something regardless of the facts, the conclusion is not based on evidence, but prejudice.

T. B. Robertson, a man of standing in the Church of England, said:

> "For eighteen hundred years the Christian Church has been unanimous in upholding the plenary inspiration, the infallibility and supreme authority of Scripture. There is no exception to this rule. All branches of the Christian Church, though wide apart in many other things, holding discordant 'Rules of Faith,' and sharply opposed on questions of church ordinances and church government, whether Roman, Greek, or Protestant, with all the various parties and sects into which they are divided, are agreed that the Sacred Scriptures are the Word and work of God.

> "If we go back to the Reformation, when there was a great spiritual earthquake, and the foundations of the Christian religion were thoroughly examined and tested, we shall find, by a study of the Articles of Faith drawn up at that time by the different reformed churches, that they are unanimous in upholding the plenary inspiration and the supreme authority of the Word of God. The importance of this unanimity cannot be overestimated when we remember the host of learned men, mighty in the Scriptures, whom God raised up at that time, and who with one voice pro-

12   Quoted from a speech given at Eagle Christian Church

claimed the infallibility of the Bible.

"If we go back to the earlier days of the church, when there was such fierce controversy waged on questions of doctrine, we shall find that all parties appealed to the Holy Scriptures as the supreme infallible authority of the Christian Church. If we examine the Christian writers, beginning with those immediately following the writers of the New Testament, we shall find a consistent and universal belief that the Bible is the Word of God, and the supreme authority in matters of Christian faith.... Thus we see that for eighteen centuries all Christian churches, by whatever name they were known, and all writers of every sect and creed, have consistently maintained that God is the Author of the Bible; that its commands are authoritative, its decisions final, and its teachings infallible. It is strange, therefore, to find in these last days that some who profess and claim themselves Christians deny all this.

"The Bible has been a subject of attack in all ages, and from time to time men have arisen who have striven to destroy its divine authority, and thus rob the world of the blessings which follow from a belief in its truths. But hitherto it has been left to infidels and avowed enemies of Christianity to deny the truthfulness of its records; but, in these last days, men calling themselves Christians are to be found who reject the plenary inspiration of the Bible, and some even the inerrancy of the statements of Jesus Christ. And so we find that in Christian colleges, candidates for the ministry are taught things which, when proclaimed by such men as Voltaire and Tom Paine, were indignantly rejected as infidelity and skepticism."[13]

13   *Jesus Christ Versus the Modernists*, by Canon T. B. Robertson,

THE BIBLE STANDS

The Bible stands like a rock undaunted
'Mid the raging storms of time;
Its pages burn with the truth eternal,
And they glow with a light sublime.

Refrain:

The Bible stands though the hills may tumble,
It will firmly stand when the earth shall crumble,
I will plant my feet on its firm foundation,
For, the Bible stands.

The Bible stands like a mountain towering
Far above the works of men;
Its truth by none ever was refuted,
And destroy it they never can.

The Bible stands and it will forever,
When the world has passed away;
By inspiration it has been given,
And its precepts I will obey.

The Bible stands every test we give it,
For its Author is divine;
By grace alone I expect to live it,
And, to prove it and make it mine.

Refrain:

The Bible stands though the hills may tumble,
It will firmly stand when the earth shall crumble;

a man of standing in the Established Church of England. This was written
about 1829 and quoted from *The Bible Champion*, February, 1930, page
105.

I will plant my feet on its firm foundation,
For the Bible stands![14]

This hymn states the fact of inspiration quite clearly. Even though critics have been diligent, the result has been a confirmed Bible. It has stood the most detailed and exhaustive efforts to prove it false. There are so many proofs for the Bible.

Christian evidences continue to be a strong witness to the inspiration of the Bible. The internal evidences for the Bible are the canonicity and credibility of the Scriptures, the miracles, fulfilled prophecy, the propagation of Christianity and its fruits in the world wherever it has been preached. The Bible is always accurate, though written by 40 writers over a period of 1,500 years; it tells the same story and is in complete harmony, has a purity of ethics, is dignified, and presents the facts of history, always pointing to the one and only God who is pure and holy and seeks reunion with His creation—mankind. This is accomplished by the death of His son, Jesus Christ, who is proven to be God in the flesh by his life, miracles, and well-attested resurrection from the dead. These and many other evidences remain proof of the inspiration of the Bible.

---

14   Haldor Lillenas, 1917. Public Domain

SECTION TWO

CANONICITY

VIII. THE CANONICITY OF THE BIBLE

The word *canonicity* may not have much meaning to many readers. Therefore a definition may be helpful. It is a term that is used in relationship to biblical inspiration. The basic meaning of the word canonicity is to measure, or that which has been measured and has met the standard. Something that has been measured and met the standard can then be called canonical.

The word "canon" is of Christian origin and is derived from the Greek word *kanon*, which probably has its roots in the Hebrew word *kaneh*, meaning a measuring rod, or ruler. The word then means:

1. A straight rod, or bar, used especially to keep things straight; a straight edge, or a bar of wood or metal having one side true to a straight line that is used for testing surfaces, edges as a ruler.

2. A measuring rod.

3. A rule or line used by carpenters and masons for measuring or for keeping things straight.

4. As a metaphor, it means anything that serves to regulate or determine other things; a rule.

5. A standard or testing rule in ethics, art, music, or language. The term in antiquity was applied to testing art, or fixing the proper length of fingers on a statue, the height of a face or the proportions of the statue.

6. A standard, or rule, of conduct, living, action, or judging.

7. A boundary line or limit.

8. In textual criticism it is used to indicate that the Bible books have been measured and met a certain standard.

The Greek work *kanon* occurs five times in the New Testament. It means:

1. That which measures, a rod or ruler, a rule. (See Galatians 6:16; Philippians 3:16.)

2. It is used of that which is measured, a fixed amount of something. In this sense it is used in 2 Corinthians 10:13−16, and while it is translated "rule" twice and "line" once in the *KJV*, yet it is more correctly translated each time "province" (margin, or limit). The meaning is that of a boundary, or fixed space, within the limits of which its power and influence is confined.

The above information helps in understanding the term canon when applied to the Bible.

1. It is the measuring rod, the straightedge, the testing rule, or critical standard by which each book of the Bible must be tested before it may be admitted as a part of the Sacred Scriptures. Those books which came up to the standard were admitted, while those books which did not come up the standard were rejected.

2. It is the name given to the collection of books which did come up to the standard, and which has

become the testing rule of faith and practice. The word "canon" was first applied to the Scriptures in the fourth century A.D. by the Alexandrian church father Athanasius (A.D. 296–373).

The Sacred Canon of Scripture is the title given to those genuine, authentic, and inspired books when, taken together, form the Holy Scriptures. Each book of this Sacred Canon must be canonical.

A book or manuscript is canonical when its contents come up to, or agree with, a certain rule or standard so that it may be admitted into the Canon.

An un-canonical book is one whose contents have not reached the standard, so that it cannot be admitted into the Canon such as 1 and 2 Maccabees, the Epistle of Barnabas, and other of the apocryphal books.

The canonical Scriptures as a whole are those books that have been proven to have the right to be in the sacred text because they have been carefully tested by and met the standard. They then have become the proven measure of faith and practice, the true test of moral and religious duty. The Scriptures have conformed to the rule or standard, therefore, they are the standard.

Here is a brief summary of the tests of canonicity. In order for a book to be acknowledged as canonical and worthy of a place in the Bible they must meet these tests:

1. Divine authorship. Inspiration: is it inspired? Was it given by God through the Spirit through men; or did it come from man alone?

2. Human authorship. Was it written, edited, or endorsed by a prophet, apostle, or spokesman for God?

3. Genuineness. Is it genuine? Can it be traced back to the time and to the writer from whom it professes to have come? Or, if the writer cannot be named positively, can it be shown to contain the same matter, in every essential point, as it contained when written? The multitude of ancient manuscripts has given us a way to show that the text has not been revised or changed.

4. Authenticity. Is it authentic? Is it true? Is it a record of actual facts?

5. Testimony. In modern times another test may be added: the testimony of the Jewish church, the early and later Christian church, the church councils, and the ancient versions of the Bible.

Each of these tests should be considered separately. The first two, however, dealing with divine authorship and human authorship and endorsement, are sufficiently strong to settle the question of canonicity and authority. And if a book is inspired of God it must be genuine and authentic; He does not inspire deceptions and falsehoods.

Here is the basis of the Canon. In order that there may be a collection of books to form the Sacred Canon, there must be these things:

1. There needs to be a selection of individual books from which to choose. It is not true that the Old Testament Canon is simply a collection of early national literature. There was extensive literature besides the biblical texts. References are made in the canonical books to fifteen or more extra-canonical books. A number of apocryphal and other books were written between the Testaments and in New Testament times.

2. A number of books having a common character. Books disagreeing in historical or doctrinal statements could not form a canon.

3. A Canon would require a common religion, as two or more religions could not be taught in the same sacred canon.

4. A nation, or a people united by common religion, and political institutions.

5. A sacred national literature.

6. A system of national belief and practice.

7. A common language.

8. The art and practice of writing. Modern discoveries have shown that a high state of civilization existed, and the art of writing was practiced in Babylonia several centuries before Abraham left Ur of the Chaldees (Genesis 11:31), and in Egypt centuries before the Israelites sojourned there. The Mosaic age was one of libraries and learning. Moses could write (Exodus 17:14; 24:4; Numbers 33:2; Deuteronomy 31:9, 24).

We need a Canon of Scripture for these reasons:

1. So that we may have a complete revelation from God. The Bible in a real sense is one book, having one author—the Holy Spirit, with one subject—salvation. This subject runs through the entire book and is not complete without all the books in their proper order. It is a complete revelation from God.

2. So that we may have the written Word of God. While the prophets and Apostles were living, and revelation was in effect, this was not so necessary, for it was easier to know what writings were and were not inspired. After these holy men died and inspiration had ceased, it was necessary to collect them into one volume to preserve the sacred writings.

3. So that the sacred writings might be collected and preserved from corruption and destruction. This was especially important in the first few centuries A.D. when so many were hostile to Christianity. In A.D. 302 the Roman Emperor Diocletian ordered all the sacred books of the Christians to be burned. It was therefore necessary to know which books were of God so as to preserve them. Diocletian's destruction of Bible books helps us understand what happened to many old, important, and well-known copies of Scripture.

4. A Canon was necessary so that they could distinguish between the true and the spurious literature that some wanted to place in the Canon. For example, Emperor Constantine ordered fifty copies of the Bible to be made and circulated around the Empire. It was necessary to know which books should be included in the Bible for the churches.

Canonization answers these questions:

1. Why was each book placed in the Bible?

2. Why have certain other books been refused a place in the Bible?

3. Why have all these books been brought together in one volume?

4. Does this volume contain all the books which properly belong there?

5. Expressed in another way, has any book been omitted?

6. Does our Bible contain any book which should not be there?

The Bible is the Holy Canon and it has been proven to contain the whole of the revelation given to us by the prophets and Apostles of the Lord. There is not too much or too little. Like Isaiah, the small Bible, which has sixty-six chapters, the entire Bible has sixty-six books. Throughout there is a red cord from beginning to end which is the red cord of redemption, or the red cord of salvation that is heard from every bleating lamb that was offered, until the perfect sacrifice should come—Jesus, the Holy Son of God. He came to reconcile the whole world to its creator and God, who made mankind to love, loved His creation and has communicated with them throughout the Bible's pages.

IX. OLD TESTAMENT DIVISIONS

The Threefold Division of the Old Testament

The Hebrew Bible, the Bible used by Christ and His Apostles, was early divided into three parts: 1. The Torah, or Law, 2. The N'bhiim, or Prophets, 3. The K'thubhim, or Writings, called in Greek the Hagiographa, or Holy Writings. This threefold division was recognized by Christ (Luke 24:44).
The Hebrew Bible contains the following 24 books, in the threefold division:

1. The Law (5 books):
   Genesis, Exodus, Leviticus, Numbers, Deuteronomy

2. The Prophets (8 books)
   a. The Former Prophets (4 books)
      Joshua, Judges, Samuel, Kings
   b. The Latter Prophets (4 books)
      Major (3 books): Isaiah, Jeremiah, Ezekiel
      Minor (1 book): The Twelve

3. The Writings (11 books)
   a. Poetical (3 books): Psalms, Proverbs, Job
   b. The Five Rolls (5 books): Song of Solomon, Ruth, Lamentations, Ecclesiastes, Esther
   c. Three historical Books: Daniel, Ezra-Nehemiah, and Chronicles

Here are some observations about the divisions. The first section, the Law, is the same as the modern Christian division, the Pentateuch.

The second section, the Prophets, is composed of four books known as the "former prophets," probably because they continue the God-guided history of the God-guided people from the Law books to the end of the kingdom (Zechariah 1:4; 7:7). They are largely historical. These are followed by four books known as "latter prophets," probably because they are later in time, being interwoven with the history of the later kings and on to the end of the Old Testament history, and because they are prophetical in character. Of the latter prophets, three were called "major," or greater in length, and one was called "minor" because it was composed of twelve short books united in a single book. These short books were called "minor," not because they are inferior in quality or authority, but because they are brief in contents. These eight books were called "prophets" because they were written by men who had the prophetic office as well as the prophetic gift.

The third section, with its eleven books, is made up of miscellaneous works, three of them being poetical, and they are grouped as "writings" probably because they were written by men who had the prophetic gift but not the prophetic office. They are in three divisions: poetical, the five rolls, and the three books. The last has no recognized name, although the books are historical in character. This third section was also called "the Psalms," a name taken from the first book of the section.

The twenty-four books in the Hebrew division contain the same material as do the thirty-nine books in the modern division, only they are arranged differently. In the *Greek Septuagint* version, the books of Samuel, Kings, Chronicles, and Ezra-Nehemiah were each divided into two, making eight books instead of four. The Twelve was divided into twelve books. This makes fifteen more books, or thirty-nine in all, but no new matter is added. The *Latin Vulgate* has the same divisions, and this has been followed by the English and other versions. The *Modern Hebrew Bible*, from A.D. 1517, has the books divided into thirty-nine, but the sections and the order of the books are the same as the ancient. It begins with Genesis and ends with Chronicles.

Various reasons have been given for why the Hebrew scholars divided the books like they did. We do not know for certain their reasons. The main fact to be remembered is that the Hebrew Bible and our own contain the same books, only arranged in different order.

X. FORMING THE OLD TESTAMENT CANON

What was the guiding principle in forming the Old Testament Canon? The Bible does not give much definite information about the canonization of any of its books, nor is there any formal historical account that tells us how it was done. There are several theories that have been promulgated by different scholars.

1. Some would say that age was the test and that the canon was made up of the oldest Hebrew literature, books that were highly prized and venerated because of their age.

This theory is refuted by the fact that some fifteen or more extra-biblical books are named in the Old Testament as existing before many of the canonical books were written, yet they are not included in the Canon.

2. Another theory is that the Canon is merely a choice collection, the gems of the Jewish classics, such as might have been made later from Greek or Latin literature.

This could not be, because the fundamental and essential character of the Old Testament Canon is thoroughly and exclusively religious; everything that went into it was for religious purposes only.

3. Others would suggest that the Hebrew language was the test.

This cannot be true since fifteen or more extra-canonical books referred to in the Bible were, of course, written in Hebrew, as were also the apocryphal books of Ecclesiasticus, 1 Maccabees, Tobit and possibly others. None of these were regarded as canonical.

4. Another idea was that its conformity to the Law of Moses was the test, the question being, "Does it agree with the Torah, the Law of Moses?"

It is true that no book that contradicted the Law of Moses would be admitted into the Canon; it is also true that the Old Testament does not contain all of the books that agree with the Law.

5. Finally, there are those that say it was the religious and moral elements of the books that were mainly considered in selecting them. At the same time they might add one or more of the above-mentioned ideas.

Some of the apocryphal books written before the Canon was closed are of a religious character. Why were none of them admitted? The question before us is why were the canonical books admitted?

The problem with these theories is that they overlook three important elements: God, inspiration, and the official position of the writer; they attempt to explain the tests of admission to the Canon on the grounds of merely human judgment and choice.

The real tests are:

1. The Bible is a revelation from God; it is God speaking through the Holy Spirit. This is inspiration.

2. God spoke through divinely inspired men, spokesmen, and prophets. The result was divinely inspired writings. These writings are profitable for doctrine, reproof, correction, instruction in righteousness, and are the complete manual for men in every good work, because they are inspired of God (2 Timothy 3:16−17). They are not inspired of God because they are profitable; they are profitable because they are inspired of God. The writers wrote not by their own will, but by the will of God (2 Peter 1:21). The divine character and inspiration of each book was clearly stamped upon it, and could be recognized and proven. The human writers were known prophets of God. The first two tests, divine and human authorship, were recognized practically as soon as the writings were produced, and the other tests—genuineness, authenticity, and testimony—could be added as verifications. The Canon

gradually grew as the inspired writers finished their work and it became known for its divine stamp. When the divine succession of prophets and divinely inspired writers came to an end, it became necessary to gather them into one book. This is how the Bible came to be.

The three steps were: 1. Divine inspiration and authority, which made them canonical; 2. Human recognition of this inspiration and authority; 3. Collection, into one book. These three steps must not be confused.

The Jews received the books of the Old Testament, and no others, as canonical. There was (and is) widespread agreement among the Jewish nation as to what was (and was not) the word of God. Looking within the biblical text, there are hundreds or thousands of claims to inspiration, too numerous to list. Not only does the Old Testament make claims of inspiration, but there are hundreds of claims of inspiration of the Old Testament in the New Testament.

The Completion of the Old Testament Canon

There is not uniformity of thought here and historical documentation is scarce. There are ancient and persistent traditions that the Old Testament books were collected together by Ezra and a band of helpers known as "The Great Synagogue." These traditions have garnered around them so much that is legendary, fabulous, over miraculous, fanciful, and contrary to known history and chronology, that they are largely discredited in their entirety, and the very existence of the Great Synagogue is denied; this, of course, is in the interest of the modern view of the completion of the Canon. Without attempting to prove the existence of the Great Synagogue as a definite institution, the following facts stand out boldly:

1. The Babylonian Exile (606–536 B.C.) was a period of punishment for disobedience to the Law of God. The period after the Return was one of confusion and reconstruction, and Zerubbabel, Ezra, and Nehemiah, with Haggai and Zechariah, were busy rebuilding the temple, city, and walls, and restoring the Mosaic laws and institutions. (See the books of Ezra, Nehemiah, Haggai and Zechariah.) There were great religious revivals and reforms that followed the public reading of "the Book of the Law" (Neh. 8–10). And the people would desire an authoritative collection of their sacred books to know the will of God and to guard against future trouble.

2. Ezra, the leader of the second group of the returning people, was not only a priest—he was also the scribe. (Ezra 7:6) He was the beginning of a guild of scribes which extended into New Testament times. The scribes were lawyers, teachers, judges, writers, and copyists, all in one person.

3. There were, near and at the close of the Old Testament times, five great inspired writers, more or less contemporaneous: Ezra, Nehemiah, Haggai, Zechariah, and Malachi. These, with or without Joshua or other high priests, could have been members of such a "synagogue." (2 Maccabees 2:13; 15:9)

4. All the Old Testament books were written before 430 or 424 B.C., Nehemiah and Malachi, contemporaries, being the last. This can be proven, higher criticism notwithstanding. It is therefore conceivable that five or more men began and completed the collection and arrangement of the Old Testament books. Doubtless, Ezra, as a scribe, was the leader in this work.

5. It was generally understood that Malachi (433−430 or 425 B.C.) was the last of the prophets, and that Old Testament prophecy (Scripture) ended with him. This fact was emphasized in Maccabean times, when the people were perplexed because there was no "prophet" among them (1 Macc. 4:46; 9:27; 14:41).

6. There existed "books" (Daniel 9:2), private and partial collections of books (rolls), and books "laid up in the temple" and carefully guarded. These were recognized as inspired and authoritative. As the line of prophets had ceased, and as it was also uniformly believed among the Jews that the Holy Spirit had departed after Malachi, there was need of an official collection and canon of these books. And as these five men (of the "Great Synagogue," if you will) were the last of the prophets (inspired spokesmen for God), it would seem to be highly probable that the Canon was collected by them, or in their time.

7. Josephus, the Jewish historian (A.D. 100), in his treatise *Against Apion*, corroborates these statements. He states clearly that the time during which the sacred books of the Jews were written extended from Moses to Artaxerxes I (who reigned 465−424 B.C.), that the number of books was 24, that nothing was added after the death of Artaxerxes (424 B.C.) This was because the line of prophets had ceased at that time. He said no one dared to make any additions, subtractions or alterations and that every Jew was not only willing to abide by them as God's commands, but he was also willing, if need be, to die for them. Josephus was a learned man of priestly origin and

he had abundant opportunity to know the history of the Old Testament Scriptures. He was arguing with a shrewd, hostile, scholarly grammarian, Apion; he was defending the accuracy and sufficiency of the Hebrew Scriptures as compared with the contradictory histories of the Greek writers and he had to be careful and accurate in his statements. He is not giving personal opinions merely; he is the spokesman of his people.[15]

8. The *Septuagint Version*, begun about 280 B.C., continued for about 100 years until about 180 B.C. Some scholars prefer a date of 250–150 B.C. This is a translation of the entire Old Testament into the Greek language. It proves that all the books of the Old Testament existed at that time and were considered canonical.

9. The *Prologue to Ecclesiasticus* was written in 132 B.C. by Jesus, son of Sirach, as a preface to his translation, from Hebrew into Greek, of the Book of Ecclesiasticus, written by his grandfather, of the same name, Jesus, son of Sirach. Twice he mentions the Old Testament as a whole, under the threefold division, "the Law, the prophets, and the others, that have followed in their steps," and "the law itself, the prophets, and the rest of the books." He says his grandfather, about 50 years before, or 180 B.C., gave a lot of time to reading "the law, and the prophets, and the other books of our fathers." Here is a historical recognition of the Old Testament Canon in its threefold, Jewish, division as far back as 180 B.C. Jesus, our Lord, gives a similar recognition to the threefold division of the Old Testament in Luke 24:44.

15   See Josephus, *Against Apion*, I, 8

10. Jesus endorsed the entire range of Old Testament Scripture, by His statement, "From the blood of Abel unto the blood of Zachariah, who perished between the sanctuary and the altar" (Luke 11:51, compare Matthew 23:36). This is from Genesis 4:10, the first book of the Hebrew Bible, to 2 Chronicles 24:20−21, the last book of the Hebrew Bible.

XI. FOUR CLASSES OF OLD TESTAMENT BOOKS

After the close of the Old Testament Canon, questions arose among some Jews: 1. Concerning certain books already contained in the Canon; 2. About some other books written later and seeking admission into the Canon. These books came to be divided into four groups of books. (1) The Homologoumena, (2) The Antilegomena, (3) The Apocrypha, (4) and the Pseudepigrapha.

The Homologoumena were the confessed and undisputed books that were at home in the Canon and no one questioned them. They are 34 in number, all but the five Antilegomena books.

The Antilegomena books were spoken against and a few people said they did not belong in the Canon. These books were disputed by some Jews. These books are five in number. See below for a discussion of these books.

The Apocrypha were hidden or had secret parts and were written after the canonical books were written, and were not admitted into the Canon. They could not have been "taken out" of the Canon, for they were never a part of it. They were of questionable value and authenticity. They were apocryphal. (See below.)

The Pseudepigrapha are those books which were written by unknown persons around the time of the birth of Christ, or between 200 B.C. and A.D. 200 and were passed on to a gullible public as the works of distinguished Bible people. The Old Testament Pseudepigrapha are all those writings which claim to have been written by Old Testament characters, whether the contents be of a Jewish or a Christian nature. It would be like a modern person writing a book and trying to sell it as having been written by Abraham Lincoln or George Washington. They would affix a famous name to the book to encourage its acceptance.

The Antilegomena books were spoken against by some scholars in the late first and early second century A.D. They were the Song of Solomon, Ecclesiastes, Esther, Ezekiel and Proverbs. The objection to the Song of Solomon was that it seemed to be a poem about merely human love. Some objected to Ecclesiastes, saying that contradicted other canonical Scriptures and favored the views of the Sadducees and tended toward atheism. They objected to Esther because it did not mention the name of God. Some said Ezekiel apparently contradicted some of the requirements of the Mosaic Law. They thought Proverbs had contradictory statements. These ideas have been adequately refuted. At a later time both Old and New Testament books will be objected to by higher critics.

These attacks would not have been made if there had not been an accepted Old Testament Canon. The objections could not prevail against the sentiments and convictions of the Jewish church. They were soon settled by councils and no other book was ever inserted or withdrawn from the Canon.

XII. THE OLD TESTAMENT APOCRYPHA

The word "Apocrypha," when applied to Scripture, means:

1. "Hidden" or "concealed" and applies to the works which were written for an inner circle of people, sometimes a heretical sect, and, which were not supposed to be understood by those outside, therefore it had the idea of secret, mysterious or occult.

The word is similar to "esoteric" and intended for those initiated.

2. A second meaning was spurious, forged, of unknown or fraudulent authorship and content, heretical.

3. In the fourth century A.D., and possibly later by Jerome himself, the word came to be used in the sense of uncanonical or unrecognized books, and was applied to those religious books which were of inferior quality and authority when compared with the inspired writings. When Jerome translated the Vulgate he translated the 24 (39) canonical books, and then said, "Anything outside of these must be placed within the Apocrypha," as uncanonical.

The contents of the Old Testament Apocrypha are fourteen in number and are given this order in the English version:

1. Esdras*
2. Esdras*
3. Tobit
4. Judith
5. The Rest of Esther**
6. The Wisdom of Solomon
7. Ecclesiasticus
8. Baruch, with the Epistle of Jeremiah (Sometimes separated, to make fifteen books.)
9. The Song of the Three Holy Children**
10. The History of Susanna**
11. Bel and the Dragon
12. The Prayer of Manasses*
13. 1 Maccabees
14. 2 Maccabees

*Not accepted by Catholics, thus making seven they accept.

**Sometimes combined with Esther & Daniel.

The Alexandrian manuscript of the Septuagint adds 3 and 4 Maccabees, making 16 books. The Vulgate does not have them. The Vatican manuscript contains none of the Maccabean books; the Sinaitic contains 1 and 4 Maccabees.

It is not our purpose at this point to discuss the Apocryphal books, we will later, but only to note that there was good reason for them not being included in the Sacred Canon. For many years it was believed that ancient books were few, but recent discoveries have proven that writing was common and that many books were in circulation, either in the form of clay tablets, cylinders, bronze or other writing materials. We will discuss writing materials in a later chapter.

The Ebla Tablets[16]

Other writings, though not apocryphal, are examples of writings not included in our Bible. At Ebla in Syria, a library of over 2,100 clay tablets was found. This proves that books were not uncommon during the time of the writing of the Bible. The Ebla Tablets have been dated as early as 2100 B.C. The ancient tablets include a bill of lading shipping goods to Sodom and Gomorrah. Eber the Hebrew is mentioned also, possibly an ancestor of Abraham. These confirm that writing was common and widespread much earlier than some have wished to acknowledge.

Writing was common very early and the Bible mentions a number of books not contained in the inspired text. It seems certain that the Bible quotes from many ancient documents,

16   *The Archives of Ebla, an Empire Inscribed in Clay*, Giovanni Pettinato, Doubleday & Company, Inc., Garden City, New York. 1981.

possibly even some that existed before the flood and may have been carried by Noah onto the ark and that survived the flood. These records could have been kept as family histories almost back to Adam. Adam lived and could have known Methusaleh and Methusaleh could have talked with Noah. People had various organized languages after the time of the Tower of Babel. Writing was common and this is illustrated by the extra canonical books we call the Apocrypha. These tablets make no pretense to be biblical and are not classified apocryphal, which classification came much later.

The Nag Hammadi Texts

Another group of ancient manuscripts has been found which fit into the New Testament period. They are of value, but definitely not scripture. They are called the Nag Hammadi texts. These texts are not a part of what is commonly considered the Apocrypha, but they are of special interest to the author, since he had the opportunity to see and photograph them while at the Coptic Museum in Cairo, Egypt.

They were found in 1945 in a cave near Nag Hammadi in southern Egypt not far from Karnak. They were found by a man who was looking for natural fertilizer. While digging in the sand he came across the cave where they were hidden. They have been called the oldest known Codex form of books. Some might suppose them to be scripture since they talk about biblical people and events.

The texts were in leather pouches that were placed in large pottery jars. They passed through several hands before ending up in the Coptic museum, where they reside today. They contain thirteen codices (books of leaves) and in these books are 52 chapters of 1,200 pages.

They fit into the category of apocryphal in that they bear a resemblance to our biblical texts and talk about biblical characters, but do not measure up to the canonical standard of our Old and New Testament books. They do have significant value.

Their value is that they talk about many of the biblical characters, Paul, James, Thomas, Phillip, John, Peter and others. They prove that Christianity was well founded in Egypt in the fourth century and before. Probably the most significant is the Gospel of Thomas.

They have been rejected as canonical for many reasons and especially because of their strong gnostic and heretical content. There is additional information about these manuscripts on line for those who wish to know more about these very old books.

The Apocrypha books can be divided into five classifications: (The Ebla Tablets and Nag Hammadi Texts are not included in the following summary.)

1. Historical. There are five historical books. Esdras is a compilation from 2 Chronicles, Ezra and Nehemiah. It was used by Josephus in writing his history. It has some value. 1 Maccabees is a historical record covering forty years from the accession of Antiochus Epiphanes to the death of Simon Maccabaeus (175–135 B.C.). It is a trustworthy account of the Maccabean War and an important history of the inter-testament period. 2 Maccabees is a fanciful and spurious book purporting to be letters to Jews in Egypt and include supernatural material of a questionable nature. 3 Maccabees is a historical romance with more romance than history. It is silly and superficial. 4 Maccabees is a philosophical book on the supremacy of pious reason.

2. Teaching. There are two didactic books. The Wisdom of Solomon, in which the writer claims to be Solomon, is an ethical work commending wisdom and righteousness and condemning iniquity and idolatry. The other is Ecclesiasticus or the Wisdom of Jesus, Son of Sirach. It is patterned after

Proverbs, Ecclesiastes, and Job. It contains a wide range of instruction about conduct and a large number of maxims, proverbs, and wise sayings collected from many sources.

3. Religious Romances. There are several religious romances. Tobit is an example during the Captivity and claims to be based on historical facts. It is not pure history, but does show Jewish life in its best forms and contains the miraculous and has a moral tone. Judith is a romance set in the time of Nebuchadnezzar and is intended to show Jewish bravery and devotion to the Law. It has little or no historical basis. It teaches that the end justifies the means.

4. Prophetic. There are three prophetic books. Baruch is a weak imitation of Jeremiah's language and claims to be written by Baruch the scribe. The Epistle of Jeremiah was appended to Baruch and is a warning to the Babylonian captives against idolatry. 2 Esdras is an apocalyptic Esdras and contains seven visions.

5. Legendary. The Remainder of Esther was written in Greek and scattered throughout canonical Esther in the Septuagint. It enlarges upon the story of Esther. The Song of the Three Holy Children is the first of three additions to the Book of Daniel. In the Septuagint it is inserted after Daniel 3:23. The History of Susanna is another religious romance of the deliverance of a pure woman from the schemes of two immoral men through the wisdom of Solomon. The idyll Bel and the Dragon, in which Daniel is the hero, is a thrilling story of the destruction of two objects of Babylonian worship

and the deliverance of Daniel from the lions' den. The Prayer of Manasses is penitential prayer of one supposed to be Manasseh, king of Judah, while in prison.

The authors of the Apocryphal books are entirely unknown, except in the case of Ecclesiasticus. This book is said to have been written by Jesus, son of Sirach, and to have been translated into Greek by his grandson, of the same name. The authors are thought to mostly have been Alexandrian Jews, with two notable exceptions which are the authors of 1 Maccabees and Ecclesiasticus, who were probably Palestinian Jews. Jewish writers, even of the canonical books, seemed to have little interest in putting their names on their books.

The language of the books is primarily Greek, although Ecclesiasticus, 1 Maccabees and part of Baruch, Judith, and Tobit were written originally in Hebrew or possibly Aramaic.

There is no way of proving the exact time of the writing of any of these books, with the possible exception of Ecclesiasticus. This is thought to have been written in Hebrew about 180 B.C. and translated into Greek about 132 B.C. Most scholars will date the Apocryphal books from 200 B.C. to A.D. 100.

Although not inspired, they do offer a contribution to the study of the nation of Israel and particularly the inter-testament period. They are a part of the literature of God's covenant people and help to fill the gap of 450 or more years between the end of the Old and beginning of the New Testament literature, when prophecy and inspiration had ceased. They provide a connecting link. The book of 1 Maccabees is especially valuable, as it throws a lot of light on the Jewish wars and the fierce struggle to throw off Greek heathenism and maintain their worship of Jehovah God. These books help us see the difference between inspired and non-inspired writing. There is a drastic difference.

Reasons for Rejecting the Apocrypha from the Canon

1. It is universally acknowledged that they never had a place in the Hebrew Canon.

2. They are never quoted in the New Testament, either by Christ or His Apostles or by any writer, much less do these ascribe to them inspiration or canonicity. They were mostly in existence at that time. Some scholars would suggest they were in the Septuagint at that time.

3. Josephus expressly excludes them, limiting the number of divinely inspired books to 24, which he lists, the same as our 39.

4. Philo, the great Jewish philosopher of Alexandria, (20 B.C.–A.D. 50) wrote prolifically and quoted largely from the Old Testament Scriptures, yet he never quoted from the Apocrypha, nor even mentions them.

5. They are not found in any catalogue of canonical books made during the first four centuries A.D.

6. Jerome declared for the strict Hebrew Canon and rejected the authority of the entire Apocrypha in a most emphatic manner. His declaration had great weight with the churches.

7. Divine inspiration and authority is claimed by none of the writers, and is definitely disclaimed by some of them.

8. They are entirely without the true prophetic element; the "succession of prophets" had ceased.

In them, no one speaks or writes with a message from Jehovah.

9. The books contain many historical, geographical, and chronological errors and distortions of Old Testament narratives, contradicting themselves, the Bible, and secular history.

10. They teach doctrines and uphold practices which are directly contrary to the canonical Scriptures. Lying is sanctioned, suicide and assassination are justified, salvation by works and by almsgiving, magical incantations, prayers by the dead and for the dead, etc., are taught and approved.

11. Their weakness of style, stiffness, lack of originality, and artificiality of expression as compared with the canonical books, is noticeable.

12. Much of the literature is legendary and the stories contain many absurdities.

13. The so-called miracles and the descriptions of the persons and deeds of their supernatural beings, contain much that is fabulous, grotesque, and silly.

14. The spiritual and even the moral level are, as a whole, far below that of the Old Testament. When one reads the Old Testament and then reads the Apocrypha, he feels that he is in a different world.

15. The books come too late for the Canon, as the Canon had been closed. Some are obviously a crude copy of the Bible books.

16. Some of them were permitted to be read for instruction, but they were not considered canonical and authoritative for doctrine by any prominent man, set of men, nor church council until the Roman Catholic Council of Trent (A.D. 1546) and then by a very small majority who anathematized any who might think differently.

17. The Christian Church, the successor and development of the Jewish Church, received from the latter the same Old Testament Scriptures.

18. There is strong presumption, from expressions of Christ and His Apostles, by their use of the word "Scripture," etc., that in their day the Old Testament Canon had long been fixed. Christ appealed to the Hebrew Scriptures as to a well-defined collection of writings held in absolute reverence. The New Testament furnishes proof that there was no question as to what was and was not Scripture.

19. The canonical books were each provided with Targums by the rabbis and paraphrases of the original Hebrew writings, and such paraphrases of the Apocrypha is entirely missing.

20. To place these books on a level with the Holy Scriptures is impossible for the historical and careful theological student. The contents of the Apocrypha are the strongest witness against them.

XIII. THE OLD TESTAMENT PSEUDEPIGRAPHA

Besides the Apocrypha, there is another collection of books of Jewish and Christian origin, written between 200 B.C. and A.D. 200. They are contemporaneous with the Apocrypha, written in Hebrew, or Aramaic, but they exist today in Greek, Syriac, Latin, Ethiopic, and Slavonic. This list of books continues to expand with new discoveries.

These books were called the "Apocrypha" by the ancient church. They are not called "Apocrypha" by the Roman Catholic Church, which accepts seven of the Apocryphal books as canonical. By the Protestant churches they are sometimes called "Wider Apocrypha," and sometimes the "Pseudepigrapha." Other times they may be called "Apocalyptic Literature." Each name has its significance.

The word Pseudepigrapha means false or spurious writings, written under a false name or names. These writings were sometimes falsely ascribed to biblical characters and to biblical times, hence spurious, and have never been accepted as canonical by any branch of the Christian Church. Whether these writings were intended to deceive or not is not certainly known, but the writers were doubtless men of piety who saw, in those dark days when Judaism was struggling either with or under foreign powers, the need of teaching or exhortation or denunciation. They thought that they could better command attention and accomplish their purposes by using the name of some eminent person or by reference to some noted event in early Jewish history.Sometimes they are called "Apocalyptic Literature" because they are composed largely of apocalypses, revelations and visions. What the book of Revelation is to the New Testament and Ezekiel, Zechariah, and especially Daniel are to the Old Testament, the Jewish Apocalypses are to the Pseudepigraphal books. As the book of Daniel was a comfort in times of persecution, these books sought to bring comfort under the rule of the Seleucidae, Antiochus Epiphanes, and during the

Maccabean periods. They offer visions of a bright future, the coming Messiah, the Messianic kingdom, and the millennium. They also sought to deal with the creation of the world, angels, with the origin of sin and explanations of evil, suffering, future destiny, and rewards.

Below is a partial list of some of the more important Pseudepigraphal books.

1. Apocalyptic (12 books)
The Book of Enoch
The Secrets of Enoch
The Apocalypse of Baruch
The Rest of the Words of Baruch
The Assumption of Moses
A Revelation of Moses
Prophecy of Jeremiah
Ascension of Isaiah
Apocalypse of Elijah
Apocalypse of Zephaniah
Apocalypse of Esdras
Sibylline Oracles

2. Legendary (10 books)
The Testament of Adam
The Book of Jubilees or the "Little Genesis"
Testaments of Abraham, Isaac, and Jacob
Apocalypse of Abraham
Testament of the Twelve Patriarchs
Life of Asenath (wife of Joseph)
Testament of Job
Testament of Solomon
The Book of Noah
Penitence of Jannes and Jambres

3. Poetical (2 books)
Psalms of Solomon (18 Psalms in Greek)
Addition to the Psalter Psalms 151; 3 apocry
phal psalms in Syriac.

4. Didactic (2 books)
Magical Books of Moses
The Story of Achiacharus, Cup-bearer to
Esarhaddon, King of Persia

Writers of no personal renown wrote things and affixed important people's names to them so that they would have credibility. They were written intending to deceive and often have. Every once in a while an unsuspecting person will run across some of the Apocryphal or Pseudepigraphical books and will think they have found additional Scripture. They can be deceived and deceive other people.

In reality the Apocryphal and Pseudepigraphical books never did meet the high standards for inspiration. They were left out for many good reasons and never achieved acceptance by the Hebrew or Christian church.

XIV. THE FORMATION OF THE NEW TESTAMENT CANON

The New Testament Canon is the collection of 27 books which we know as our Scripture. They have been accepted by the church down through the centuries. These books all existed at the end of the first century A.D. and were spread over a wide territory, probably from Babylon in the east to Rome in the west. They had been received by the churches to which they were sent, were circulated to other churches, and treasured along with the Old Testament and recorded the life, work, and words of Jesus and His Apostles (Romans 1:10; 11; 15:28; 1 Corinthians 4:17; 11:23; 1 Thessalonians 2:13; 2 Thessalonians 2:15; Colossians 2:7 and so on).

The New Testament Canon was formed much as had been the Old Testament Canon. During the time from the beginning of the second century and beginning of the fourth, the works were recognized as the words of God and gathered together into one volume. As early as 2 Peter 3:15 the works of Paul were admitted to exist and to be considered Scripture, along with other New Testament writings. The New Testament books were being grouped together as early as the middle of the second century when the Gnostic Marcion put together a mutilated Gospel of Luke and ten of Paul's epistles.

By the time of Emperor Constantine, the New Testament books were gathered together and published in 50 copies of the New Testament which were circulated around the Empire. It is possible that either the Vaticanus or Sinaticus manuscripts could be one of these.

Paul seems to acknowledge Luke's Gospel as Scripture in 1 Timothy 5:18. In this same century, Clement of Rome (A.D. 96) quotes the Lord Jesus from Matthew and Luke. He shows familiarity with Romans, 1 Corinthians, Ephesians, 1 Timothy, Titus, Hebrews, and 1 John.

The Epistle of Barnabas, written somewhere between A.D. 70 and 100, probably earlier than later, abounds in quotations from the Old Testament and at least two from the New. He quotes from Matthew 22:14 and gives what may be the earliest reference to our New Testament books as "Scripture."

The Didache, or Teaching of the Twelve, is usually dated about A.D. 100 or earlier. It quotes the New Testament 23 times, mostly from Matthew and Luke.

Polycarp (A.D. 69—155), a disciple of the Apostle John, in a letter to the Philippians (150 or earlier) quotes freely from the New Testament, using Matthew, Luke, John, Acts, ten of Paul's epistles, with no fewer than eleven references to 1 John and treats them all as Scripture.

The "Second Epistle of Clement" dates about A.D. 120—140, and quotes extensively from the New Testament, especially from Jesus, with such comments as "The Lord saith in the Gospels," "the Lord said," and "God said." Twice he says, "the Scripture saith," quoting from Matthew and Luke.

Justin Martyr (A.D. 100—140) in his great "Apologies," or Defenses of Christianity, quotes from Matthew about 43 times and from Luke 19 times; he also quotes from John, and probably from Mark. His quotations are more numerous and more elaborate than those of any preceding writer and they are, from the nature of his subject matter, mostly taken from the Gospels. He shows familiarity with Acts, and at least six of Paul's Epistles, 1 John and Revelation. He says the "Memoirs of the Apostles" were called "Gospels" and that they were read on Sunday when the church gathered. They were accepted as equal with the Old Testament.

Irenaeus (A.D. 130—202), bishop of Lyons, Gaul, wrote extensively, but nearly all his writings are lost, except his great work *Against Heresies*. He is said to be the first writer to make a full use of the New Testament, making 1,800 quotations and references in his extant works, and using them in such a way as to imply that they had for some time been considered as of unquestioned authority. He refutes Gnosticism and other heresies from Scripture. He says that there were four Gospels and only four. He especially quotes from the Gospels, Acts, thirteen Pauline Epistles, 1 Peter, 1 John and Revelation. He considers them as inspired, canonical, and authoritative in the fullest sense and in every way equal to the writings of the Old Testament.

Clement of Alexandria (A.D. 150—217), scholar, bishop, teacher, and writer, quotes from and acknowledges as canonical the four Gospels, Acts, Pauline Epistles, 1 Peter, 1 John, Hebrews, James, Jude, and Revelation. He speaks more than once of the "Old and New Covenants Testaments" in such a way as to leave no doubt as to his meaning. He calls the New Testament books "the divine Scriptures," and "the holy books."

Tertullian (A.D. 150—220) the great North African teacher and writer, quotes more than 1,800 different passages from the New Testament, making 7,200 references, 2,800 from the

Gospels, 2,600 from Matthew, Mark, and John alone. He uses as inspired Scripture, 22 or 23 New Testament books, and also the words "each instrument, or Testament," "both Testaments," and "the New Testament."

The heretics also offered strong evidence as they attacked the New Testament, which called for strong defenses. It has been said heresy spoke louder than orthodoxy in defining what was considered Scripture. The debate between Origen (A.D. 185—254) and Celsus (third century) is an example. In the debates and writings of Origen and Celsus, it is clear that Celsus was attacking the canonical books, not the apocryphal books. It is said that if all of Origen's writings were still in existence that he had quoted the entire New Testament several times. He wrote so much that he employed seven scribes to record his writings. One of Origen's works was the Hexapla, which gave six different Greek and Hebrew versions of the Old and Testament side by side.

Included in the heretical individuals and sects were the Ebionites, Gnostics, Simon Magus, Cerinthus, the Ophites, Basilides, Valentinus, Hedraclion, Marcion, the Montanists, and many others who show familiarity with our New Testament and sought to argue its teachings. They used the canonical books in their writings, not the apocryphal books.

Many other writers could be cited as evidence for our present canon, and people of great scholarship and renown give similar views during the period from the first to fourth centuries. Such people as Dionysius the Great, Cyprian, Eusebius, Cyril of Jerusalem, Athanasius, Chrysostom, Jerome, and Augustine quote the New Testament.

We could add to this list as proof of our present canonical books the ancient versions or translations of the Scripture. Two examples of this are the Old Latin and Jerome's Latin Vulgate. The purpose of this book is not to cover all existing evidence, but only to show that the evidence is conclusive and there can be no doubt that from the very time of their writing, the Gospels, Acts of the Apostles, the Epistles, and Revelation were considered by the church to be the inspired words of God—Scripture. I believe we have proven this point beyond any reasonable doubt.

By the end of the fourth century, the entire Church was practically unanimous as to the canonicity of our 27 books to the exclusion of all other writings. The books had been tested and found acceptance by the whole church, not merely by a single synod or council, but by the whole church around the world.

XV. FOUR CLASSES OF NEW TESTAMENT BOOKS

As is true of the Old Testament Canon, there were also four classes of books in the New Testament. There are three principle classes and one less important. We call them the homologoumena, the antilegomena, and the Apocrypha, and the fourth is the pseudepigrapha.

While the church was young, the number of local congregations was small and more widely scattered. Since the process of copying by hand was slow and expensive, the means of communicating between churches was also slow. This explains why there were not so many copies as we have today with Bibles everywhere.

The Gospels are larger and contain the work and teachings of Christ. Acts describes the work and the spread of the gospel. Great practical doctrinal issues are addressed in the Epistles of Paul. They are addressed to prominent churches and pastors. First Peter is addressed to a large area. First John supplements the Gospel of John. Philemon is a personal letter and a companion piece with Colossians. Philemon and Colossians would naturally be more widely known, copied, and circulated; hence they would be received first. Their apostolic authorship or endorsement, and authority would be more commonly known. These are the twenty homologoumena books and they are found in practically all early lists.

There were seven other books, the antilegomena, or disputed books, those about which certain questions arose, and which were not admitted to the Canon until a bit later. The seven anti-legomena were questioned but for various reasons: 1. Hebrews was questioned slightly on the matter of doctrine, but largely as to the point of authorship. Some thought that Paul wrote it, others did not, others were uncertain. The Eastern Church considered apostolic authority sufficient and the West also stressed apostolic authority. Later the church East and West came to agreement, largely through the influence of Jerome, Athanasius and Augustine, and Hebrews was declared canonical. 2 James was questioned largely because of the supposed conflict with Paul on the doctrine of Justification by faith. Some also questioned the authorship—if by "James," which one? 3. Second Peter was questioned as to who wrote it, and when? It differs somewhat in language, style, character, and structure of words; could it be that Peter wrote it? 4—5. Second and Third John are personal and comparatively not so important, and they claim to have been written, not by an Apostle, but by an "elder" whose name is not given. Who was the writer? Was it John? If so, which John? 6. Jude was rejected by some as unauthoritative because of its reference to Enoch, a pseudepigraphical book. The question of authorship also appeared. Is the book apostolic? What is its relation to 2 Peter? 7. Revelation. This was one of the first books to be received, and it was the last to be doubted. It was received, doubted, and then received. Dionysius of Alexandria (A.D. 250) was the first to question its apostolic authorship, largely because of "dogmatic prejudice," disliking its Christology and chiliasm. It appeared to him to be different from the Gospel of John and I John. Dionysius thought someone holy and inspired wrote it, but he did not know who. His teaching did not have much effect on the discussion.

In summary, some of the Antilegomena books were short, personal, and obscure as to authorship, hence in those days they were considered comparatively unimportant for copying and circulation. Others created objections which had not yet been answered. Some were unknown to some churches; others to other churches. Hence the lists from different parts of the world differ as to contents. Some omit them entirely, some omit one or more, others omit another. These are the antilegomena books. Later, by the middle of the fourth century, with more centralization and greater interchange of opinion among the churches; practically all except Revelation were accepted. By the end of the century Revelation also was almost universally accepted, completing the list of 27 books.

The Homologoumena, or acknowledged books, were those over which there was little or no dispute. These are the four Gospels, the Acts, thirteen Pauline Epistles from Romans to Philemon, 1 Peter, and 1 John, twenty in all.

The question of authorship was prominent regarding each of the seven disputed books. These epistles were addressed either to Christians in general or to private persons, not to specified churches—Revelation being the exception. Therefore, there may have been less interest in their circulation. By the end of the fourth century the doubts were removed and the seven Antilegomena books were accepted.

The Apocrypha were the rejected books, the spurious books. The word is used here in the sense of extra-canonical, non-canonical or not in the New Testament, but without implication that their contents are necessarily false or spurious.

Why were the Apocryphal books written? 1. Possibly it was an effort to give more information about Christ and His teachings than was available. 2. Or a desire to expand on material already given in the four Gospels. 3. Some were written to enforce some unsound doctrinal ideas or teachings. 4. The Apocryphal Acts arose before the canonical Acts was fully accepted. The effort was to tell what other Apostles did, rather than the two (Peter and Paul) who were primarily the center of action in the canonical Acts. 5. They glorify true Christianity but by pious fraud. The Apocryphal books seem to be an effort to fill in lacking material in the Canonical books. They may have been well intentioned, but were not inspired works.

Examples of some Apocryphal epistles are these: 1. The Teaching of the Twelve Apostles. 2. The Epistle of Barnabas.

3. The First and Second Epistle of Clement. 4. The Shepherd of Hermas. 5. The Gospel of Nicodemus. 6. The History of Joseph the Carpenter, and many others.

In a pseudepigraphical book the author attached some well know biblical person's name in an effort to find more acceptance for the writing. Some examples of New Testament pseudepigraphical books are: 1. The Gospel of Andrew. 2. The Gospel of Bartholomew. 3. The Gospel of Barnabas. 4. The Gospel of Matthias. 5. The Acts of John, Paul, Peter, Andrew, Thomas, Matthias, Philip, Thadaeus, and many others.

These books did not measure up to the canonical standard tests and although interesting, can easily lead the unsuspecting astray. These books were called by Eusebius "spurious," which they in truth were—illegitimate and counterfeit. Some apostolic fathers included some pseudepigraphal books briefly, such as the Didache, 1 Clement, Barnabas, and Shepherd of Hermas.

The apocryphal and pseudepigraphal books were of an inferior quality and did not measure up to the standard of the canonical books, and were not accepted by those church leaders in the time in which they were written, nor by the church since. Most all were rejected, and there is a striking difference between them and our Bible.

Their value may be to offer some historical insight and help us know the ideas, fears, hopes and imaginations of those who wrote them. But for very good reasons they have been rejected because they were not inspired books. They have some value as folklore and of value to those of us who love medieval literature. We who love theology cannot afford to neglect them.

SECTION THREE

THE GENUINENESS AND AUTHENTICITY OF THE SCRIPTURES

XVI. DEFINING TERMS

The word *genuine* means actually belonging to, or proceeding from, the reputed source, origin, or author; having the origin or character which it appears or is claimed to have; not counterfeit, spurious, false, or adulterated. A genuine text is one which has the date, authorship, etc., which it purports or claims to have (Webster, New International Dictionary).

A book or manuscript is *genuine* when it can be traced back to the writer or writers from whom it professes to have come, and to the time when it is claimed to have been written; that is, when its claims concerning its authorship are true; secondarily, when the matter which it now contains is the same in every essential point as it was when the author wrote it. If each biblical book or manuscript should contain the writer's name or positive evidence as to who he was, the first part of the definition would be sufficient. Since certain books do not contain this information, yet they seem to be the production of an inspired writer, authentic and authoritative, the second part of the definition would prove their genuineness and would be needed.

When we talk of the genuineness of the Scriptures it means that we know they were written by the writers whose names they bear and about the time that has been assigned to them; or, as containing the same matter, essentially, as was originally given by their writers.

A book or manuscript is *authentic* when it relates facts as they really occurred—when its statements may be relied upon as true. The authenticity of the Scriptures is the right they have to be considered as a record of actual facts.

Genuineness has to do with truth in authorship, or origin;

76

authenticity with truth in facts. A book may, therefore, be genuine without being authentic, or authentic without being genuine. The professed author may not be the real one, yet the contents may be true—then it would be authentic but not genuine. The professed author may be the real one but the contents may not be true—then it would be genuine but not authentic. It will be shown that our Bible is both genuine and authentic.

These terms may be reversed by some persons, but the above definitions are those in common use today.

A book or manuscript is "forged" or "spurious" when its statements concerning its authorship are false.

A book or manuscript is corrupt when its text has in any way been changed. The credibility of the Scriptures is the right they have to be believed and received because of their absolute truthfulness. The integrity of the Scriptures deals with the fact that they have come down to us in a practically unchanged, uncorrupted, or unadulterated form from the original authentic copies. It is the unaltered condition of the text.

Is the Bible Genuine?

There are six ways, reaching from the beginning to the present day, to prove the genuineness and integrity of our Bible.

1. The original manuscripts.
2. Ancient versions, 280 B.C. to A.D. 870.
3. Quotations of the Fathers, A.D. 96—600 and onward.
4. Manuscript copies, 350 B.C. to A.D. 1450.
5. Printed copies of the original texts, A.D. 1477 until today.
6. Modern versions, A.D. 1380 until today.

Additional proofs of the genuineness of the Scriptures include: 1. The quotations or allusions to the Scriptures by the heretics and enemies of Christianity, which help confirm the time, authorship and facts of the various books of the Bible. 2. The Targums (a paraphrase) of the Old Testament.[17] 3. The Talmud and Midrashim of the Old Testament. 4. The quotations from and references to the Old Testament by Jesus and the New Testament writers.

Original Manuscripts

A manuscript is a document written by hand, as opposed to a printed copy. An original manuscript is the one first in existence, the one which came from the hand of the author, an "autograph."

No original manuscript of any book of the Bible now exists, as far as is known; they are all lost. It is not known just how they became lost, but several causes may be suggested, such as decay and other natural causes, the wear and tear of the fragile papyrus, destruction by enemies, war, and persecution and the burning or burial of worn or soiled manuscripts by friends.

Jewish law required that worn manuscripts were to be burned or buried near the synagogue. Next to the Synagogue on Masada such a manuscript burial ground has been found. Destroying old, unclear manuscripts was so that an old, not clearly readable text would not be copied incorrectly. They were to keep clear, certified, and correct manuscripts so as not to lose even one letter of the revelation.

Why did God not cause the original manuscripts to be preserved? The answer is not known, but ideas have been suggested.

1. Their preservation was not necessary, because there is abundant proof of what was written—copies, versions, quotations, commentaries, harmonies, quotations by enemies, lists, catalogues, etc. What was originally written is not in doubt.

---

17   The Targums were translations or paraphrases of some parts of the Old Testament Scripture into the Aramaic language. The word *targum* means to interpret, explain or translate.

2. They might have been worshipped. People have a tendency to revere old things, like bones, relics, ashes of saints, splinters from the cross, etc. No material Bible objects have been preserved. If the very handwriting of Moses, David, Isaiah or Paul existed, some would be worshipping it and thus detracting from the true worship of God.

Manuscript Copies

A Bible manuscript is a copy written by hand and in the original biblical languages, Hebrew and Greek. There are two kinds of Bible manuscripts: uncial and minuscule.

An uncial Greek manuscript is one written in capital letters, each formed separately. It is sometimes called a "majuscule" (somewhat great) manuscript. These manuscripts are the earlier, extending from the fourth century A.D. or earlier, to the tenth century.

A minuscule manuscript is one written in small letters. The word means rather small. These manuscripts extend from the ninth to the fifteenth century. There is some overlapping of words. A minuscule manuscript is sometimes called a "cursive." While some minuscules are cursives, having the letters joined in a more or less running hand, not all are, and the term is inaccurate. Uncial letters also might be joined.

Manuscript copies are those of the Hebrew and Greek Testaments which are transcribed, or copied, from the original manuscripts, whether immediately or more or less removed. They are the known manuscripts now in existence and being used, to a large extent at least, in determining the text of our Bible. They are the manuscripts which we will discuss in detail in a later chapter.

A codex manuscript is in book or leaf form, rather than a roll.

XVII. AGE, PREPARATION, AND PRESERVATION OF MANUSCRIPTS

With the Old Testament it is not always easy to know the age of existing manuscripts. Some of them are "dated," that is, they contain notes telling who copied them and the date. This information is not always certain, because the means of dating may be uncertain. Today we have a more uniform system of dating, while they did not. It is thought that some inaccurate dating was purposely used. The size and shape of the letters is not very helpful with Hebrew, since the letters are mostly square. This is not to suggest there is no way to determine the ages of manuscripts.

With New Testament manuscripts it is somewhat easier. Some manuscripts have a known and recorded history or tradition. Other things are helpful: the size and form of the letters, punctuation, divisions, etc., can be considered. These things have helped competent scholars to be pretty good at setting the actual dates. Here are some of the many tests they use:

1. The means of dating is helped by the material on which it is written and in this order: a) Skins, large and heavy; b) Papyrus rolls; c) Papyrus codices, (book or leaf form) as we have learned from modern discoveries; d) Vellum, thin and fine; e) Parchment, thicker and coarser, somewhat stained; f) Paper made from hemp or flax; g) Paper made from linen rags; h) Sometimes redressed parchment, called palimpsest, meaning it was erased and something else was written over it. Generally speaking skins were probably used for the Old Testament; papyrus rolls for the original Septuagint, made in Egypt, and for writing until the first century A.D.; papyrus codices were used from the second to the fourth centuries; vellum and parchment from the fourth to the eighth centuries, flax from the eighth or ninth to

the twelfth or thirteenth centuries; and paper from linen rags from the fourteenth century. Vellum continued with paper until about the fifteenth century, when it was entirely displaced.

2. The size and form of the letters help to determine the age of the manuscript. In the Greek the uncials, all capitals, were used before the tenth century and minuscules thereafter. The height, shape, slanting, and shading of the letters are also helpful in determining age.

3. Punctuation. At first the words were written without spaces between them. Then a space came to indicate a pause. Then came spaces between words and a dot to indicate a pause. Then came in succession: commas, colons, interrogation points, and systematic punctuation. Accents and breathing marks were introduced in about the seventh to eighth centuries and were perfected gradually with the use of the minuscule text.

4. Text divisions came as early as the fourth century when the Gospels were divided into long and short sections. In 458 the Epistles of Paul were divided into sections for public reading. In 590 the Acts and General Epistles were divided. In the seventh century lectionaries were made. All of this helps us date the age of biblical manuscripts.

5. Other things are helpful, such as the use of capital letters, flourished letters, ornamentation, spelling, the color and kind of ink, and the color of the writing material or parchment. Various forms were popular in different areas of the world helping to know the place of origin of the manuscript.

Preparation of the Manuscripts

With the Old Testament there were two kinds of manuscripts: 1) Synagogue rolls, or sacred copies, and 2) Private, or common copies. The Synagogue rolls were read in the public services. They contained the Pentateuch on one roll, the corresponding sections from the Prophets on another roll and the Megilloth, or "five rolls," each on a roll by itself. The Megilloth consisted of the Song of Solomon, Ruth, Lamentations, Ecclesiastes and Esther. These manuscripts were made extremely carefully. The Talmud tells of the rules to be followed:

1. The parchment must be made from the skin of clean animals and be prepared by a Jew only, and the skins must be fastened together by strings made from clean animals.

2. Each column must have no less than 48 or more than 60 lines. The entire copy must be first lined, and if three words were written in it without the line, the copy was worthless

3. The ink must be of no other color than black and it must be prepared according to a special recipe.

4. No word, nor letter, could be written from memory; the scribe must have an authentic copy before him and he must read and pronounce aloud each word before writing it.

5. He must reverently wipe his pen each time before writing the word for "God" and he must wash his whole body before writing the word "Jehovah," lest the holy name be contaminated.

6. Strict rules were given concerning the forms of the

letters, spaces between letters, words and sections, the use of the pen, and the color of the parchment.

7. If a scroll needed to be revised, it must be done within 30 days after the work was finished, otherwise it was worthless. One mistake on a sheet condemned the sheet; if three mistakes were found on any page, the entire manuscript was condemned.

8. Every word and every letter was counted and if a letter were omitted, an extra letter inserted, or if one letter touched another, the manuscript was condemned and destroyed at once.

Some of these rules may appear extreme and absurd, but they show how important the scribes knew the sacred text to be. This helps us to understand how the Scriptures could have been copied for so many years without error.

This gives us a better understanding of why one group was often referred to as "scribes," since they played such an important role and had to be highly qualified to be trusted with the copying of Scripture.

Private copies were not subject to such strict rules and vary in size, form, material, color of ink, etc. Yet the private rolls were prepared with great care and were often beautifully adorned with large initial letters to begin a section. Sometimes they were scrolls, but often they were in codex or page form. A few of these private copies contain the entire Old Testament

The papyrus sheets, upon which some of the New Testament possibly was originally written, were tender; hence, the original manuscripts doubtless soon perished. During the first three centuries, copies were carefully prepared and guarded. There were at least a dozen times of severe persecution under at least ten different Roman Emperors. Probably the worst was under Emperor Diocletian, who ordered all the Christian Scriptures to be destroyed. During this period many copies were burned. To escape death, a few Christians gave up their copies, but many manuscripts were concealed and preserved and the work of multiplying them continued. New churches were being rapidly formed in various parts of the Empire and the demands for the Scriptures were increasing. Papyrus was giving way to vellum.

After Constantine accepted Christianity in A.D. 312, he ordered 50 vellum copies to be made for the churches of Constantinople, one or two of which may have survived until today. More will be said about that later. Other cities of the Empire must have wanted many more. Under government protection, copies could be safely and carefully made, and they were.

After Monasticism arose, the monks became the leading scribes and copied with similar precision as did the previous scribes. With the invention of the printing press came a great wave of biblical manuscripts copies as well as versions of the Bible. We have such an abundance of manuscripts and printed copies over the centuries, there can be no doubt as to the accuracy of our Old and New Testaments.

Preservation of the Manuscripts

Both Old and New Testaments were carefully preserved. The Hebrews considered their Scriptures the very words of God, as did the Christians.

With the Old Testament, it is commonly believed that Ezra and The Great Synagogue gathered into one the 33 Hebrew books (39 Christian books) of the Old Testament. The difference in number only means that the Hebrews put some books together that the Christians separated; they are the same books and material. It is believed that there was a "master" copy kept and used to accurately maintain the Scriptures.

Moses received the Law from God, handed it down to Joshua and the High Priests, to the prophets and finally to the Great Synagogue. Josephus, about A.D. 95, says the books were "justly believed to be divine," and no one would be bold enough to try to add anything to them or try to take anything from them. These same attitudes remained during the Talmudic and Masoretic times and until today.

The New Testament was being bound together as one volume from the fourth century onward. The number of Greek manuscripts continued to grow and there are more than 5,000 that are fairly widely known. In recent years the author has discovered that many more exist in old monasteries and libraries, particularly in Greece. More will certainly be found in coming years.

Variant Readings of New Testament Manuscripts

It is true that there are thousands of variant readings among the more than 5,000 Greek New Testament manuscript copies. Some writers have exaggerated this number with a goal of discrediting the accuracy of our Greek text today. Although the author has not compared many of these copies with our United Bible Societies' text, he has studied one of the oldest manuscripts of the Gospel of John, P66, or the Bodmer II text. It was loaned to the Vatican Library and on display there. The author saw it and purchased a photocopy. This photocopy was carefully compared and translated into English. The most significant variation was that the account of the woman caught in the act of adultery, John 7:53—8:11, is not found. Another frequent variant reading is that the word for God, *theos*, is abbreviated to "*ts*" but leaves no doubt as to what is meant in the context. The conclusion was that there is no real cause to doubt what was written due to variant readings.

As Dr. John Trever said after he examined the Dead Sea Scroll copy of Isaiah, the variant readings were so minute as to be of interest only to scholars and did not affect the meaning. This very old Gospel of John (A.D. 200) confirms the accuracy of the Greek text we use today.

There is considerable discussion about the Majority Text and Minority Text of the Greek Text, sometimes called the Eastern or Western Text (the Eastern Text coming from

Alexandria, Egypt and the Western Text from Rome or Constantinople). What can be learned is that there were separate streams of copying the text and the variant readings help us know which stream they are from.

There are hundreds of thousands of variant readings, but since they follow a pattern, a variant reading could in reality be only one, since it appears in all of the manuscripts from the stream of the text it represents. When the number of Greek manuscripts is more than 5,000, one variant reading between each would make 5,000, and 100 variant readings would amount to 500,000. When it is realized that many counted variant readings are similar and when the nature of the variant readings is considered, it leaves only a few New Testament passages in question. When one passage is questioned and another passage that teaches the same or a similar teaching is not questioned, we are left with no doubt as to what was originally written. The actual teachings brought into question by a textual problem, result in no New Testament teachings left in doubt.

Additional manuscripts continue to be found, catalogued and studied. The text continues to be refined. Although some still insist on the Nestle Greek Text, while others the United Bible Societies' Greek Text, looking at the translations that come from these two sources indicate that scholars are not in doubt about the actual text of our New Testament. A comparison of how the different translators have done their work will prove this point. This comparison chart is found on page 133.

XVIII. OLD TESTAMENT MANUSCRIPT COPIES

As late as 1956, known manuscripts of the Old Testament were neither plentiful nor old. More than 1,300 years separated when the last Old Testament books were written and when we had copies of them. The earliest dated Old Testament manuscript was A.D. 916, while with the New Testament only about 150-200 years existed between the writing and when we have manuscripts of them; the Chester Beatty manuscripts are dated around A.D. 135−250. The Bodmer II text of the Gospel of John is dated A.D. 200. There was less than 250 years between the writing of the New Testament books and when we had full copies of them all grouped into one codex book. Before 1956 we had manuscripts of the New Testament which were about 700 years older than those we had of the Old Testament. This is no longer so, as will be explained shortly.

Why was there such a shortage of manuscripts?

1. A primary cause of the loss of Old Testament manuscripts was the apostasy and persecutions under Kings Ahaz, Manasseh, and Amon; another cause was the captures of Jerusalem by Nebuchadnezzar (606−56 B.C.) and by Antiochus Epiphanies about 170-165 B.C. (who destroyed the biblical scrolls found in the Temple in Jerusalem); scrolls were likely lost during the Maccabean persecutions (170−165 B.C.), and by Titus who captured Jerusalem and destroyed the Temple in A.D. 70; scrolls were likely lost during the revolt under Bar Cochba A.D. 132−135; New Testament manuscripts were lost due to efforts to wipe out Christianity under the persecutions of the Roman Emperors, especially Diocletian, wars and many kinds of disasters caused the destruction of other manuscripts. Especially harmful were times when men like Diocletian made it their aim to wipe out the Hebrew and Christian faiths and this resulted in widespread destruction of all but a few manuscripts.

2. A second cause was the jealous tenacity with which the Jews clung to and treasured their Scriptures, so that when a copy became worn out, mutilated, useless, or condemned because of some slight error in copying, it would be reverently buried, stored

with manuscripts no longer considered useful, or burned. This was so that an old, not clearly readable manuscript might not be preferred to a later one and allow errors into the text.

3. It is believed by some that after the Masorites (about A.D. 600–700) standardized the Hebrew text, they destroyed all that were considered inaccurate.

Before 1956 there were about 1,700 Old Testament manuscript copies and more have been discovered since. This leads us to probably the greatest manuscript discovery of all time, The Dead Sea Scrolls.

The Dead Sea Scrolls[18]

From 1946-1956, the Dead Sea Scrolls were discovered. They received their name from having been found near the Dead Sea. There were 972 manuscripts and among them many copies of Old Testament books, originally it was thought there were 330 Old Testament books, but eventually this number grew to 380 Old Testament books, including all but the Book of Esther. There were multiple copies of Genesis, Exodus, Deuteronomy, Psalms, and so on. Found were 38 of our 39 Old Testament books. These manuscripts are dated from 225 B.C. to A.D. 50. One Dead Sea Scroll is thought to be 368 B.C. Many of the Old Testament biblical manuscripts date well before the birth of Christ.

Most of the Dead Sea Scrolls were found near Khirbet Qumran in twelve caves. The author has visited several of these

18   Suggested reading: 1. *The Dead Sea Scrolls*, LaSor, William Sanford, Moody Press, Chicago. 1956. 2. *The Message of the Scrolls*, Yigael Yadia, A Touchstone Book, Simon and Schuster, New York, New York. 1957. 3. *The Mystery of the Dead Sea Scrolls*. Allegro, John, Gramercy Publishing Co., New York, New York. 1956. 4. Read online about The Dead Sea Scrolls. There are volumes of material. 5. Trever, John C., three books. See Bibliography.

caves and the ruins of Qumran many times. Qumran is near the northwest edge of the Dead Sea, not far from Jericho.

The area is one of the most arid places on earth and perfect for the preservation of ancient manuscripts. When the Essenes saw the invasion of the Roman Generals Titus and Vespasian, about A.D. 70, they took it upon themselves to preserve their most treasured possessions—their library with its old books. Without a doubt they intended to reclaim them, but they may have been among the casualties at Masada or Gamla, fortresses which were totally wiped out by the Romans.

The author has often thought that it was in the great plan of God to provide a latter day witness to people separated from the Old Testament events by hundreds of years of what really happened and was written and thereby confirm the biblical text. Many of these scrolls predate the birth of Christ. This is especially significant with books such as Daniel and Isaiah, which had so often been attacked due to their clear prophecies of Christ. They have now been shown to be, in fact, prophecies. The Isaiah Scroll is dated 225 B.C. We now know for certain that Daniel and Isaiah's prophecies were precisely that—prophecies.

1.   How the Scrolls Were Discovered

The initial discovery was made in 1946–1947 by Bedouin shepherd Muhammed Edh-Dhib, his cousin Juum'a Muhammed, and Khalil Musa. The shepherds discovered them housed in a cave at what is now known as the Qumran site. Dr. John C. Trever reconstructed the story of the scrolls from several interviews with the Bedouin Edh-Dhib's cousin.

The story is told about how the scrolls were found. The shepherd boy was looking for a lost sheep and, as boys are known to do, was throwing rocks and he heard a jar break. The scrolls had been sealed in large pottery jars. Trying to find what had broken, he found the main scroll cave and retrieved several manuscripts, among which were the Isaiah Scroll, Habakkuk Commentary, and the Community Rule scroll. These he took back to his camp where he showed them to his family. They kept them at their tent hanging on a tent pole. Contrary to a popular rumor, none of them were destroyed but they did show them to family and friends.

2.   Metropolitan Samuel Buys Scrolls

Eventually the family tried to sell them to a Bethlehem dealer named Ibrahim 'Ijha, who said they were worthless. Later they found a Syrian Christian named Metropolitan Samuel, who bought them for $29 U.S.

Not too long after, in 1972, I visited with Metropolitan Samuel in his office and he described the purchase and his loaning the Isaiah scroll to Dr. Trever, who took it back to the United States and discovered how old and valuable it was. I saw the original Isaiah scroll before it was replaced by a repro-duction, which is what is now on display at the Shrine of the Book museum. Metropolitan Samuel still had several scroll jars and fragments in his possession. We talked at length about the whole process of buying the scrolls and how the discovery of their great antiquity and value took place.

3.   Additional Discoveries Made

When the value and antiquity of the manuscripts was learned, this spurred on many Bedouins to search for more of them and using more systematic efforts led to the discovery of additional scrolls. From 1948-1956 additional manuscripts were found in caves near Qumran and as far away as Masada, where some were found buried near the Synagogue, in a manuscript burial gravesite.

It is not the purpose of this book to elaborate on the details of the Dead Sea Scrolls, which can easily be found by searching the subject of Dead Sea Scrolls on line. The matter under dis-cussion is the importance of the Dead Sea Scrolls to the subject of our Bible's accuracy.

4. Origin of the Scrolls

A positive answer as to the origin of the scrolls cannot be given and the debate continues. One suggestion is that they have an early Christian origin traced to James the Just and Paul the Apostle. This seems to be wishful thinking on the part of some and leaves many questions unanswered.

There is the Jerusalem theory that has somewhat more plausibility. It is suggested that with the impending destruction of Jerusalem by the Romans, wise Rabbis took their most precious scrolls and put them in a safe place. This would explain the variety of styles of writing and varieties of thought. It may be true that some of the manuscripts did come from Jerusalem, which seems plausible.

But the most logical explanation is that most came from the library of the Essenes at Qumran. The Essenes were a monastic community who clearly saw the difference between light and darkness and who saw much of what was happening in Judah and Jerusalem as being of the darkness. They had drawn aside to the wilderness to preserve righteousness and to study the Holy Scriptures. In the Qumran ruins there were scriptoriums, where they copied and worked with the manuscripts, places to make and fire the scroll jars, places near the scriptorium for the ritual baths required in copying Scripture, and places for storage of water and food.

The Essenes lived near the oasis of Jericho where a plentiful supply of food was to be had. The weather would be terribly hot in summer months and they had swimming pools to keep cool. Even on very hot days, with plenty to drink, shade, and a breeze, the weather is tolerable. People have lived nearby in Jericho for millennia. The Essenes spent their time studying and copying Scriptures. Their most valuable possessions were their books, and they preserved nearly 1,000 of them. The most valuable of this number were the 330–380 Old Testament scrolls, containing all but one Old Testament book, Esther.

There may have been Christians among the Essenes, and some have suggested that even John the Baptist was of their number. The Olivet Discourse (Matthew 24) was understood by Christians to indicate a terrible time of trouble that was coming soon, advising Christians to depart from Jerusalem when they saw the invasion (what Jesus called "the abomination of desolation"), the coming of the Roman generals Titus and Vespasian.

Nevertheless, the Essenes did see that the Jews were doomed and they found a way to preserve their library, hiding it in multiple caves and sealing it in. Most manuscripts were within sight of their community. Along the western side of the Dead Sea there are thousands of caves, making discovery nearly impossible, especially since they covered over the entrances to the caves.

These are the three main theories, but there are several others that do not seem worthy of consideration. It is most likely that the Qumran community made the proper-sized jars that fit the manuscripts and sealed them inside, providing for us today a confirmation of our Old Testament text.

Another valuable consideration is that the climate there is very conducive to preservation of the manuscripts. It is one of the driest spots on earth, with infrequent rain storms, sometimes not coming for months or even years. The arid climate, and the scrolls being sealed in fired pottery jars, left the scrolls wonderfully preserved over the nearly two thousand years. Some have conjectured that this was God's way of giving us additional proof of our Scriptures to further confirm His Word.

5.   Date of the Dead Sea Scrolls

The parchment of the Dead Sea Scrolls were carbon dated and most of the biblical texts showed dates from the first two centuries B.C. Analysis of handwriting is called paleography and by this means suggested a date of 225 B.C. to A.D. 50. A third method of dating used was radiocarbon, and this dating method showed dates from 385 B.C. to A.D. 82. There is wide agreement that many of the biblical manuscripts date well before the birth of Christ. The Isaiah manuscript remains dated at 225 B.C.

Other Hebrew Texts and Conclusions

Before the Dead Sea Scrolls, our oldest Old Testament manuscript was the *Leningrad Codex*, dated A.D. 919, which is in the Royal Library at Leningrad, Russia. It is written on vellum, with three columns of twenty-one lines each to the page. It has vowel points and accents above the line. This manuscript is not complete.

Our next oldest manuscript has the entire Old Testament. It is dated 1008 and is also in the Royal Library at Leningrad. This means that the Dead Sea Scrolls take us back more than 1,200 years for all but the book of Esther.

There is a copy of the Pentateuch called *Oriental 4445*, in the British Museum in London, which is believed to date about A.D. 820–850. This date is questioned by some and this manuscript covers only the first five books of our Bible.

There are some very old papyrus fragments that are dated A.D. 150., and if this date is true they are the oldest we had before the Dead Sea Scrolls.

From this it is apparent how valuable the Dead Sea Scrolls are in proving the accuracy of our Old Testament. Dr. John C. Trever said, after he carefully examined the Isaiah scroll, that he was disappointed, because over a period of over 1,000 years, the variant readings were so few and of such insignificance as to be of interest only to scholars and did not affect the meaning. The words of Jesus have been proven true. "Not one small stroke or letter will pass from the Law until all things are accomplished" (Matthew 5:18).

The Higher Critical scholars are in reality modern false prophets who like to question the integrity of our biblical Hebrew text, they have been proven wrong in their attacks on biblical accuracy.[19]

Many comments come from the author's personal observation in talking with the prime person, Metropolitan Samuel, and visiting the sites and seeing the manuscripts first hand. The bibliography of this section can be very extensive, as one can learn looking at the Wikipedia web site.

Old Testament Versions and Commentaries

1. The Samaritan Pentateuch is sometimes called the Samaritan Torah. It is a separate stream of the Old Testament's first five books. It is written in the Samaritan alphabet and was used by them as their entire Bible.

   When Solomon died, his son Rehoboam became king over all Israel. Instead of listening to the old and wise counselors of his father, David, he took the advice of his younger friends and raised taxes and made more strict laws. The result was that under Jeroboam ten tribes broke away from Israel and made their new capital in Samaria. They set up a place of worship in Samaria, in place of the Temple in Jerusalem, not wanting their people going there and possibly wanting to reunite the nation. This new place of worship made it possible to really separate from Judah. They also had their own scriptures, the Pentateuch, now called the Samaritan Pentateuch.

   This separate stream of Scripture has survived until today. It is slightly different in some respects from the Masoretic text or the Greek Septuagint. The nearly six thousand variations are mostly spelling of words or grammatical constructions, but the more serious differences are efforts to endorse their worship at Mount

---

19   For additional information on this subject, see Wikipedia, Dead Sea Scrolls.

Gerizim rather than Jerusalem.

The Samaritan text has been the source of serious debate as far back as the seventeenth century. But today, after the Dead Sea Scroll discoveries, we have come to realize that the Samaritan Pentateuch provides us another authentic ancient textual tradition despite that there are some variant readings introduced by the Samaritans.

As to the date of the Samaritan Pentateuch, the copies we have today probably come from about 432 B.C. when Manasseh, the son-in-law of Sanballat, founded a community in Samaria. You can read about this in Nehemiah 13:28 and also in Josephus, *Antiquities XI.7.2:8.2*. All of this is to say that the date of origin is uncertain and may be older than some presently believe. For those who desire to know more about this subject, you can find it under "Samaritan Pentateuch," from Wikipedia on your computer.

The conclusion to the matter is that the Samaritan text gives us another way of establishing what was in the first five books of our Old Testament. It is in substantial agreement with our ancient Hebrew texts, the Leningrad texts and the Dead Sea Scrolls. In doctrinal matters there is substantial agreement.

2. The Targums were translations or paraphrases of some parts of the Old Testament Scripture into the Aramaic language. The word *targum* means to interpret, explain or translate. After the Jews returned from Babylonian captivity, Hebrew nearly ceased to exist as their popular language. It became necessary, in the public reading of the Scriptures, for the reader, or his assistant, to give a paraphrase, or interpretation, of the same in the

Aramaic language, which was in use. This custom was in use from Ezra's time forward about 444 B.C., as is seen in Nehemiah 8:8, R.V. margin.

There are Targums of the entire Old Testament except for Daniel, Ezra and Nehemiah, of which some portions were already written in Aramaic. There are three main Targums, one of the Pentateuch, another of the prophets and the third of the Hagiographa, or Holy Writings.[20]

Here again, we have strong evidence of what was in our Old Testament Scriptures, giving additional proof of what was written by Moses and the prophets. It is clear why Lower Critics, those who believe the Bible to be the Word of God, are so sure of what the biblical text actually says.

3. The Talmud and Midrash are neither translations nor paraphrases, but still are important Jewish biblical literature and are conveniently treated in connection with the Targums, as contemporaneous literature.

What exactly are they? They contain the civil and religious laws not found in the Pentateuch, with commentaries upon and illustrations of these laws. The words "Talmud or Midrash" come from a root meaning "teaching or doctrine." The Talmud represents the learning, teaching, opinions, and decisions of the Jewish teachers for about 800 years, 300 B.C. to A.D. 500. They give the Jewish interpretation of the Law. It is the source of Jewish law.

There are two parts to the Talmud: the Mishna,

---

20   For additional information on this subject, see H.S. Miller, *General Biblical Introduction,* pages 215-217.

which was the oral or spoken law; and the Gemara, the commentaries and illustrations. The Gemara is the Talmud proper, but both terms apply to the Talmud.

This gives us another way to find out what was written in the Pentateuch or first five books of the Bible, as well as other Old Testament books.

4. A fourth way that the Old Testament accuracy can be established is the *Septuagint* version or translation of the Old Testament. When Alexander the Great conquered the world in the fourth century B.C. (around 330 B.C.), Greek became the language of the world, similar to what English is to the world today. It was the language of commerce and civilization.

Alexander founded the great city of Alexandria in Egypt, and it became a literary center of the world, boasting the greatest library, museum, and college, which were some of the finest in the world. Alexander was friendly to the Jews because of their intelligence and industry and many of them immigrated to Alexandria.

Not only was there a large community of Jews in Alexandria but others spread throughout the Greek Empire. Greek became the common language, creating a need for the Old Testament in Greek, thus the *Septuagint* version.

The name *Septuagint* comes from a Latin word that means seventy. This name comes from the ancient tradition of how the Septuagint came into existence. A letter, supposedly written by Aristeas, who claimed to be a high official in the court of Philadelphus, to his brother Philocrates says, "Demetrius Phalarius, librarian of the royal library at Alexandria, suggested to the king the importance of having in the library a Greek translation of the Hebrew Law. The king was pleased with the idea, released certain Jews who were in bondage in Egypt in order to gain favor at Jerusalem, and sent an embassy of which Aristeas was one, with costly gifts and a letter to the high priest Eliazar at Jerusalem, asking him to send to Alexandria a copy of the Law and six men from each of the twelve tribes of Israel who were competent to translate it. The request was granted and seventy-two men were sent, with a copy of the Law written in gold. A seven-day banquet was given, at which time the king tested them with difficult questions and was astonished by their wise answers. Three days later they were taken to a conveniently furnished home on the quiet island of Pharos and the work of translation was begun. The seventy-two worked together, compared notes, and finished their work in seventy-two days. The finished work was read to an assembly of Jews, who gave to it their enthusiastic approval and pronounced a curse upon any one who should ever make any change in that which was so sacredly and accurately done. They asked that a copy be given to their leaders. Next it was read to the king, who was delighted, and he gave orders that the books be preserved with great care. The translators were sent back to Palestine laden with presents for themselves and for the high priest."[21] This narrative may have some truth in it, but is not consistent with the fact that the translation was done over many years as earlier stated.

This tradition was repeated by others: Aristobulus, Philo, and Josephus. Some of the Church Fathers accepted the theory without question. Others said the translators worked independently of each other in sev-

21   *Ibid*, p 221

enty-two cells and when they compared their work they were exactly alike. Jerome was the first to question and ridicule these later inventions. As with most folklore, there is likely a thread of truth to this fictitious account.

It was most likely the work of Alexandrian Jews, rather than Palestinian Jews. First, it shows an imperfect knowledge of Hebrew; second, it contains words and phrases which are peculiar to the Greek used in Alexandria; third it contains a liberal amount of Egyptian words; fourth, it contains errors regarding names of places in Palestine. The translation in many places is a free one which often departs from the Hebrew text which the Jews held so literally. A good Palestinian Jew would have abhorred the very thought of translating their Holy Scripture into another language.

What we can glean from all of this are these points. The version was made in Alexandria, Egypt. It was done by Alexandrian Jews. It was begun about 280 B.C. The Hebrew Law, in an authorized copy, was brought from Jerusalem. When completed, an authorized copy was placed in the Royal Library at Alexandria, although its purpose was to provide it for the Jews in Egypt. It was almost certainly the work of several different Jewish scholars. It is probably safer to say that it was begun about 280 B.C. and completed by 180 B.C.[22]

The *Septuagint* version provides for us additional proof of our Old Testament Scriptures. It also helps us know what was then accepted as Scripture, to know that some sacred books, questioned by the higher critics and unbelievers, were in existence long before they believe they were. It helps us know that the marvelous

---

22   For additional information, see H.S. Miller, *General Biblical Introduction*, pp 222–223.

prophecies of Isaiah, Daniel, and other prophets were really prophecies, not written after the fact, which some unbelievers have claimed.

Modern technology has helped in the comparing and examining of all of the different evidences that support the biblical text we have today. What Jesus said has been again affirmed: "For truly I say to you, until heaven and earth pass away, not the smallest letter or stroke shall pass away from the Law, until all is accomplished" (Matthew 5:18). The Old Testament was always worthy of our trust, but today we have conclusive proof why.

What Happened to the Original Old Testament Manuscripts?

The practice of Israel and the scribes was to preserve correct copies and when old manuscripts became worn or unclear they were to burn or bury them. There is some evidence as to what happened to old and very valuable Old Testament manuscripts. It is plausible that the original copies of the Prophets would have been highly valued and thus preserved.

When the Jews returned from Babylon, they brought with them the sacred writings. These must have been treasured by them. A possible explanation of what happened to these valuable old Scriptures can be found in I Maccabees 1:55–58, when Antiochus Epiphanes conquered Jerusalem, burned the city, and desecrated the Temple. "And when they had rent in pieces the books of the law which they found, they burnt them with fire. And whenever anyone was found with any the book of the testament, or if any consented to the scriptures, the king's commandment was that they should put them to death. Thus they did by their authority unto the Israelites every month, to as many as were found in the cities."

It was quite possible that at that time the original copies of

Ezra, Nehemiah, and the later prophets were still in existence. Copies that survived were likely spirited away by the priests and scribes that survived, but the most sacred and valuable were destroyed.

Later a similar thing happened to New Testament Manuscripts in the time of Emperor Diocletian, who made a concerted effort to destroy all of the Christian Scriptures.

XIX. NEW TESTAMENT MANUSCRIPT COPIES

Our next consideration is an examination of what sort of evidence there is for the accuracy of our New Testament Scriptures. Since the New Testament manuscripts are much younger than the Old Testament manuscripts, it is understandable that there are many more copies available. In fact, the number today is something over 5,000. Others are being found from time to time and this number will continue to increase.

The manuscripts can be divided into four categories: uncial, minuscule, papyrus fragments, and lectionaries. The uncial manuscripts have capital letters, while the minuscule is written in small letters. The papyrus manuscripts are written on a type of paper made from a reed that grows along the Nile River in Egypt. This thick reed is cut into strips that are laid crisscross and the natural gluey paste that is secreted when the reed is cut makes a strong bond and durable paper. The product is sanded and turns into a very durable paper, due to the fibers in the papyrus plant. This paper was widely used for many years and is today again being produced, mainly for works of art. These old New Testament manuscripts, written on papyrus are called "P" manuscripts. The lectionaries were sections of Scripture, made into manuscripts and read in church gatherings. Although they were not complete copies, they do allow us to check various sections of Scripture against other manuscripts we have.

Uncial Manuscripts

In the early part of the fourth century (A.D. 313) there came a change in matters pertaining to the Bible and the Church. The great persecutions under the Roman Emperors, Nero (64–69), Domitian (95, 96) Aurelius (163–177), Severus (202–211), Decius (250), Valerian (258), Diocletian and his successors (303–311), had hindered the circulation of the sacred books. Diocletian especially had ordered churches demolished and all copies of the Scriptures destroyed.

The next emperor, Constantine (A.D. 313–337), publicly acknowledged himself a convert to Christianity, stopped all persecution, made Christianity the religion of the Empire, became a friend of the bishops and a student of the Scriptures, and even composed and delivered religious discourses. He ordered churches rebuilt and copies of the Scriptures multiplied. He ordered that fifty copies of the Bible be produced. He moved the capital from Rome to Constantinople (330), and aimed to make this a Christian city. He built the first "St. Sophia" church in Constantinople, which later burned, was rebuilt, and then burned again. The one that stands today was built by Emperor Justinian (A.D. 537). Some believe that two copies of Constantine's fifty Greek Bibles have survived until today, the *Vaticanus* and *Sinaiticus*, which we will discuss a bit later. He ordered Bishop Eusebius to prepare these Bibles for public use in the churches.

Another important change in New Testament manuscripts came about at this time. The use of vellum, (leather) in place of papyrus as the writing material and the use of codex (book) form in place of the roll form made it possible to bring together the writings in one volume. The rise of controversies in the church made it necessary to know what was and was not Scripture, requiring the proliferation of Bibles.

The two great libraries of the time were in Alexandria, Egypt, and Pergamum in Asia Minor, which today is Turkey. There was rivalry between the two cities to have the largest library in the world. Alexandria, in Egypt, was able to discontinue shipping papyrus to Pergamum, which necessitated another type of writing material, and vellum came to the forefront for important documents.

Number of Uncial Manuscripts

Today there are at least 322 known uncial manuscripts. About 300 uncial manuscripts have been used in making the American Bible Society's Greek New Testament. Of these only one, the Sinaitic, now contains the entire New Testament. The others, which have suffered some mutilation, for certain, originally contained all of it and still contain most of it. The great age of these manuscripts has resulted in some pages being lost, and wear to some still existing pages. Having personally seen these manuscripts, they are clear and quite readable.

The *Sinaiticus*, (A.D. 325) is listed by the Hebrew letter for "A," while the rest are listed with the English letters of the alphabet. These are the (A) Alexandrian (A.D. 440); (B) The *Vaticanus* (A.D. 325); (C) Ephraem (A.D. 445), which is Palimpsest Rescriptus; and many later ones. Of the 300, 57 contain a substantial part of the New Testament, of which nine have the Gospels complete, seven the Acts, nine the General Epistles, seven the Pauline Epistles, and four have the Revelation. The rest are fragmentary and some are very small.

Eight of the Oldest Manuscripts

1. The Sinaitic: *Codex Sinaiticus*
    The Hebrew letter Aleph is the code used to identify it. It is dated around 325–340 and contains the Old Testament in the Septuagint translation, including the Apocrypha and the entire New Testament and adds the Epistle of Barnabas and most of the Shepherd of Hermas. Its language is Greek and it is located in the British Museum in London, England. It is owned by the

British Government. It omits about one half of the Old Testament and the Apocrypha, also Mark 16:9−20 and John 7:53—8:11, the passage that tells of the woman caught in the act of adultery.

The manuscript contains 346½ leaves, 199 of the Old Testament and 147½ of the New. This, with the 43 leaves at Leipsic, makes a total of 389½ leaves. The pages are 13½ by 14 7/8 inches. Each page contains four columns about 2½ inches wide, except in the poetical books of the Old Testament, where there are two wider columns to the page. Each column has 48 lines. The writing is large, clear, and good. The material is excellent vellum, made from the finest skins of the antelope.

This manuscript, although considered one of the earliest known, was discovered quite recently. It was found in the Monastery of St. Catherine at Mt. Sinai, where the name "Sinaitic" came from. In 1844 Dr. Constantin Tischendorf, a German biblical professor and scholar, who had given his life to the search and study of ancient manuscripts, especially biblical manuscripts, was visiting this convent. He saw in the hall a basket filled with parchment, waiting to be used to light the monastery fires. He was told that already two full baskets had been burned. Such was the ignorance of these monks. He found in the basket 43 leaves of vellum containing a portion of the Septuagint translation of the Old Testament. Since they were considered valueless, he was given them.

During his first and second visits to the monastery he found almost nothing. Then on his third visit in 1859, fifteen years later he was more successful. This time under the commission of the Czar of Russia, Alexander II, he was about to leave without any new discovery, when in conversation with the steward concerning the Septuagint, the latter remarked that he also had a copy of the Septuagint. Tischendorf followed the steward into his room, where he showed him a bundle wrapped in a red cloth. Soon there lay before their eyes, not only the Old Testament, but also the New Testament, complete along with some other writings. He was permitted to examine the manuscript in his room that night. He spent all night in copying. Later he was able to secure a temporary loan; then in the same year, 1859, it was given as a "conditional gift" to the Czar of all the Russians, for the purpose of publication. Tischendorf published it. In 1933 it was sold to the British Museum for L100,000 (in today's value, over $1,000,000). It is one of the greatest book purchases of all time.

The author felt a great sense of history and appreciation at being able to view this priceless old copy of our Bible. It just may have been one of the fifty Bibles Emperor Constantine had prepared for the church of Constantinople. While at the Monastery of St. Catherine, we were permitted to enter the library and on display there are the letters between Dr. Tischendorf and the monastery. Many other copies of the Greek New Testament reside there.

This monastery was built by Emperor Justinian in A.D. 527. It is probable that this manuscript was given to the monastery by Justinian.

2. The Vatican: *Codex Vaticanus*

The English letter B is used to identify this fourth century manuscript, which has been dated A.D. 325−350, but possibly closer to 325. It contains the Old Testament, *Septuagint*, along with the Apocrypha, except for the books of Maccabees and the Prayer of Manasses; and it contains the New Testament.

The language is Greek and its present location is in the Vatican Library in Rome, Italy. It is owned by the

Catholic Church. It has some missing parts: most significant is that it is missing from Hebrews 9:14 to the end of the New Testament. It has the General Epistles, which are placed after Acts.

It is on vellum and has 759 leaves, 617 of the Old Testament and 142 of the New. The writing is small, clear uncial. A more complete description can easily be found on line today for those who are interested.

Its early history, like the Sinaitic, is uncertain. There are evidences that would suggest Egypt or Caesarea as its source. It probably was made in Egypt, in some connection with the Alexandrian Library, or possibly at the Christian church in Caesarea. It could be that it was written in Egypt and showed up later in Caesarea. It showed up first in later history in the catalog of books in the Vatican Library in 1481, about the time the Vatican Library was founded. At that time there was not much interest in studying old biblical manuscripts. Erasmus, in 1533, knew of its existence, but neither he nor Luther were permitted to study it.

A lot of intrigue surrounds the middle history of it, but in 1957 and 1959 Pope Pius IX had it photographed and published. These two editions were, probably, purposely inaccurate and differing so as to not let the actual text be known for certain. It was not until 1989-90 that finally the Catholic Church made an accurate copy available.

In 1972, while visiting the Vatican, I asked if I might see this manuscript. My guide said, "You are in luck, it is on public display." He took me to it and turned his back while I took pictures of it. He also pointed out that "P 66," the Bodmer II text of John, was on display, which he also let me photo. More will be written about this later.

3. The Alexandrian: *Codex Alexandrinus*

This manuscript is identified by the English letter "A." It contains the Old Testament, Septuagint, with the Apocrypha, and the New Testament. At the end of the New Testament, I–II Clement and the Psalms of Solomon are added.

It has been dated around A.D. 450.

It is written in Greek and is in the British Museum in London, England. It belongs to the British Government. It has a few omissions in both Old and New Testament, but not many.

It has 773 leaves—639 of the Old Testament and 134 of the New Testament. More information on it can be found in *General Biblical Introduction*, by H. S. Miller, page 195.

Its history suggests that although it has been dated in the middle of the fifth century A.D., it is most likely much older. It probably came from Alexandria Egypt, therefore its name. It traveled around from Alexandria, to Constantinople and finally was given to King James I of England. Unfortunately for King James, he died before it reached him and too late to be used in making the first *King James Version*. It was placed in the British Museum, where it resides. It is available by photo-reproduction. While in London I had the chance to look at it and photograph it. This was the first biblical manuscript to be used by scholars.

4. The Ephraem: *Codex Ephraemi Rescriptus*

This manuscript is identified by the English letter "C" and is dated around 450. It also could be earlier, but certainly not later. It is a copy of the Greek Bible, both Old and New Testaments. There are a number of omissions: the greater part of the Old Testament, except for parts of Job, Proverbs, Ecclesiastes, Song of Solomon, and the apocryphal books of Wisdom of Solomon and Ecclesiasticus. In the New Testament, 2

Thessalonians, 2 John and some parts of other books are missing.

The manuscript is a palimpsest, which means rubbed away or erased and another subject written over it. Vellum parchments were scarce and expensive. Often the same parchment was used twice, the first writing being erased and the same sheets used the second time. Due to the ignorance during the Middle Ages, a valuable writing was often covered by something of little value. The Syrian Father Ephraem (299-378), whose writings apparently were considered of more value than the Holy Scriptures, erased the Bible and wrote his sermons over them. This explains the name of the manuscript. During this use by Ephraem, many of the leaves were lost or discarded. There remain 64 leaves of the Old and 145 of the New Testament, for a total of 209.

This manuscript was also probably written in Alexandria and brought to Italy by John Lascaris around 1500, when Greek scholars and manuscripts were being welcomed in the West. It was owned by Pietro Strozzi and later by Catherine de Medici, who wanted it so she could read the sermons of Ephraem. It came to the National Library in Paris, which now owns it. A seventeenth century student saw traces of writing beneath the sermons of Ephraem. Investigation proved this to be true, and underneath was found this very old copy of our Bible. By chemical means the original was restored, and in 1840 Tischendorf more fully restored it. He was the first to read it successfully. I saw this manuscript when it was on display in the British Museum in London.

5. The Beza: *Codex Bezae*

This manuscript is identified by the English letter D. It is often dated around A.D. 550. It contains the Gospels, 3 John 11−15, and Acts of the Apostles. It is written in Greek and Latin. It is in the Library of Cambridge University, Cambridge, England. There are many omissions and some variations from the accepted text.

This manuscript has 406 leaves, each eight by ten inches. The Greek text is on the left page and the Latin on the right page. This manuscript is unique because it is the oldest known manuscript of the New Testament containing two languages. It is often dated in the sixth century, but there are reasons to believe it may have came from the fifth. It is written on a poor quality of vellum.

It is thought to have been written in France or possibly Lyons, but some suggest Italy. It was found in 1562 in the Monastery of St. Irenaeus at Lyons, by Beza, the great French biblical scholar and thus its name. He became an assistant to John Calvin and succeeded him in Geneva. Beza gave it to the University of Cambridge. Most of these manuscripts have been copied and can be purchased.

6. The Claromontanus: *Codex Claromontanus*

This manuscript is identified by the English letter "D2" or "D Paul." It is dated around 550 and contains Paul's Epistles, complete, including Hebrews, and is written in Greek and Latin. It is found in the National Library in Paris, France. My son Steven and I set off to find it while in Paris and rode the rail clear out into the country where it was supposed to be, just to learn it had been moved back to central Paris near where we started. We returned 15 minutes too late to see it. We were within 100 feet of it, but the museum was closed. We left Paris the next morning before the museum opened.

It is called D2 because together with D they cover the greater part of the New Testament in Greek and

Latin. It is from the same period as D, but does have some omissions. The Greek text is more accurate than the Latin.

It is thought to have had its origin in Italy, or possibly Sardinia. It was found in 1562 by Beza in the monastery at Clermont, France. Beza used it during his lifetime, and after his death it came to the National Library in Paris.

7. The Washington: *Codex Washingtoniensis*

This manuscript is identified by the letter "W" and is dated in the fourth or fifth century. It contains the four Gospels and portions of all of the Pauline Epistles from 1 Corinthians onward, including Hebrews. It also contains the Old Testament books of Deuteronomy, Joshua, and Psalms.

Its language is Greek and it is in the Smithsonian Library, in Washington D.C., and is the property of the United States Government. This ancient and important manuscript contains 187 leaves or 374 pages with the page size being 5 5/8 by 8¼ inches. Each page has a single column of 30 lines and is written on good vellum in a small, clear sloping uncial hand. Interestingly, the Gospel of Mark chapter 16 has the long ending with verses 9–20.

This manuscript was purchased in 1906 with three others, from an Egyptian antiquities dealer by the name of Mr. C. L. Freer of Detroit, Michigan. Because of this they are sometimes called the "Freer Manuscripts."

8. The Koridethi Gospels: *Codex Koridethi*

This manuscript is identified by the Greek letter *theta* and dates in the eighth or ninth centuries. It contains the four Gospels and is written in Greek. It is in the Library at Tiflis, capital of Georgia, formerly a part of the Soviet Union. They were discovered at Koridethi

Monastery in the Caucasus region near the east end of the Black Sea. It is a rough uncial, unattractive copy. Although not of great value, it does add additional evidence of what was in our New Testament.

Early Papyrus Manuscripts

Even though the papyrus documents are normally older than the vellum manuscripts, they are being considered next since they are not as complete, nor plentiful. This is not to suggest that they are not tremendously important, because they are.

Papyrus, made of reeds that grow along the Nile River of Egypt, is a very durable paper that was used for important documents during the time of the church founding and for several centuries thereafter. It is again being made and used for art work.

There are now 127 papyrus manuscripts that are used by the United Bible Societies to form the Greek text for our New Testament today. These are identified by "P1, P2, etc." and date from the second century until as late as the eighth century. Daniel Wallace claims six or seven new ones have been discovered from the second century and one from the first. These are of varying quality, but many are as readable as a modern newspaper. Here are a few of those used to help determine the Greek New Testament we use today. Six more papyrus biblical manuscripts have been found and were scheduled to be published in 2013. The author at this writing does not know if this took place.

1. The Bodmer II text of the Gospel of John (P66). It was written about 200 and is nearly complete and clear copy. I have personally seen this manuscript, purchased a photocopy and translated it into English. It was on display at the Vatican Library in Rome, Italy. It is remarkable proof that our Scriptures have not been changed. There are many other early papyrus documents of great value, too numerous to discuss here.

In "P 66" there are some minor variations from our

present Greek texts. It does not have the account of the woman taken in the act of adultery who was brought to Jesus, when Jesus wrote in the sand. It abbreviates the Greek word *theos* to two letters, *theta sigma* (no scholar should doubt the meaning), but demonstrates the accuracy with which our New Testament has been transmitted.

2. The Chester Beatty Papyri were purchased by Mr. Chester Beatty of London, England and were announced to the world November 19, 1931. The collection contains three portions of the New Testament, eight of the Old, and a part of the apocryphal book of Enoch, with a Christian homily. All are on papyrus, in codex form and of an early date—from the second to fifth centuries. (Remember, the second century is from A.D. 100−200.)

   They contain parts of Matthew, Mark, Luke and John, and sections of Acts—30 leaves (60 pages). There are 86 leaves (172 pages) of Paul's Epistles and about one third of the book of Revelation. There are eight Old Testament portions having parts of the books of Law and Daniel. Daniel's portion is taken from the Septuagint.

   These papyri are very important because they extend the time backward in the period between the original manuscripts and our full New Testament Greek copies. These take us back 100−150 years earlier. We have 15 of the New Testament books and nine of the Old Testament, which take us back to as early as the second century. There are five more that take us back to no later than the third century.

   Have many plain and precious truths been removed from Holy Scripture? No. The Bible has been miraculously maintained and preserved.

3. The Rylands Fragments of the Gospel of John. Among

the Rylands Fragments manuscripts was found a most precious fragment of John's Gospel, written in a style suggesting the second century, before A.D. 150. (Deissmann says 138 others 125). It is a mere fragment, giving John 18:31−33 on the front and John 18:37-38 on the back, but it is in codex form and shows how early the codex form for manuscripts was used and that the Gospel was in circulation within less than fifty years of its writing.

Of the 127 papyrus documents used in our United Bible Societies' Greek text, many more are worthy of consideration, but this is the not the purpose of this book. The early and voluminous nature of our Greek manuscripts proves to us that we can trust the Bibles we use today. We have been considering our uncial manuscripts; now let us turn our attention to the minuscule.

Minuscule Manuscripts

The uncial manuscripts extended from the third to tenth centuries. But there are some overlappings of uncial and minuscule copies. As the demand for copies of Scripture increased and books began to multiply and economy in time and space were needed, minuscule writing came into use. The large characters, written separately and slowly, gave way to the smaller, more or less connected letters which could be written more quickly. Beginning in the 8th and 9th century and by the eleventh century the uncial had been replaced almost completely by the minuscule.

The exact number of minuscule manuscripts changes from time to time due to additional manuscript discoveries. It is also difficult to get exact counts of what is in various libraries. My son Dr. Steven Crane and I were at the Monastery of St. Catherine and wished to visit their library, which has many minuscule manuscripts. When I asked to see them I found resistance, saying that it was not possible. I explained that I was the head of a college that taught "clergy" and that the study of biblical manuscripts had been a lifetime endeavor. In addition I was willing to pay up to $1,500 for the right to examine the library. Seeing my interest, the head bishop wrote a letter of permission and one of the Greek Orthodox priests took us up the several flights of steps to the library.

We entered through a door that resembled something from a school of the 1940s or 1950s. The room was a couple of hundred feet long and quite wide, with stacks of books that were many shelves high, with a long ladder on rollers that could be moved back and forth to reach the higher shelves.

We did not make an exact count but were shown what the priest said were 2,775 ancient Greek books of the New Testament. This was the library that Dr. Constantin von Tischendorf visited and from which the Siniatic Codex came. Copies of Dr. Tishendorf's correspondence with the monastery were on display in glass cases. These Greek copies of the New Testament are in codex form, the print clear, and mainly on vellum.

When H. S. Miller wrote in 1956, he stated that the number of minuscules was about 3,000. The minuscule manuscripts are listed by number, while the uncial manuscripts are listed by letters. The value of the minuscule to the study of the biblical text is much less than the uncials due to their later date. There are exceptions to this rule because a twelfth-century copy may be made from a fourth century one, and thus confirm what was written from 300-400. The question is not how many years have passed, but how many times it has been copied. For example, minuscule 1 (an eleventh century document), is almost identical to the Vatican and Sinaitic, therefore a very valuable witness to the original text.

While traveling in Greece a very few years ago I was discussing with our guide about New Testament Greek texts. He told me that there were three very old monasteries on the eastern coast of Greece where he had seen many very old Greek Bibles. He has offered to take my son Steven and me there on our next visit. It is reasonable to expect that more ancient minuscule, or even some uncial manuscripts, may be found in the future.

As a review, here is a list of the Greek texts that have been used in making our United Bible Societies' Greek text: 116 papyri manuscripts, 44 lettered uncials, 256 numbered uncials and 2,818 numbered Greek minuscules. Greek lectionaries are also used to check the text's accuracy. This will be discussed in an upcoming section, as well as how the Latin versions have also been used to confirm textual accuracy.

The result is a very pure text. Yes, there are thousands of textual variant readings, but when the number of manuscripts is realized, when the kinds of variant readings are found, the end result is a pure text in which no New Testament teaching can be brought into question because of textual variant readings. An example of variant readings could be given using P−66 as an example. The Bodmer II text of the Gospel of John has many differences. But these variations are not bothersome. The word for God is always abbreviated using theta sigma. There is no question as to what was in the original, but the scribe used an abbreviation for a very commonly used word.

Some very old manuscripts do not have a verse or a few verses that are in later copies, but often when something is not there in one Gospel, the same thing is found in another. Each time we face a textual issue it does not result in a question of what is taught, as another passage that is not doubtful teaches the same thing. Significant textual issues with our New Testament are less than 20, none of which are of doctrinal significance. As Jesus said, "The Scriptures cannot be broken" (John 10:35).

XX. OTHER EVIDENCES FOR OLD AND NEW TESTAMENT ACCURACY

Of the many other ways we have of checking the accuracy of both our Old and New Testament Scriptures, we will look at three more. They are the ancient papyri fragments, old lectionaries, and various inscriptions. These give us the opportunity to spot check our ancient manuscripts, both Old and New Testament. The papyri are just fragments, the lectionaries only quote parts of the text, and the inscriptions also are usually brief.

1. Papyrus fragments. Some old fragments have been found in other places than Egypt, but most come from there. This is reasonable for several reasons. First, much of Egypt is very dry. Second, papyrus had its origin in Egypt. Third, Egypt was the literary capital of the world for several of the early centuries, most important for preservation of the biblical manuscripts.

   While doing archaeological excavating near Alexandria, Egypt in 1900, Grenfell and Hunt's team came upon another cemetery of sacred crocodiles. Crocodiles were buried with people as some sort of talisman of good for the future. They were embalmed and their heads and bodies were stuffed with old waste papyrus documents, invoices, copies from old books, or whatever was at hand.

   One of Hunt's men angrily threw the old crocodile against a rock and it burst open, and he noticed the documents within, leading to the discovery of many important old documents. Some of these were just funeral documents. But some were important old papyrus fragments. These fall into three main categories.

   a. Texts of classical literature from authors like Homer, Plato, Demosthenes, Herodotus, Lysias, and many others.

   b. Biblical and theological texts.

   c. Non-literary, such as invoices, public records, and funeral brochures. (A funeral document was purchased by Joseph Smith Jr., the Mormon prophet, from archaeologists who were traveling through where he lived. Because ancient Egyptian was not readable at the time, he was temporarily safe in trying to translate it. He claimed it was something written by Father Abraham himself, while in reality it was just a document from a funeral.)[23]

Let us turn our attention to the theological papyri now. About thirty small fragments of the Septuagint have been found and are dated from the third to seventh centuries. They can be used to check the accuracy of our present Septuagint text.

In 1925 Robertson listed 34 fragments of the New Testament.[24] Later this number came to be 70, and today more have been found. Although these are just small parts of our overall New Testament text, they do give us the chance to spot check what text was in the period of A.D. 250. These fragments give us portions of Matthew, John, and Hebrews.

The theological fragments give us quotations of the "Sayings of Jesus" from the early third century. Others found were of acts, epistles, apocalypses and sermons. Many other subjects are covered in these very old papyrus fragments. This discussion does not take into consideration the much more complete papyrus documents like the Chester Beatty Papyri, already discussed, but is limited to small fragments.

The value of papyrus fragments is great because they often let us check various biblical books 100–150 years earlier than when our more complete vellum manuscripts were written. Sometimes they help us con-

---

23   He translated about seventy Egyptian characters into over 4,000 words, turning one letter into seven names and seventy words. This is one of hundreds of proofs that Joseph Smith was a false prophet.

24   Robertson, *Introduction to Textual Criticism*, pages 76-78.

firm an uncertain word that later manuscripts may not agree about. Some of these fragments are from scrolls, but others are of the codex (book) type and help us establish when the codex form began to be used. The fragments are probably from private copies of Scripture, which helps us to know that the Bible books were circulated more widely among the general population than was previously thought.

2. Lectionaries are service books, or volumes containing excerpts that were read during the church year in public assemblies. The number of lectionaries that are known is about 2,200. These contain collections of passages, complete but not continuous; some from the Gospels, some from Acts, some from the Epistles. The Greek texts were copied quite faithfully, reach back to a very early time, and furnish proof of what the biblical manuscript then in use contained.

3. Ostraca and inscriptions are writings on pieces of broken pottery, or possibly metals, upon which small portions of Scripture were written, as a rule, in the Koine Greek. Inscriptions on pottery were an inexpensive way for poor people to take to their homes portions of Scripture when they could not afford the more expensive papyrus or vellum copies. We have about twenty of these ostraca and date them about the seventh century A.D. They represent the most unique copies of any manuscript ever written and indicate how valuable the Scriptures were to them.

   There are also copies of Scripture on church walls, monuments, pillars, coins, metal, and other ways to make Scripture available to the general public.

What can be learned from all of the above information? We can know for certain that our biblical texts of both Old and

New Testaments have been faithfully preserved for us today. When supposed experts or modern-day false prophets criticize the Bible's accuracy, they show their ignorance and that they really are not true, but false prophets.

We can know that not one doctrine of the Old or New Testament can be brought into question because of a slight textual variant reading. Jesus' words have been vindicated: "The Scriptures cannot be broken, nor will one letter or word pass away as long as there is heaven and earth." The Psalmist was right, "Forever thy word has been settled in heaven." Psalm 119:89

4. Quotations of our New Testament as proof of their existence and content.

A whole book could be written on this subject alone, but we will just summarize the information. We have already established what the biblical text was for both the Old Testament and New Testament. Now let us turn our attention to how it was used by the early church fathers. We will begin in the fourth century A.D. and move backward to the early second century.

a. During the fourth century at least ten men made catalogs of the twenty-seven books of our New Testament. They were Augustine, Ufinius, Jerome, Philastius, Gregory, Nazianzen, Ephihanius, Athanasius, Cyril, and Eusebius. Together in their writings they quoted the whole New Testament. St. Augustine wrote one book that had seven hundred sermons based upon the sacred Scriptures.

Eusebius was born A.D. 260 and became an Elder and Bishop of Caesarea. He became noted for his scholarship and books and is named "Father of Church History." He completed his church history in ten books in A.D. 325. He confirms that when he wrote there were only four Gospels. Second, that they bore the names of Matthew, Mark, Luke and John, and they and the rest of the New Testament books were authoritative when he wrote.

b. During the third century there is solid evidence for the existence of the New Testament and what it contained. The decisive writer during this period was Origen of Alexandria. Alexandria was the literary capital of the world at that time. He was born in Egypt in 186 and died in A.D. 253. Among both the Christians and heathens he was held in the highest esteem morally and his veracity is never questioned. He wrote a three-fold exposition of all the books of the New Testament. He testifies to the existence of every one of our New Testament books.

Origen was the most prolific of the church fathers. He is said to have written 6,000 books, which includes tracts, homilies and letters. His monumental work is the Hexapla. He wrote commentaries on nearly all the books of both Testaments and these contain a wealth of original suggestions as well as some interesting interpretations.

Concerning the Gospels, Origen says, "As I have understood from tradition respecting the four Gospels, which are the only undisputed ones in the whole church of God throughout the world, the first is written according to Matthew, the second is according to Mark ... the third is according to Luke ... and the last of all, the Gospel according to John."

Eusebius says concerning Origen: "If we had all his works remaining, We should have before us almost the whole text of the Bible." Dr. Keith gives the following enumeration of his quotations from the four volumes of Origen: He quoted Matthew 1,352 times; Mark 195 times; Luke 649 times; John 775 times; Acts 147 times; Romans 731 times; 1 Corinthians 620 times; Galatians 130 times; Ephesians 135 times; Philippians 68 times; Colossians 94 times; 1 Thessalonians 48 times; 2 Thessalonians 36 times; 1 Timothy 92 times; 2 Timothy 55 times; Titus 19 times; Philemon 3 times; Hebrews 153 times; James 18 times; 1 Peter 48 times; 2 Peter 5 times; 1 John 77 times; Jude 5 times, and Revelation is quoted 60 times. No one can doubt the existence of the New Testament in its present form at that time. He is credited with nearly 18,000 quotations from the New Testament.[25]

But, Origin is not the only writer from the third century A.D. who verifies the existence of our New Testament. There is Julius Africanus, Ammonius, Caius Romanus, Cyprian, Firmilian, Apolonius, Dionysius of Alexandria and Malchion, who all quote from the New Testament, not only showing its existence but its importance as scripture at that time. This information is accepted by Christian and unbeliever alike.

   c. Now consider the evidence for the existence of the New Testament from the last half of the second century, that is, from A.D. 150−200. First, consider that they were so widely ac-

---

25   H. S. Miller, *General Biblical Introduction*, Page 259.

cepted in the third century and that they could not have just burst on the scene. But here are five witnesses to their existence.

First, consider Clement of Alexandria. He converted from Platonic philosophy to Christianity by reading the New Testament books and their teaching. He lived from A.D. 160−220, the last half of the second and early third centuries. He was a man of wide and great learning and his testimony as to the New Testament's existence during his life is unimpeachable. He refers to them as "Holy Books, Divine and Inspired Scriptures." "There is but one God which is proven by the Law and the prophets and the four Gospels." Clement quoted no less than 189 times from twenty-one of our New Testament books.

Second is Turtullian, from the last half of the second century. He lived from A.D. 140 to 210. He lived and worked in Carthage, of Northern Africa. He had been a Roman lawyer and a pagan. He became a staunch believer and defender of the "Faith," converted by the New Testament. His greatest work now in existence is, *Against Marcion*. In it he uniformly recognizes the four Gospels as written by the evangelists, and distinguishes Matthew and John as Apostles from Mark and Luke, whom he designates as "Apostolic Men." He quoted 1,802 times from 24 of our New Testament books and many times these quotations are long and formal. He never quotes from the apocryphal books which were added to the Bible much later.

Third in the list is Irenaeus. He was born at Smyrna, and lived from A.D. 120−202. He gives testimony from the West, like Clement and Tertullian did from the East. He was martyred for his testimony, which shows that he believed the scriptures sincerely enough to die for them. He wrote many books, but only five of his books *Against Heresies* remain in existence. In these volumes he refutes the "Gnostics." His most famous quotation is, "So firm is the ground upon which these Gospels rest, that the very heretics themselves bear witness to them, and starting from these documents, each one endeavors to establish his own peculiar doctrines. For the Ebionites, who use Matthew's Gospel only, are refuted out of this very same, making false suppositions in regard to our Lord." He quoted from the New Testament as we know it 767 times, missing only 3 John. Between Clement, Tertullian, and Irenaeus, they quote the New Testament over 3,000 times.

We can add many to this list of second century writers who quote from our New Testament: Athanagoras (A.D. 117), Claudius Apollinaris (A.D. 161—180), Dionisius, Bishop of Corinth, and Melito. During this period the Muratori Canon was produced; scholars agree that it was produced A.D. 160.

d. Next we will look at the evidence that comes from the first half of the second century, A.D. 100—150. Remember that the New Testament books were in existence and in high regard in the last half of this century. In the period of A.D. 100—150 it is estimated that there were more than three million Christians in the Empire. It is estimated that 60,000 copies of the New Testament were in use. They were quoted and appealed to across the Empire. Notice the testimony of four men of this period.

First, consider the testimony of Justin Martyr at Rome in A.D. 167. He was a Greek scholar and philosopher before he became a Christian. Among all the defenders of the faith up to this time, he is possibly the most widely known. His two most famous works preserved for us are *Two Apologies* and *A Dialogue*. The longest dialogue was presented to Emperor Antonius in A.D. 139, and the shorter one was given to Marcus Aurelius in A.D. 163. He bears witness to the Gospels in this passage: "And the messenger then sent to a Virgin announced to her the glad news, saying, 'Behold, thou shalt conceive thru the Holy Spirit, and bring forth a son, and he shall be the Son of the Most High; and thou shalt call his name Jesus; for he shall deliver his people from their sins'; as those who have written memoirs concerning everything relating to our Savior, Jesus Christ, have taught, whom we believe."

In his account of the Lord's Supper, Justin Martyr says they met each first day of the week to celebrate this feast. He says when they met, they "read from the memoirs of the Apostles and prophets as long as time would allow." Here is a brief summary of his testimony: 1. He had in his possession written histories of the ministry of Jesus. 2. His blessed citations can all be found in our New Testament. 3. He has forty quotations from the book of Matthew. 4. He quotes twenty times from Mark and Luke. 5. John is quoted substantially also. 6. He quotes 125 times from the New Testament.

Second, let us look at the testimony of Papias, who also worked and wrote in the first half of the second century. He was a contemporary of the Disciples of the Apostles. Eusebius says of him, "But Papias himself, in the preface of his discourse says that he was by no means a hearer and an eye witness of the Holy Apostles, but that he received the doctrines of Faith from intimate friends of the Apostles." He, by his writings, shows he had an extended acquaintance with the four Gospels.

The third witness from this period is Basilides, who lived until A.D. 130. He wrote a "24-book commentary" on the Gospels. He quotes from Romans, Ephesians, Colossians, 1 Timothy, and 1 Peter.

Finally, Diognetus, speaks to us from this period, writing at about A.D. 117. His letter still exists in its original Greek form. He was familiar with John's Gospel, and with Paul's letters. He makes other references to Romans, 1 Corinthians, Galatians, Acts, Ephesians, Philippians, 1 Timothy, Titus, and 1 Peter. This proves to us conclusively that the New Testament literature was not only known in the second century but was widely used and known right after the year A.D. 100.

e. Now we turn our attention to quotations from or in regard to the New Testament Canon from the first century.

Our first witness is Clement of Rome, A.D. 30–100. His first letter to the Corinthians is admitted as genuine and the date assigned is A.D. 96.[26] He shows familiarity with Peter's and Paul's writings and imitates their style of

26 H. S. Miller, *General Biblical Introduction*, page 262.

writing. He is familiar with John's Gospel and quotes from it. His allusions to the Hebrew letter are numerous. Lardner cites thirty-one quotations from seventeen of the New Testament books.

Witness number two is from the apostolic era—Barnabas. His books and writings were doubted by some until 1859 when Dr. Tischendorf discovered the Greek Text of the "Epistle of Barnabas" and since that time it is admitted to be authentic. He quotes Jesus saying: "As it is written in Scripture, 'Many are called but few chosen!'" This is a quote from Matthew 22:14 and is the first time the New Testament is quoted and called "Scripture." In his writing he also alludes to Matthew 1:13 and 20:16. He distinguishes between the true Lord's Supper and the Judaizing element in the early church, showing knowledge of Paul's writings. Twenty-four times he quotes from twelve of the New Testament books.

The third witness, from the apostolic period, is Hermas. He probably wrote under Emperor Hadrian. He is quoted by Irenaeus, Tertullian, Origen and Eusebius. Lardner cites twenty-three quotations from fourteen books of the New Testament in his writings.

Next is Ignatius, who was bishop of Antioch of Syria and lived from A.D. 37–108. He wrote seven short epistles in the Greek language and quoted nineteen times from our New Testament.

Finally, our last witness is Polycarp, who had personal contact with John the Apostle. He was a disciple and pupil of John. He wrote a letter to the Philippian church. He makes forty quotations from what we know as the New Testament books. This takes us back to the very days of the Apostles themselves, to the fountain of inspired purity and gives importance to 2 Timothy 3:16: "All Scripture is given by inspiration of God ..."[27]

Therefore, we have solid proof of the accuracy of our Old and New Testaments. With the Old Testament we have the *Samaritan Pentateuch*, the *Septuagint*, Ancient Hebrew versions and the Dead Sea Scrolls. We can look further into the Targums, Talmud, and ancient quotations to establish what was written by the prophets.

With the New Testament, proof is considerably more voluminous, with the uncials, minuscules, papyrus fragments, lectionaries, ancient inscriptions, and finally with the multitude of quotations from the Church Fathers.

There can be no doubt about any teaching in our Bibles. As the song writer said, "The Bible stands like a rock undaunted 'mid the raging storms of time ... Its truth by none ever was refuted, and destroy it they never can ..."[28]

f. There is more evidence for our Bible and that is found in the ancient versions. A version is a translation of Old or New Testament into languages other than in which they were written.

We have additional proof of the genuineness and authenticity of the Scriptures and the New Testament text in the ancient versions. An ancient version is, in general, one which was made before the invention of the printing press,

27   The above information about ancient quotations of our New Testament comes from a small pamphlet written by Archie Word, Sr., entitled *How—When, and Where We Got Our Bibles*. Written by Archie Word, Evangelist, and Editor of *The Church Speaks*, 550 N. E. 76th Avenue, Portland, Oregon, 1956.
28   Haldor Lillenas, 1917. Public Domain

or before A.D. 1450. After 1450 the term modern version is used.

Ancient versions were needed as the gospel spread to other lands where Greek and Hebrew were not well known. The fact that the Scriptures were translated into other languages is additional proof of their importance and wide acceptance.

The gospel spread from Jerusalem on the day of Pentecost immediately to many different nations because of all those represented at Pentecost. It spread to Asia Minor, Egypt, Ethiopia, North Africa, Macedonia, Greece, Italy, India, and beyond. Sinners were saved and churches established. This created the need for the Bible in their own languages.

It is not our purpose to give an exhaustive discussion of the ancient versions, only to make the reader aware of their existence and importance to this discussion.

Of the Old Testament there were these versions translated from Hebrew: 1) The *Samaritan Pentateuch* (430 B.C.); 2) The Aramaic Targums for the Aramaic speaking Jews of Palestine (450 B.C. onward); 3) the *Greek Septuagint* (280-180 B.C.) 4) *Aquila's Greek* version for the anti-Christian Jews (A.D. 128); 5) Theodotion's versions for Christians (A.D. 180); 6) Symmachus' version for Christians (A.D. 200); and finally, 7) Origen's Hexapla (A.D. 250).

Ancient versions with both Old and New Testaments: 1) The Syriac for the Christians churches of Syria (about 150 A.D. onward); 2) Latin, the Old Latin, the Italic, for the churches of Italy; the Vulgate for the western churches (A.D. 383-405); 3) The Egyptian or Coptic, for the churches of Egypt (about A.D. 250); 4) The many others were the Ethiopic, Gothic, Armenian, Georgian, Arabic, Slavonic, and Persian.

As the evidence for biblical accuracy is known, it becomes apparent why the competent theologian views attacks on the Bible as signs of ignorance. There can be no doubt that our Bible has come down to us with a multitude of evidence to prove its accuracy.

XXI. THE HEBREW KITTEL TEXT, THE NESTLE GREEK TEXT; AND THE UNITED BIBLE SOCIETIES' GREEK TEXT

The Hebrew Old Testament Text

When biblical scholars want to study the original language text of the Old Testament they commonly use *Biblia Hebraica*, edited by Rudolf Kittel and published by Wurttenmbergische Bibelanstalt, Stuttgart, Germany.

This is the seventh edition and does benefit from some of the variant readings that come from an examination of some of the Dead Sea Scrolls. The finding of the Dead Sea Scrolls did not alter the text in any significant way as was indicated by Dr. John C. Trever, who said, "The variant readings were minute and of interest primarily to scholars."

Kittel's text contains the 39 books of the Old Testament and makes it possible for biblical scholars to check what was actually written by the prophets. Biblical Hebrew, being a dead language, is static and the meaning of words is fixed. With a good knowledge of biblical Hebrew and the use of a lexicon, a scholar can understand what was written in the original language. This is the Bible I use when seeking to understand what was written. Today we can be assured that the Old Testament Scriptures have not been tampered with or changed.

The Greek New Testament Text

In A.D. 1522, the *Complutensian Polyglot*, which had the Greek and Latin texts side by side, was an effort to provide a standardized Greek text. (The Greek New Testament was completed in 1514 but not published until 1517 after Erasmus' death) Others like the *Textus Receptus* followed. Then next in order came the *Nestle's Greek Testament*, based on the works of Dr. Tischendorf, Westcott-Hort and Weymouth. Each was a progression towards a more accurate Greek text of our New Testament Scriptures. Today the United Bible Societies' Greek text is commonly used, and the latest editions of the Nestle-Aland and UBS have the exact same text.

The United Bible Societies' text is based on 133 papyri manuscripts, 42 lettered uncials, 108 numbered uncials, and 62 Greek minuscule, and another 204 numbered Greek minuscules are used only when significant for certain variant readings. Old Greek lectionaries have been used to help confirm the Greek text. These are numbered and preceded with the letter "L" for lectionaries. Numerous lectionaries are used to confirm the exact text. Also considered to confirm the text have been the Latin versions, both Old Latin and the Vulgate. The Church Fathers' writings are also considered to further confirm the text.

The end result is that we have positive proof of what was written by the inspired New Testament writers. When people criticize the accuracy of our modern Bibles, they are speaking out of ignorance, not from understanding the subject. Although there are variant readings we now know what was written.

Reading the original language texts takes more than a casual knowledge of how to use a Hebrew or Greek lexicon and is not the task for someone who has only been shown how to use a diaglot or Vine's Expository Dictionary. Yet, for those who devote enough years of study, Greek can be mastered. This helps the careful student to have a fuller understanding of the biblical text.

Biblical Hebrew, being a dead language, leaves our biblical text unchangeable. Hebrew is a rather difficult language to learn, with the Hebrew verb forms containing 21 kinds of verbs, each being written in 176 ways, and with affixes and suffixes added can be written nearly 800 different ways. The noun forms are fairly simple. When these languages are understood an accurate translation can be achieved, which is what we have today.

Greek is a very precise language, and Koine Greek, being also a dead language, protects the exact meaning of words and makes our Scriptures secure and unchangeable over the past centuries and in the years to come. Few, if any languages are more suited to accuracy and the security of the text, than Greek and Hebrew. It seems providential that these were chosen to secure our Old and New Testaments. That Greek rose to world acceptance and then died also seems providential, and leaves us without doubt as to what was written by the inspired writers.

SECTION FOUR

TEXTUAL CRITICISM

XXII. THE HISTORY OF TEXTUAL CRITICISM

The Bible has had many friends, but also many enemies. Dr. Dinesh D'Souza is correct in his analysis of this problem when he says, "The objections to Christianity are often more moral than intellectual." This does not mean that those who have sought to destroy the Bible were not very intelligent people; many have been. It only means that they have not wanted the restraints placed upon them that believing brings. They may have been intelligent, but are for some reason or other predisposed to disbelieve. They begin their study with the goal of disproving rather than proving the Bible. Those who begin with ulterior motives may not be objective investigators.

It is probable that some who have sought to destroy the Bible have done so out of honest motives, brought about by ignorance of the facts of the matter or by having been taught to mistrust the Bible in their higher education training. On many occasions it has become clear that people's objections have come due to lack of correct information.

There are two main divisions to Textual Criticism: Higher Criticism and Lower Criticism. While both Higher and Lower Criticism are legitimate ways to study the biblical text, generally Higher Criticism seeks to destroy the Bible while Lower Criticism seeks to show the Bible's accuracy. One often is destructive the other constructive.

1. Higher Criticism.

When scholarly judgment is applied to the genuineness of the biblical text, it is classified as "higher" or "historical" criticism. This study is applied to the date of the text, its literary style and structure, whether it is historically accurate and who actually wrote the documents.[29]

After the Reformation, when people again had the Scriptures in their possession, they learned of their sinful behavior. This led to rebellion on the part of carnal people who did not want the restraints that Christianity placed upon them. This is not a blanket denunciation, but what appears to have been a predominant cause. In Europe, primarily in Germany and France, there arose a movement to disprove the Bible. This proved to be disastrous to both countries. Nevertheless the movement was real and proved very destructive as its advocates were often brilliant and influential. This led to empty churches, the breakdown of marriage, widespread immorality, and made possible the French Revolution and the death camps of Auschwitz and Dauchau.

While it was the "in" thing for many American theologians to travel to Europe to study, they became infected with what was called "German Rationalism." This was founded on the idea that there could not be miracles, they were unscientific, nor prophecy, since no one knows the future. During the scientific revolution these ideas became widely accepted and brought about efforts to explain the Bible on purely scientific grounds. This produced a flood of teaching and books seeking to disprove the Bible. These were some of the roots of destructive Higher Criticism.

Not all Higher Criticism was destructive; some came from efforts to defend and explain the origin

---

29   For a fuller discussion of this matter see *A General Introduction to the Bible,* Norman L. Geisler and William E. Nix, Moody Press, 1975, pages 376-ff.

and history of the Bible, and to defend it.

In Old Testament studies this brought about Julius Wellhausen's attempt to mediate between traditionalism and skepticism. He wanted to date the Old Testament books much later than thought. "This theory was based largely upon the argument that Israel did not have writing prior to the monarchy, and that an Elohist (E) Code and a Yahwist (J) Code were based on two oral traditions about God … to these were added the Deuteronomic (D) Code … and the so-called (P) or Priestly Codes."[30]

This was then defined as the J, E, P, and D codes that divided the Pentateuch into sections, not written by Moses, but were said to be a collection of traditions handed down from generation to generation.

Out of this school of thought came late dating of books and the effort to de-supernaturalize the biblical text. Removing miracles and prophecy from the Bible leads to the questioning of Jesus' miracles and of the greatest of all miracles—the resurrection of Jesus. The results were destructive to Christian faith.

Our effort here is not to examine these theories in detail, only to make the reader aware that there have been many efforts to discredit our Bible.[31]
Out of Higher Criticism came Source, Form and Redaction Criticism.

    a.   Source Criticism sought to learn the sources of the writer's material. If ancient writers had footnoted their material, as is com-

30   *Ibid*, page 377.
31   For a fuller study, read Roland Kenneth Harrison's *Introduction to the Old Testament*, Eerdmans Publishing Company, 1975; or Donald Guthrie's *New Testament Introduction*, InterVarsity Press, 1974; or Geisler and Nix's *A General Introduction to the Bible*, Moody Press, 1975.

mon today, it would have been helpful. While it is true that the writers had other sources for their writing, to suggest there was no supernatural source leaves many difficult questions unanswered.

b.   Form Criticism studied the written form with an effort to suggest more than one author. For example, Isaiah was first thought to have two authors and then later three. These were called "Deutero-Isaiah" and later "Trito-Isaiah." A more careful look at Isaiah demonstrates that Isaiah wrote with a style that might be called "Trinity" with three sections of the book and each section having three sections.[32]

c.   Redaction Criticism sought to reduce the biblical text to its basic essence. The critic did not believe much of the Bible actually to be historical. Thus, they removed the parts they felt were added later or were mythical. One of several authors suggested that there were very few actual statements of Jesus in the Gospels. They had redacted it down to nothing.

What have we learned from all of this? The destructive Higher Critics' arguments forced the Lower Critic to seek answers to their arguments. With each attack came further research into what the Bible actually said. The end result has been positive. The supposed problems in the Bible have continued to

---

32   See *Studies in Isaiah*, by F. C. Jennings, Loizeauz Brothers, Neptune, New Jersey, 1982.

be reduced and in each occasion the Bible has been shown to be accurate, while the destructive Higher Critics have been left with "egg on their faces."

Higher Criticism has shed some light on our Bibles, but for the main part, their efforts have been more destructive than constructive. The disastrous results in Germany and France, resulting in World Wars I & II, show them for what they were—faith wrecking and society ruining. Men without God often end up as inhumane beasts. Faith, morals, families, society, and nations are wrecked. Faith sustains and builds families and nations.

2.   Lower (Textual) Criticism.

This has been the main thrust of this writing, to show the accuracy of our biblical text, and to authenticate its antiquity and accuracy. At the same time the Lower Critic shows the foundation for the Scripture by the acronym MAPS.

a.   **M**anuscript evidence has conclusively proven the accuracy of our Old and New Testament texts. The LXX and Dead Sea Scrolls have proven that prophecies were just that—prophecies.

b.   **A**rchaeology has proven over and over again the biblical record. If it is in the Bible, eventually it will be found. Old libraries, like the one found at Ebla in Syria, have proven that writing was widespread long before 2200 B.C. Most of the places mentioned in the Old Testament have been found. You can go to Babylon, Nineveh, Jerusalem and Jericho. Many of the people who were said by the Higher Critic to have never existed have been found.

c.   Biblical Prophecies have been shown to be just that. There was a time when questioning the antiquity of Daniel may have had a sound of intelligence, but no longer. With the Septuagint having been completed around 180 B.C., with Daniel in it, Daniel's astounding prophecies have been shown to be what they claimed. Daniel's seventy-week prophecy accurately predicted when Jesus would be crucified over 500 years before the event. The book is full of amazing prophecies about nations and kingdoms. Also found among the Dead Sea Scrolls was Daniel, dated long before the birth of Christ. A prophecy given, whether 100 or 500 years before, is just that—a prophecy.

With the finding of the Dead Sea Scroll book of Isaiah that was copied in 225 B.C. we have another whole group of prophecies proven to be just that—prophecies. There were 20 other copies of Isaiah found among the Dead Sea Scrolls. Add to this the other 38 of 39 Old Testament books, found among the Dead Sea Scrolls, with their hundreds of prophecies of the future and the supernatural nature of the Bible has been well documented. The total number of Old Testament books found among the scrolls was 380.

d.   Statistics prove the Scripture. The chance that 330 prophecies about Jesus would all be fulfilled in one person, Jesus, is astounding. For there to be hundreds of other prophecies given throughout the Bible shows its inspiration. That the virgin birth would be predicted in Genesis 3:16 and Isaiah 7:14, is truly remarkable. Humanly virgin births are impossible. History records no other proven virgin birth.

"The Bible stands like a rock undaunted 'mid the raging storms of time ... Its truth by none ever was refuted and destroy it they never can ..."[33] "Forever, O Lord, Thy word is settled in heaven" (Psalm 119:89). "The sum of Thy word is truth and every one of Thy righteous ordinances is everlasting" (Psalm 119:160). Jesus said, "The Scriptures cannot be broken" (John 10:35).

XXIII. HOW ACCURATE ARE OUR MODERN VERSIONS?

Most translations of our Bible have sought to faithfully transmit into another language what was actually written in the Hebrew and Greek texts. Not all translations have been created equal and vary according to the language skills and understanding of the biblical content by the translators. For the most part, old and newer translations have been done by some of the most competent people of the period in which they were done. Whether it was the *Old Latin*, Jerome's *Latin Vulgate*, the *Douai*, or those done by Wycliffe, Tyndale or Luther, each represents their best effort to communicate the Word of God in the language of the people.

Translations have differing purposes. Some translations seek to translate the ideas word for word, while others seek to get across the general ideas contained in the Hebrew or Greek texts. Some are literal, and others seek to communicate the thoughts or ideas.

People who are reading the Bible for the first time are often confused by reading a literal, word-for-word translation, but find understanding when they have a modern speech translation. Actually both have their place and can be used to enhance understanding.

33   Haldor Lillenas, 1917. Public Domain

As Christians mature, they may be left confused by "translation frustration." One person wrote a note to our minister, Dr. Steven Crane, recently and said, "I love it that you take us to the original languages to get the exact meaning of what God was saying! But which translation is most exact? I want to read a translation that stays with the true intent of God's original word! No transliteration, or do I mean paraphrases? I want just exactly what God said. I guess what I am saying is that I would love to know which translation is the closest to the original languages ..."

This is a great question. Visit any local Christian bookstore and you will see shelf upon shelf of various Bible translations. There are a multitude of different versions. In fact, there have been about fifty new versions in the last fifty years. How are we to know which one is best to choose?

The short answer to this is that most all of the mainstream translations are wonderfully done. They are, for the most part, all very good and there is an amazing consistency and accuracy among all of them. Sure, there are exceptions. We could give for an example The *New World Translation*, sponsored by the Jehovah's Witnesses, which appears to be an effort to prove their false doctrines rather than to faithfully present what the Hebrew and Greek texts actually say. But, for the most part, modern versions are pretty good, done by people who love God's Word, yet most translations may have some, or several weak spots.

Critics of the Bible use the multitude of translations as an avenue of attack on the integrity of the Bible. They claim the existence of these various works show that the Bible is somehow inconsistent or even contradictory. Actually, their critique shows that they do not understand the nature of translation, or biblical languages. Anyone who has learned a foreign language, or studied how language is used, knows that there is not always a word-for-word equivalent when moving from one language to another. Every language contains figures of speech and idioms that cannot be translated directly. Word morphology also necessitates changing vocabulary to express a more precise meaning. Often what is easy to say in a word in one language, might necessitate several words or an entire phrase to convey the same meaning in another language, or vice-versa. A translator's job is to communicate, in the most accurate way possible, the intended meaning of the author, or speaker, to the intended audience. Here are several common questions and their answers.

Question One: Why is translation necessary? To make God's Word understandable.

We have all probably heard the joke about the well intentioned man who insisted on the use of the *King James Bible.* When presented with other translation options he would reply, "If the *King James Bible* was good enough for the Apostle Paul, it is good enough for me!" The poor man did not understand that the Bible was primarily written in two languages: Hebrew and Greek. There are a few Old Testament passages believed to have been written in Aramaic. These original languages are useless to most people in the world today, which is why we need good translations. Even those people who live in Greece today do not understand Koine Greek, nor do those speaking modern Hebrew understand biblical Hebrew. Most people depend on translations.

Translations are not only necessary for English speaking people, but also for the people around the world who do not speak English, the people of the 6,500 different languages spoken around the world today.

Question Two: Why do we need updated translations? The answer is that it is necessary to make God's Word understandable for us today.

While God's Word does not change, language does. Here are a few examples of how languages change. If it were said that a person made a lot of "dough," would you conclude that he was a baker? This is an example as to how our speech changes meaning over time. Another is that we say something is "bad" and this no longer means bad, but good! In the early *King James Versions* the word "let" was used to mean restrain or prohibit, with just the opposite meaning today.

Words change meaning in a living language. Fortunately, both biblical Hebrew and Greek, the languages of the Bible, are both dead and unchanging today.

With additional old manuscripts being found we can now further refine the Greek and Hebrew texts and make even more accurate translations. As previously mentioned additional manuscripts will continue to be found like those in Eastern Greece. This will help confirm the accuracy of our biblical text. Our hope is to examine these soon.

Question Three: Why don't we just stick with the Authorized Version, the King James?

We might ask, which one, since there have been at least eleven different updates of the 1611 *King James Version*? Each has helped keep the *KJV* up to date with common English usage.

On the surface this may have some appeal, especially for those of us who are older and reluctant to accept change. The question, though, shows a lack of understanding of the *King James Version*. For its day it was the best available. The question does not take into consideration who "authorized" it and its history. King James authorized it, not God. King James was not a model of Christianity. It was commendable that he wanted the English-speaking people to have a good translation. His instruction to the translators was, "You must be faithful to the biblical text and not contradict the teachings of the church. This left the translators in a difficult position. Some words were not translated at all but they just put the Greek words into the English (transliteration), leaving confusion and helping false doctrine to continue.

Another problem with the *King James Version* was that it was not based on the most important Greek and Hebrew texts that were found later. It was primarily based on Tyndale's work and a few old texts.

This question also does not take into consideration which *King James Version* is to be used, as it has been revised many times. Not many of us would understand the first or even later editions of the King James. If it is all right to revise the King James, why not turn our best biblical scholars loose to make a remarkable and up-to-date version, which is what has been done?

Another reason for us to move to more modern translations is that grammar changes with time. We no longer use words like "ye, thee, thou, and doest." When older folk read these words they understand, but the younger generation just tunes out and stops reading or listening.

Question Four: Why do we need so many translations?

The answer is that it is necessary to make the Scriptures understandable to as many people as possible. Different translations speak to the hearts of different people. Those who study Scripture find that different translations open new vistas of understanding, when the same thing is said in a different way. The main difference in translations is that they may be literal, word for word, free, or dynamic, thought for thought. These should not be confused with translations which are called "paraphrases" which seek to explain or summarize the text, but which are not translations at all. We will discuss each of these types a bit later.

Some would advocate only the literal, word-for-word translation. While the literal translations definitely have their place, it is not really possible to make a truly literal translation that is understandable. All good translations need to communicate the thoughts and facts of the original. Sometimes the literal translations are wooden, rigid, and not very understandable, while a more fluid translation may communicate the writer's true intent much better. Certainly there is a place for both approaches. I like the literal translation for careful research, and the more dynamic translation for the overall understanding of the context. Both serve a real purpose.

142

Very early in the history of the church the value of different versions was found important, with works like Origen's Hexapla, which had several versions of Scripture side by side. Today similar types of Bibles are available.

A good translation takes more than just knowing how to translate word meanings properly. Good translations must put the proper words in an understandable progression. It requires the knowledge of grammar and syntax. This is the danger caused by only using an interlinear and *Vine's Expository Dictionary of New Testament Greek Words* or Davidson's *Analytical Hebrew Lexicon*. Poor Greek and Hebrew skills have led to dangerous heresies such as are taught by the Jehovah's Witnesses today.

Possibly a few examples would be helpful to illustrate translation problems here.

"The liquor is great, but the meat is lousy."

From this would you understand Jesus' words, "The Spirit is willing, but the flesh is weak." (Matthew 26:41). Both are literally accurate, but both do not convey the intended meaning.

Just because a word *could* mean something, does not mean it *does* mean something. The degree of accuracy is not in whether it is literal or dynamic, but in how well it communicates the meaning of the original to the specific audience. For example, 1 Kings 20:11 will illustrate the point.

"Let not him that girdeth on his harness boast himself as he that putteth it off" (*KJV*).

"Let not him who girds on his armour boast like him who takes if off" (NASB).

Both are literal renderings of the original text. But if a dynamic translation is compared with the KJV or NASB, the dynamic will be more easily understood by people today. All may be true to the text but the dynamic is most readable.

"A warrior still dressing for battle should not boast like a warrior who has already won" (NLT).

"Don't brag about a victory before you have even dressed for battle" (God's Word).

The question is which conveys the meaning best to a modern audience?

Question Five: What are the marks of a good translation?

The answer is that it communicates the author's intended message to those who read or hear it. It must do several things to be a good translation.

1. A good translation must be faithful to the original text. How can you know if it is? You say, "I don't know Hebrew or Greek." Check to see who did the translation. One well-known translation, widely used, leaves who translated it blank. Frankly, the translator should not have been ashamed of it. Very few translations are like the *New World Translation* which seeks to prove false doctrine and not translate accurately. Most are a genuine effort to translate carefully.

2. Is it readable? Do you read and comprehend what is written? For some, the *KJV* is a clear and understandable translation—fine, use it. For others, especially the younger generation, they read the *KJV* and do not have a clue what it is talking about and end up walking away from Christ and the church. As you read the text does it arouse interest and stimulate you to read more? Does it lead you to faith and action? If your Bible reading bores you, maybe checking a more dynamic version would remove the boredom. Try a reputable, but different

translation.

3. Is the translation God and Christ honoring? There are some translations that are too casual, flippant and do not represent a high view of God and Scripture. Some try to make the Scripture gender neutral, or speak of God in a casual or too intimate way.

In summary, most modern-day Bibles are very good. You can rest assured that what you have is what God intended you to have. Here are some recommendations that may be helpful. The literal translation will be helpful for careful Bible study and research, while a dynamic version can be great for personal devotional and inspirational reading.

The author used the *NASB* (*New American Standard Bible*) for Bible study and also recommends the ESV (*English Standard Version*). While studying Hebrew and Greek, the author placed several popular versions along the top of his desk. When finished with his own translation and checking the others, he found that the *NASB* was almost always exactly what the original text said.

Two very good dynamic versions for today are the *NLT* (*New Living Translation*) and another is *GW* (*God's Word*). While these are not literal, word-for-word translations, they do a very good job of conveying the intended meaning of the text.

The use of a paraphrase for Bible study is discouraged, since they are more a commentary on the writer's view than actual translations of the text. One well-known paraphrase was done by a man who had no knowledge of Hebrew or Greek. It may be like the blind leading the blind and not advisable for personal study of Scripture.

Our purpose is not to be exhaustive in our coverage of the many translations done over the centuries, but to examine some of the most common and widely used versions available and most commonly used in the American church today.

Literal Word-for-Word Translations.

1. The *King James Version*

A brief history of the *Authorized King James Version* is helpful. It was not the first English version of our Bibles. The first *King James Version* was translated in 1611. Before it, there were the *Wycliffe Bible* (1382), the *Tyndale Bible* (1526) the *Coverdale Bible* (1535), the *Geneva Bible* (1557) and the *Bishops' Bible* (1568).

The *King James Version* has undergone many revisions and the ones used today are very different from that "authorized" by King James. Actually there were two 1611 translations and major revisions in each of the following years: 1612, 1613, 1616, 1629, 1638, 1650, (6x), 1660, 1683, 1727, 1762, 1769, 1873, and 1888. All of them were an attempt to put God's Word in the common vernacular. We now have a *New King James Version* and even the most often used version of the KJV is not the most recent of the previous revision efforts, but one of the earlier renditions. People who insist on KJV only, normally have no idea which of the revisions they are insisting everyone should use.

What does this mean? The work of providing a good Bible translation, for people with a living language, is a never-ending task. As our language progresses so must the translation.

Those who insist on the *Authorized King James Version* would be at a loss to understand the one actually "authorized" by King James, the original Authorized Version of 1611.

It could be that they are more concerned about not having to deal with a more modern version, since they have memorized so much out of the old. We older folks must not selfishly insist on never moving ahead, leaving the new generation without an understanding and missing out on the salvation we have.

When I was a child the *KJV* was used in our church. It was replaced by the *ASV* (*American Standard Version*). This was used in Bible college. At seminary the *NASV* (*New American Standard Version*) was used. I can recite passages from three different versions. Actually the newer versions have helped to expand my understanding. If we are too old to change, we may just be too old.

If you read and understand the *KJV*—fine, use it, but don't refuse to accept a version that may aid your understanding, and that of the younger generation.

We now have the *New King James Version*, which combines accuracy with a more readable style. In the author's opinion it may be high on the list of desirable translations.

2. The *Revised Standard Version*

The *Revised Standard Version* came as a result of the revision of the *King James* done in England in which an American committee participated. The two committees had agreed that the American Committee would not publish a conflicting version for ten years. Many of their suggestions were vetoed.

The American group wanted a number of changes that the British committee did not want. They sought to have their suggestions added as an appendix or noted in some other manner. Finally the British revision committee disbanded without acting on the American scholars' suggestions. Therefore, the Americans waited to honor their commitment.

The *Revised Standard Version* was copyrighted in 1901 by Thomas Nelson and Sons publishing. This version was also an effort to update the *King James Version*. Their stated purpose in brief is:

"In the Bible we have not merely an historical document and a classic of English literature, but the Word of God. The Bible carries its full message, not to those who regard it simply as a heritage of the past or praise its literary style, but to those who read it that they may discern and understand God's Word to men. And men need the Word of God in our time and hereafter as never before. That Word must not be disguised in phrases that are no longer clear, or hidden under words that have changed or lost their meaning. It must stand forth in language that is direct and plain and meaningful to people today. It is our hope and our earnest prayer that this *Revised Standard Version* of the New Testament may be used by God to speak to men in these momentous times, and to help them to understand and believe and obey His Word."[34]

The newer version followed several helpful suggestions, such as to use the word Jehovah instead of Lord. They wanted to use the more meaningful reading "Holy Spirit"

34   Revised Standard Version, 1946, preface, pg. vi, Norwood Press, J. S. Cushing Co. –Berwick & Smith, Co. Norwood, Mass., USA.

rather than "Holy Ghost." They wanted to use the word "Covenant" rather than "Testament." These, along with many other changes, would have made the version more understandable. The result of the action of the British committee was to have a competing version come a little more than ten years after theirs. (For a more complete discussion of this subject see *General Biblical Introduction*, H. S. Miller, pg. 379-381.)

3. The *New American Standard Bible*

The *New American Standard* was copyrighted in 1960 by the Lockman foundation of LaHabra, California. The stated purpose was this: "The *New American Standard Bible* has been produced with the conviction that the words of Scripture as originally penned in the Hebrew and Greek were inspired by God. Since they are the eternal Word of God, the Holy Scriptures speak with fresh power to each generation, to give wisdom that leads to salvation, that men may serve Christ to the glory of God." The Editorial Board had a twofold purpose in making this translation: to adhere as closely as possible to the original languages of the Holy Scriptures, and to make the translation in a fluent and readable style according to current English usage.

The *NASB* has become a favorite with those who read Hebrew and Greek because of its faithful and accurate adherence to the original texts. It is probably the most nearly exact rendering of the biblical text we have today."[35]

35   The foreword in NASB, pg. v.

Like most literal translations it can be *wooden*—different from the way the average person talks. And for the new Christian it may not always communicate as clearly as it might. Nevertheless, it is probably the very best we have today for a good study Bible or from which to teach.

A negative is that the owners of the copyright are very reluctant to let it be quoted liberally for use in projection in churches or in writing. This has forced some churches to turn to other translations for use in their public worship.

4. The *New International Version*

The *New International Version* (*NIV*) full Bible was first published in 1978 and has been updated from time to time, the last time in 2011. It was initially conceived at a meeting in 1965 at Trinity Christian College in Palos Heights, Illinois, at a meeting of the Christian Reformed Church, National Association of Evangelicals, and a group of international scholars. The core translation group consisted of 15 biblical scholars. The translation took ten years and involved as many as 110 scholars from the USA, Canada, the United Kingdom, Australia, New Zealand, and South Africa. There was a wide range of denominations represented among the translators: Anglicans, Assemblies of God, Baptists, Christian Reformed, Lutheran, Presbyterian, and others.

The translation sought to provide a balance between word-for-word and thought-for-thought. Recent archaeological and linguistic discoveries helped in understanding passages that had traditionally been difficult to translate. Familiar spellings of older translations were generally retained.

Today it is the most popular, best-selling English translation, with more than 215 million copies worldwide. It can be purchased in all sorts of styles and with various kinds of helps.

The *NIV*, like most other translations, has been criticized by some scholars. In some places in the 2011 edition, the effort to make the translation gender neutral has caused it to be rejected. The Old Testament seems not to have been quite up to the standard of the New. All-in-all it is a very readable and useful translation. For critical Bible study it still has not matched the *NASB* in the author's opinion. (If a more complete review is desired, check on line for the *New International Version*.)

5. The *English Standard Version*

The *ESV*, copyrighted in 2001, seeks to be faithful to the text and is vigorous in the pursuit of accuracy—at the same time striving for simplicity, beauty, and dignity of expression. The goal has been to carry on the long legacy of the great translations of the past, yet for modern readers.

The words and phrases in the *ESV* have been carefully weighed against the original Hebrew, Aramaic, and Greek texts. Every effort has been made to not over or under-translate and not to miss any nuance of the original text. The wordings and phrasings themselves grow out of the Tyndale/ King James, word-for-word legacy and, most recently, out of the *RSV*, with the 1971 *RSV* text providing the starting point for the work. Archaic language has been brought up to date and significant corrections have been made in the translation of key texts. The effort has been to retain the depth of meaning and enduring language that have made their indelible mark on the English-speaking world and have defined the life and doctrines of the church for over four centuries.

The *ESV* is essentially literal, and as far as possible, seeks to capture the precise wording of the original text and the personal style of each Bible writer. It seeks to be faithful to the original text, letting the reader see as directly as possible the structure and meaning of the original.

The *ESV* is another recommended translation that can be helpful, whether for personal devotional reading or for deeper Bible research. (More information can be found on line, under Bible Study Tools.com, *English Standard Version Bible*, "ESV.)

Literal Thought-for-Thought Translations

From an effort to make the Bible more understandable for the average reader came the more fluid and easily understood versions. This does not necessarily mean that the translators have a low view of the original texts, but because they love the Word, they want to make it understood more clearly. This is a valid goal of translation and helpful for most who love and read the Bible.

A lengthy discussion of this kind of Bible is not the purpose here, but to make the reader aware of this additional helpful source for study, devotion, or preparation to teach, or to aid the beginning student of Scripture.

Many thought-for-thought translations are available, but there are three common ones that can be suggested. One is called *God's Word*, another *The New Living Translation*, and a third is called *The New Century Version*.

Many people find that sticking with one translation will over time bring them to steady Christian growth and maturity in Christ. Yet, others are benefited by seeing the same teachings expressed in a different word pattern that possibly helps their understanding.

Paraphrases

Paraphrases are not translations at all. They might be styled as running commentaries on the written word. They often bring with them the interpretation of the writer. Caution should be used when reading them, remembering that they may contain ideas that are not in the Hebrew or Greek texts, but express the theological view of those who wrote them.

One of the most popular of these is called *The Living Bible* and was done by Dr. Kenneth Taylor. This paraphrase became very popular during the 1970s and 1980s. He did not at first consult the original languages, but took a reliable translation, the *ASV*, and sought to make it clearer. Later he employed a group of 90 Greek and Hebrew scholars to revise the text and make it more accurate. The original work did express Taylor's doctrinal views as would be the case with almost anyone who undertook such a project.

Paraphrasing is rewording the text with the effort to make it clearer and more easily understood. Taylor did not intend for his work to be used as a primary text for serious Bible study or for scholars. His purpose was to make the Bible understandable for the average reader.

After many years, in1996, this work was published as the *Holy Bible: New Living Translation.*

Other similar works are, *Good News for Modern Man,* and *The Message.* Paraphrases do have a valuable place for Christians and especially for those who are just beginning to read the Bible.

Two Charts that Show the Position of Various Translations and the Paraphrases.

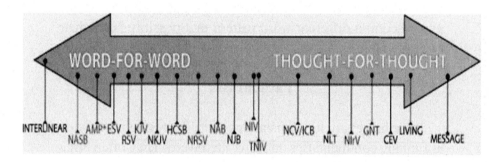

Above chart taken from http://www.zondervanbibles.com/translations.htm <link no longer active>

NASB New American Standard Bible (1971; update 1995)	NIV New International Version (1984)
AMP Amplified Bible (1965)	TNIV Today's New Internation Version (NT 2001, OT 2005)
ESV English Standard Version (2001)	
RSV Revised Standard Version (1952)	NCV New Century Version
KJV King James Version (1611; significantly revised 1769)	NLT New Living Translation (1st ed. 1996, 2nd ed 2004)
NKJV New King James Version (1982)	NIrV New International readers Version
HCSB Holman Christian Standard Version (2004)	GNT Good News Translation (also Good News Bible)
NRSV New Revised Standard Version (1989)	CEV Contemporary English Version
NAB New American Bible (Catholic, 1970, 1986(NT), 1991 (Psalms)	Living Living Bible (1950). Paraphrase by Ken Taylor. Liberal treatment of 'blood.'
NJB New Jerusalem Bible (Catholic, 1986; revision of 1966 Jerusalem Bible)	Message The Message by Eugene Peterson (1991-2000s)

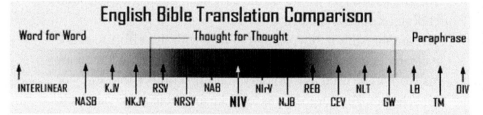

English Bible Translation Comparison chart taken from http://www.gospelcom.net/ibs.bibles/translations/index.php

Translations not identified in previous list

OIV Oxford's Inclusive Language Version-revision to NRSV to be more gender neutral and politically correct.

GW God's Word to the Nations. Translation/paraphrase by William Beck. Little known.

REB Revised English Bible

Translation Comparison of Selected Passages

	KJV	NASB	ESV	NIV	NLT[2]	Message
Proverbs 18:24	A man that hath friends must shew himself friendly; and there is a friend that sticketh closer than a brother.	A man of many friends comes to ruin. But there is a friend who sticks closer than a brother.	A man of many companions may come to ruin, but there is a friend who sticks closer than a brother.	A man of many companions may come to ruin, but there is a friend who sticks closer than a brother.	There are "friends" who destroy each other, but a real friend sticks closer than a brother.	Friends come and go, but a true friend sticks by you like family.

Comments: The KJV follows the Septuagint (Greek OT) rather than the Hebrew text. The meaning of the Hebrew text conveyed by the NASB, ESV, NIV, and more or less the NLT. The Message is completely out in left field. I see no legitimate connection between the concept communicated by the Hebrew text and the text of The Message.

	KJV	NASB	ESV	NIV	NLT[2]	Message
Romans 3:25	Whom God hath set forth to be a propitiation through faith in his blood, to declare his righteousness for the remission of sins that are past, through the forbearance of God;	Whom God displayed publicly as a propitiation in His blood through faith. This was to demonstrate His righteousness, because in the forbearance of God He passed over the sins previously committed;	whom God put forward as a propitiation by his blood, to be received by faith. This was to show God's righteousness, because in his divine forbearance he had passed over former sins.	God presented him as a sacrifice of atonement, through faith in his blood. He did this to demonstrate his justice, because in his forbearance he had left the sins committed beforehand unpunished—	For God presented Jesus as the sacrifice for sin. People are made right with God when they believe that Jesus sacrificed his life, shedding his blood. This sacrifice shows that God was being fair when he held back and did not punish those who sinned in times past,	God sacrificed Jesus on the altar of the world to clear that world of sin. Having faith in him sets us in the clear. God decided on this course of action in full view of the public—to set the world in the clear with himself through the sacrifice of Jesus, finally taking care of the sins he had so patiently endured.

Comments: KJV is the most literal here. There is disagreement about whether the word paresis means "remission, forgiveness" or "passing over, leaving unpunished." This explains the difference between the KJV and all cited modern versions. Interesting to see the NIV agree with the KJV against the NASB and ESV's treatment of the phrase 'in his blood.' Original text data missing from The Message: no mention of blood or of God's self-justification. Confusing terminology: What does it mean to "set the world in the clear with himself?" And what is the "altar of the world?"

	KJV	NASB	ESV	NIV	NLT[2]	Message
Romans 8:35-37	Who shall separate us from the love of Christ? shall tribulation, or distress, or persecution, or famine, or nakedness, or peril, or sword? 36 As it is written, For thy sake we are killed all the day long; we are accounted as sheep for the slaughter. 37 Nay, in all these things we are more than conquerors through him that loved us.	Who shall separate us from the love of Christ? Shall tribulation, or distress, or persecution, or famine, or nakedness, or peril, or sword? 36 Just as it is written, "For Thy sake we are being put to death all day long; We were considered as sheep to be slaughtered." 37 But in all these things we overwhelmingly conquer through Him who loved us.	Who shall separate us from the love of Christ? Shall tribulation, or distress, or persecution, or famine, or nakedness, or danger, or sword? 36 As it is written, "For your sake we are being killed all the day long; we are regarded as sheep to be slaughtered." 37 No, in all these things we are more than conquerors through him who loved us.	Who shall separate us from the love of Christ? Shall trouble or hardship or persecution or famine or nakedness or danger or sword? 36 As it is written: "For your sake we face death all day long; we are considered as sheep to be slaughtered." 37 No, in all these things we are more than conquerors through him who loved us.	Can anything ever separate us from Christ's love? Does it mean he no longer loves us if we have trouble or calamity, or are persecuted, or hungry, or destitute, or in danger, or threatened with death? 36 (As the Scriptures say, "For your sake we are killed every day; we are being slaughtered like sheep.") 37 No, despite all these things, overwhelming victory is ours through Christ, who loved us.	Do you think anyone is going to be able to drive a wedge between us and Christ's love for us? There is no way! Not trouble, not hard times, not hatred, not hunger, not homelessness, not bullying threats, not backstabbing, not even the worst sins listed in Scripture: They kill us in cold blood because they hate you. We're sitting ducks; they pick us off one by one. None of this fazes us because Jesus loves us.

Comments: I was flabbergasted at the audacity of The Message. This is nothing less than adding to God's Word support for one's theological position. Paul would never have said such a thing: (1) the worst sin listed in Scripture is unpardonable and, therefore, would without remedy separate one from Christ; (2) There is not one single passage of Scripture that supports the contention that no sin is capable of separating a believer from Christ. This is Eugene Peterson writing his own scripture; it is not God's Word.

	KJV	NASB	ESV	NIV	NLT[2]	Message
Colossians 2:9-10	For in him dwelleth all the fulness of the Godhead bodily. 10 And ye are complete in him, which is the head of all principality and power:	For in Him all the fullness of Deity dwells in bodily form, and in Him you have been made complete, and He is the head over all rule and authority;	For in him the whole fullness of deity dwells bodily, and you have been filled in him, who is the head of all rule and authority.	For in Christ all the fullness of the Deity lives in bodily form, and you have been given fullness in Christ, who is the head over every power and authority.	For in Christ lives all the fullness of God in a human body. So you also are complete through your union with Christ, who is the head over every ruler and authority.	Everything of God gets expressed in him, so you can see and hear him clearly. You don't need a telescope, a microscope, or a horoscope to realize the fullness of Christ, and the emptiness of the universe without him. When you come to him, that fullness comes together for you, too. His power extends over everything.

Comments: I like the NLT's paraphrase here. I think it captures nicely what the text is teaching. And again, The Message is way out in left field. A horoscope! Besides the text says nothing about realizing the fullness of Christ. Rather, Paul asserts that the fullness of the divine nature or of deity dwells in him.

Translation Comparison Chart from Zondervan

(with their spin, slightly modified)

Version	Reading Level	Readability	Number of Translators	Translation Philosophy	Example Verse
NASB [apb1]New American Standard Bible (1995)	11.00	Formal style in modern English but more readable than the King James Version.	54	Word-for-word	But we will not boast beyond our measure, but within the measure of the sphere which God apportioned to us as a measure, to reach even as far as you. 2 Corinthians 10:13 (NASB)
AMP [apb2]Amplified	N/A	Expanded and "amplified" by means of a system of brackets and parentheses, which sometimes make for fragmented reading	Frank E. Siewert, plus 12 others	Word-for-word plus additional amplification of word meanings.	We, on the other hand, will not boast beyond our legitimate province and proper limit, but will keep within the limits [of our commission which] God has allotted us as our measuring line and which reaches and includes even you. 2 Corinthians 10:13 (AMP)
ESV [apb3]English Standard Version	8.0	Literal style, but more readable than the King James Version	100+	Word-for-word	But we will not boast beyond limits, but will boast only with regard to the area of influence God assigned to us, to reach even you. 2 Corinthians 10:13 (ESV)
KJV [apb4]King James Version	12.00	Difficult to read due to 17th-century English vocabulary and word order	54	Word-for-word	But we will not boast of things without our measure, but according to the measure of the rule which God hath distributed to us, a measure to reach even unto you. 2 Corinthians 10:13 (KJV)
NKJV [apb5]New King James Version	9.0	Easier word usage, but somewhat choppy because it maintains 17th century sentence structure	119	Authors used the original KJV as a benchmark, while working to produce an accurate and modern word-for-word translation	We, however, will not boast beyond measure, but within the limits of the sphere which God appointed us--a sphere which especially includes you. 2 Corinthians 10:13 (NKJV)
HCSB [apb6] Holman Christian Standard Bible	N/A	A highly readable, accurate translation written in modern English	90	Balance between word-for-word and thought-for-thought	We, however, will not boast beyond measure, but according to the measure of the area of ministry that God has assigned to us, which reaches even you. 2 Corinthians 10:13 (HCSB)
NRSV [apb7]New Revised Standard Version	10.40	Contemporary, dignified with generic language in reference to humans	30	Attempts a balance between word-for-word and thought-for-thought	We, however, will not boast beyond limits, but will keep within the field that God has assigned to us, to reach out even as far as you. 2 Corinthians 10:13 (NRSV)

NAB [apb8]New American Bible (Roman Catholic)	6.60	A clear and straightforward translation that reads smoothly. Written in basic American English.	55	Word-for-word	But we will not boast beyond measure but will keep to the limits God has apportioned us, namely, to reach even you. 2 Corinthians 10:13 (NAB)
NJB [apb9]New Jerusalem Bible (Roman Catholic)	7.4	A highly readable, accurate translation written in modern English	36	Balance between word translation and meaning	By contrast we do not intend to boast beyond measure, but will measure ourselves by the standard which God laid down for us, namely that of having come all the way to you. 2 Corinthians 10:13 (NJB)
NIV[apb10] New International Version	7.80	An accurate and smooth-reading version in modern English	115	Attempts to balance between word-for-word and thought-for-thought	We, however, will not boast beyond proper limits, but will confine our boasting to the field God has assigned to us, a field that reaches even to you. 2 Corinthians 10:13 (NIV)
TNIV [apb11] Today's New International Version	N/A	Same as NIV	115	Balance between word-for-word and thought-for-thought. Deliberate attempt to be gender neutral	We, however, will not boast beyond proper limits, but will confine our boasting to the sphere of service God himself has assigned to us, a sphere that also includes you. 2 Corinthians 10:13 (TNIV)
NLT [apb12]New Living Translation	6.3	A readable translation; uses vocabulary and language structures commonly used by the average person	90	Translators were involved in bringing the classic Living Bible from its status as a paraphrase to a thought-for-thought translation of Scripture.	But we will not boast of authority we do not have. Our goal is to stay within the boundaries of God's plan for us, and this plan includes our working there with you. 2 Corinthians 10:13 (NLT)
CEV [apb13]Contemporary English Version	5.4	Clear, simple English that a child can understand, but with a mature style that adults can appreciate	100+	Thought-for-thought	We don't brag about something we don't have a right to brag about. We will only brag about the work that God has sent us to do, and you are part of that work. 2 Corinthians 10:13 (CEV)
NIrV[apb14] New International Reader's Version	2.9	Easy to read and understand; uses simple, short words and sentence	11	Balance between word translation and meaning, with an emphasis on meaning where necessary for simplification	But I won't brag more than I should. Instead, I will brag only about what I have done in the area God has given me. It is an area that reaches all the way to you. 2 Corinthians 10:13 (NIrV)
GNT [apb15]Good News Translation, formerly Today's English Version (TEV) and Good News Bible (GNB)	6.0	Very simple, readable version without jargon. Uses a limited vocabulary.	R. Bratcher (NT) Bratcher lus six others (OT)	Thought-for-thought	As for us, however, our boasting will not go beyond certain limits; it will stay within the limits of the work which God has set for us, and this includes our work among you. 2 Corinthians 10:13 (GNT)
The Message[apb16]	4.8	An easy-to-read, modern-language paraphrase	Eugene H. Peterson AMP [apb2] Amplified	Thought-for-thought. Converts the original languages into the tone and the rhythms of modern-day American speech while retaining the idioms and meaning of the original languages.	We're not, understand, putting ourselves in a league with those who boast that they're our superiors. We wouldn't dare do that. But in all this comparing and grading and competing, the quite miss the point. We aren't making outrageous claims here. We're sticking to the limits of what God has set for us. But there can be no question that those limits reach to and include you. 2 Corinthians 10:13 (The Message)

[apb1]A highly respected formal translation of the Bible. Purpose of the work was to update the American Standard Version into more current English. Published in 1971. Updated in 1995. The most literal is now more readable.

[apb2]A popular translation used to understand the hidden meaning of Greek and Hebrew words. Published in 1964 (updated in 1987). Break through the language barrier.

[apb3]A literal update of the Revised Standard Version, seeks to produce word-for-word correspondence. Published in 2001.

[apb4]Traditionally loved and accepted by all Christians. Purpose in translation was "to deliver God's book unto God's people in a tongue which they can understand." Published in 1611. Timeless treasure.

[apb5]A modern language update of the original KJV. Purpose was to update and modernize the original KJV but preserve the KJV as much as possible. Published in 1982.

[apb6]A new translation that attempts to combine both formal and dynamic equivalence. Published in 2004.

[apb7]A widely accepted translation in the tradition of the King James Version. Purpose was to "make a good one better." Published in 1990.

[apb8]Published under the direction of Pope Pius XII, this Catholic version of the Bible represents more than 25 years of effort by the Catholic Biblical Association of America. All editions include the Deuterocanonical/Apocryphal books. Published in 1970.

[apb9]An updated version of the 1966 Jerusalem Bible. The New Jerusalem Bible is the official English language text used in Catholic liturgy outside the United States.

[apb10]A best-selling translation, widely accepted by evangelical Christians. Purpose in translation was to "produce an accurate translation, suitable for public and private reading, teaching, preaching, memorizing, and liturgical use." Published in 1978.

[apb11]Based on the NIV, the most read and most trusted translation. Combines uncompromising accuracy with the clarity of contemporary language. New Testament published in 2001; Old Testament published in 2005. The classic translation in today's language.

[apb12]The New Living Translation is a dynamic equivalence translation based on the work of 90 Bible scholars and a smaller team of English stylists. These scholars and stylists went back to the original languages and sought to produce the closest natural equivalent of the message in natural, contemporary English. Published in 1996.

[apb13]Written at an elementary-school reading level, the CEV is readable and understandable for the modern reader. Published in 1995.

[apb14]A thorough, scholarly simplification of the NIV, the NIrV was specifically designed to help young children and new readers understand the Bible for themselves and create an easy stepping-stone from a children's Bible to an adult Bible. Published in 1994. Updated in 1998

[apb15]"A translation intended for people everywhere for whom English is either their mother tongue or an acquired language." Published in 1976. The Good Book that reads like a good book.

[apb16]This paraphrase was translated using the rhythms and tone of contemporary English to communicate to the modern reader. New Testament published in 1993, Old Testament in 2002.

SECTION FIVE

CONCLUSIONS

Next to the Bible itself, the study of the biblical background has been the most useful and productive study aid to the author in a long and productive ministry. The reason is that efforts to discredit the Bible are really attacks on the credibility of Jesus, the Living Word, known to us through the written Word—the Bible. Unless we are prepared to show that the Bible is the inspired Word of God, our message is discredited.

When talking with an unbeliever, they need to know the Bible can be trusted. Many cultish religions discredit or try to twist the Bible. They cannot be taught from the Bible until they realize that it is the inspired Word of God.

Even for the "born again" Christian, learning biblical backgrounds leads to deepened faith and commitment. The information supporting the Bible as the Holy Word of God is conclusive. There can be no doubt that the Bible is a divinely inspired book. Inspiration as defined by H. S. Miller as, "The inbreathing into man, by God, thus qualifying them to receive and communicate Divine truth." There can be no other explanation as to how the Bible came into being.

How could one of the Earth's most ancient books always be historically, archaeologically, medically, and scientifically accurate? Why has it been vindicated time after time? Why has it survived every attack? Why do its critics so often end up as its most dedicated advocates? It is an inspired book.

We have talked about Divine authorship, human authorship, and Old and New Testament inspiration. We have discussed canon and canonicity, how the Old and New Testaments were formed. We have learned why some books were included and others excluded. Such subjects as the Apocrypha, Pseudepigrapha, Homologomena, and Antilegomena have been examined.

We have learned how the Bible is genuine and authentic. We have learned why the Bible was able to be copied century after century and not be corrupted. And we have learned about the guilds of the scribes and their important part in biblical preservation.

The ancient manuscripts of the Old Testament, the Dead Sea Scrolls, and the many other ways we have to prove the accuracy of what was originally written have been examined. The huge number of New Testament manuscripts has given us today the most pure Greek text the church has enjoyed in nearly two millennia. Those who have criticized the Bible as being full of errors, or that many truths have been removed from it have been shown to be misinformed.

Believing biblical scholars have been diligent in answering the negative Higher Critics' efforts to discredit the Bible. Those who have sought to destroy the Bible, in reality have destroyed themselves and the civilizations who have listened to them. We know that the nation that forgets Jehovah God cannot prosper, as demonstrated by ancient Israel and more recently in pre-Second World War Germany and France. We must learn that when America puts God, the Bible, and Christian values out of our schools, colleges, universities, and the public square—our nation cannot prosper. Take God out of a tree and it dies. Take God out of our education and it is dead. Take God out of our national life and the result is destruction, decline, and the breakup of the family and culture.

What we must have is a return to Holy Scripture—the Bible. It is the only solution for our failing nation. No democratic republic can long survive without Christian faith. This faith must be built upon the impregnable rock of Holy Scripture—the Bible.

EXHIBIT ONE

POPULAR MODERN VERSIONS[36]

King James Version

- Forty-seven men divided into six groups. Inaugurated by King James, carried out by leading church authorities and scholars.
- Date: First published in 1611 with many other additions.
- Textual basis: *Textus Receptus* (Beza, 1604)
- Type of translation: Literal, but in the King's English.
- Accuracy: Beautiful, but accurate only to a point. Many more manuscripts have been found since its translation. Uses many words that are now obsolete (carriages means baggage; scrip means wallet, fetched a compass means sailed) or different in meaning (letteth means restrain, prevent means precede, conversation means conduct). Some passages are unnecessarily obscured (2 Corinthians 10:15-16). Language is inconsistent (Jeremiah, Jeremias, and Jeremy are used for the same name. Areopagus and Mars Hill are used for the same place.)
- Theological background: Church of England and Puritan theology of the 17th century.

New King James Version

- One-hundred-thirty people contributed as editors and an overview committee.
- Date: 1982
- Textual basis: For the most part is an updating of the *King James Version* based on the *Textus Receptus*, but does use material from the *Biblia Hebraica*.

36   Dr. Steven A. Crane

- Type of translation: Remains close to the original *King James* in rendering the Greek, but does bring an updating in many areas.
- Accuracy: The body of the translation still follows the *Textus Receptus* and is not as accurate as it could be. While it is easier to read and has seen a great improvement in clarity, it has lost the most important element from the *King James Version*—its charm.

New American Standard Bible

- Fifty-eight scholars sponsored by the Lockman Foundation
- Date: First published in 1971
- Textual basis: Kittel's *Biblia Hebraica*: Nestle's *Greek New Testament*, 23rd edition.
- Type of translation: Accurately described as both a revision of the *American Standard Version* (1901) and a fresh translation based upon the *ASV*.
- Accuracy: Excellent. Great balance of closeness to the original text and good expression in English that convey the true meaning of the original. Because it is a literal translation, it can be more stiff in its reading and the careful distinction in translating tenses of Greek verbs can make it wooden. Its extreme consistency of using the same English word every time an original word is used leads to some inferior renderings. The literal translation of the NASB provides the basis for solid biblical studies and is a superior study Bible.
- Theological background: Evangelical. Each translator shared the conviction that the words of Scripture as originally penned in the Hebrew and Greek were inspired by God.

The *New International Version*

- Over one hundred participants divided into translation teams: An O.T. Committee, a N.T. committee, a General Editiorial Committee, a Translation Committee, and Consultants.
- Date: First published in 1978.
- Textual basis: Eclectic: Kittel's Nestle's, and United Bible Societies' texts.
- Type of translation: Blend of literal and free.
- Accuracy: Although it is a free translation, it does attempt to acknowledge each Hebrew or Greek word—if not by a word in the English, then at least by word order, punctuation, or some other literary device. It is contemporary in selection of words and its meaning is usually clear. Its weakness lies in its attempt to be both contemporary and literal. Some words are rendered in newer ways (propitiation becomes sacrifice of atonement), while in other places difficult words are left in the text (tetrarch). At some points, the *NIV*'s renderings are more of an interpretation than a translation. One example of this is the word for flesh in Greek, *sarx*. The *NIV* often inserts the phrase "sinful nature" in its place. Other problems have arisen from a desire at times to become more gender neutral. The *NIV* in recent years has been the most widely read of the modern versions.
- Theological background: Evangelical. The translators are committed to the full authority and complete trustworthiness of the Scriptures which they believe to be God's Word in written form.

The Living Bible

- **History**: First published in 1971, *The Living Bible* (*TLB*) is a version of the Bible created by Kenneth N.

Taylor, the founder of Tyndale House, a major Christian publishing company. *The Living Bible* is not a translation of the Bible; it is a paraphrase. (See Translation Method.) In 1962, *Living Letters*, Taylor's paraphrase of the epistles, became available. *The Living Bible* was very popular in the 1970s and was, in fact, the best-selling book in America in 1972 and 1973. By 1997, 40 million copies of *The Living Bible* had been sold. In the late 1980s, Taylor and his colleagues at Tyndale House Publishers invited a team of 90 Greek and Hebrew scholars to participate in a project of revising the text of *The Living Bible*. After many years of work, the result was an entirely new translation of the Bible. It was published in 1996 as the *Holy Bible: New Living Translation*.

- **Translation Method**: Dr. Taylor employed the method of paraphrasing to create *The Living Bible*. While direct translation involves using a thought-for-thought or a word-for-word recreation of the text from original Greek and Hebrew manuscripts, paraphrasing uses the "in other words" method of restating a previously translated manuscript, in this case the *American Standard Version of 1901*. Paraphrasing is essentially rewording the text with the intention of making it clearer and more easily understood. Taylor never intended for his paraphrase to be used as the reader's only source of biblical knowledge, or as the primary text for scholars. Rather, his goal was to put the basic message of the Bible into modern language that could readily be understood by the typical reader without a theological or linguistic background.

- **Pros and cons**: As is true with any paraphrase, putting the Bible "in your own words" runs the risk of enabling your own biases, thoughts, and preferences to influence what the Bible says. This is impossible to avoid. The primary problem of any paraphrase of the

Bible is that it inputs far too much of a person's opinion of what the Bible says, instead of simply stating what the Bible says. There is nothing inherently wrong with a paraphrase, as long as users of the paraphrase understand exactly what it is—not a Bible translation, but rather an interpretation/commentary on what the Bible says.

- **Sample verses:** John 1:1-2, 14— "Before anything else existed, there was Christ, with God. He has always been alive and is himself God. And Christ became a human being and lived here on earth among us and was full of loving forgiveness and truth. And some of us have seen his glory— the glory of the only Son of the heavenly Father." John 3:16— "For God loved the world so much that he gave his only Son so that anyone who believes in him shall not perish but have eternal life." John 8:58— "Jesus: 'The absolute truth is that I was in existence before Abraham was ever born!'" Ephesians 2:8-9— "Because of his kindness, you have been saved through trusting Christ. And even trusting is not of yourselves; it too is a gift from God. Salvation is not a reward for the good we have done, so none of us can take any credit for it." Titus 2:13— "looking forward to that wonderful time we have been expecting, when his glory shall be seen – the glory of our great God and Savior Jesus Christ."

- **Recommended Resources:** How to Choose a Translation for All Its Worth: A Guide to Understanding and Using Bible Versions by Gordon D. Fee & Mark L. Strauss and Logos Bible Software.

English Standard Version (ESV)

- The *English Standard Version* (*ESV*) stands in the classic mainstream of English Bible translations over the past half-millennium. The fountainhead of that stream was William Tyndale's New Testament of 1526; marking its course were the *King James Version* of 1611 (*KJV*), the *English Revised Version* of 1885 (*RV*), the *American Standard Version* of 1901 (*ASV*), and the *Revised Standard Version* of 1952 and 1971 (*RSV*). In that stream, faithfulness to the text and vigorous pursuit of accuracy were combined with simplicity, beauty, and dignity of expression. The goal has been to carry forward this legacy for a new century. To this end each word and phrase in the *ESV* has been carefully weighed against the original Hebrew, Aramaic, and Greek, to ensure the fullest accuracy and clarity and to avoid under-translating or overlooking any nuance of the original text. The words and phrases themselves grow out of the Tyndale/King James legacy, and most recently out of the *RSV*, with the 1971 *RSV* text providing the starting point for our work. Archaic language has been brought to current usage and significant corrections have been made in the translation of key texts. But throughout, the goal has been to retain the depth of meaning and enduring language that have made their indelible mark on the English-speaking world and have defined the life and doctrine of the church over the last four centuries. The *ESV* is an "essentially literal" translation that seeks as far as possible to capture the precise wording of the original text and the personal style of each Bible writer. It seeks to be transparent to the original text, letting the reader see as directly as possible the structure and meaning of the original.

- **Copyright and Usage Information:** The *ESV* and *English Standard Version* are trademarks of Good News Publishers. Use of either trademark requires the permission of Good News Publishers.

EXHIBIT TWO

THE DEAD SEA SCROLLS[37] [38]

The Dead Sea Scrolls are a collection of 981 texts discovered between 1946 and 1956 at *Khirbet Qumran* in the West Bank. They were found inside caves about a mile inland from the northwest shore of the Dead Sea, from which they derive their name.[1] Nine of the scrolls were rediscovered at the Israel Antiquities Authority (IAA) in 2014, after they had been stored unopened for six decades following their excavation in 1952.[2][3] The texts are of great historical, religious, and linguistic significance because they include the earliest known surviving manuscripts of works later included in the Hebrew Bible canon, along with deuterocanonical and extra-biblical manuscripts which preserve evidence of the diversity of religious thought in late Second Temple Judaism.

The texts are written in Hebrew, Aramaic, Greek, and Nabataean, mostly on parchment but with some written on papyrus and bronze.[4] The manuscripts have been dated to various ranges between 408 BCE and 318 CE.[5] Bronze coins found on the site form a series beginning with John Hyrcanus (135–104 BCE) and continuing until the First Jewish-Roman War (66–73 CE).[6]

The scrolls have traditionally been identified with the ancient Jewish sect called the Essenes, although some recent interpretations have challenged this association and argue that the scrolls were penned by priests in Jerusalem, Zadokites, or other unknown Jewish groups.[7][8]

Due to the poor condition of some of the Scrolls, not all of them have been identified. Those that have been identified can be divided into three general groups: (1) some 40% of them

---

37   From Wikipedia, the free encyclopedia p.p. 169-235
38   The count of biblical texts found among the Dead Sea Scrolls varies from some reports to others. This is likely due to additional manuscripts being found after earlier counts. It appears that the number of biblical books found is 330–380 at this time.

are copies of texts from the Hebrew Bible, (2) approximately another 30% of them are texts from the Second Temple Period and which ultimately were not canonized in the Hebrew Bible, like the Book of Enoch, Jubilees, the Book of Tobit, the Wisdom of Sirach, Psalms 152–155, etc., and (3) the remaining roughly 30% of them are sectarian manuscripts of previously unknown documents that shed light on the rules and beliefs of a particular group or groups within greater Judaism, like the Community Rule, the War Scroll, the Pesher on Habakkuk and The Rule of the Blessing.[9]

Contents

Discovery

See also: Qumran

Qumran cave 4, where ninety percent of the scrolls were found.

The Dead Sea Scrolls were discovered in a series of twelve caves around the site known as Wadi Qumran near the Dead Sea in the West Bank (of the Jordan River) between 1946 and 1956 by Bedouin peoples and a team of archeologists.[10]

Initial discovery (1946–1947)

The initial discovery, by Bedouin shepherd Muhammed Edh-Dhib, his cousin Jum'a Muhammed, and Khalil Musa, took place between November 1946 and February 1947.[11][12] The shepherds discovered 7 scrolls (See Fragment and scroll lists) housed in jars in a cave at what is now known as the Qumran site. John C. Trever reconstructed the story of the scrolls from several interviews with the Bedouin. Edh-Dhib's cousin noticed the caves, but edh-Dhib himself was the first to actually fall into one. He retrieved a handful of scrolls, which Trever identifies as the Isaiah Scroll, Habakkuk Commentary, and the Community Rule, and took them back to the camp to show to his family. None of the scrolls were destroyed in this process, despite popular rumor.[13] The Bedouin kept the scrolls hanging on a tent pole while they figured out what to do with them, periodically taking them out to show people. At some point during this time, the Community Rule was split in two. The Bedouin first took the scrolls to a dealer named Ibrahim 'Ijha in Bethlehem. 'Ijha returned them, saying they were worthless, after being warned that they might have been stolen from a synagogue. Undaunted, the Bedouin went to a nearby market, where a Syrian Christian offered to buy them. A sheikh joined their conversation and suggested they take the scrolls to Khalil Eskander Shahin, "Kando," a cobbler and part-time antiques dealer. The Bedouin and the dealers returned to the site, leaving one scroll with Kando and selling three others to a dealer for GBP7 (equivalent to US$29 in 2003, US$37 in 2014).[13] The original scrolls continued to change hands after the Bedouin left them in the possession of a third party until a sale could be arranged. (See Ownership)

In 1947 the original seven scrolls caught the attention of Dr. John C. Trever, of the American Schools of Oriental Research (ASOR), who compared the script in the scrolls to that of *The Nash Papyrus*, the oldest biblical manuscript then known, and found similarities between them. In March the 1948 Arab-Israeli War prompted the move of some of the scrolls to Beirut, Lebanon for safekeeping. On 11 April 1948, Millar Burrows, head of the ASOR, announced the discovery of the scrolls in a general press release.

Search for the Qumran caves (1948–1949)

Early in September 1948, Metropolitan bishop Mar Samuel brought some additional scroll fragments that he had acquired to Professor Ovid R. Sellers, the new Director of ASOR. By the end of 1948, nearly two years after their discovery, scholars had yet to locate the original cave where the fragments had been found. With unrest in the country at that time, no large-scale search could be undertaken safely. Sellers attempted to get the Syrians to assist in the search for the cave, but he was unable to pay their price. In early 1948, the government of Jordan gave permission to the Arab Legion to search the area where the original Qumran cave was thought to be. Consequently, Cave 1 was rediscovered on 28 January 1949, by Belgian United

Nations observer Captain Phillipe Lippens and Arab Legion Captain Akkash el-Zebn.[14]

Qumran caves rediscovery and new scroll discoveries (1949–1951)

A view of the Dead Sea from a cave at Qumran in which some of the Dead Sea Scrolls were discovered.

The rediscovery of what became known as "Cave 1" at Qumran prompted the initial excavation of the site from 15 February to 5 March 1949 by the Jordanian Department of Antiquities led by Gerald Lankester Harding and Roland de Vaux.[15] The Cave 1 site yielded discoveries of additional Dead Sea Scroll fragments, linen cloth, jars, and other artifacts.[16]

Excavations of Qumran (1951–1956)

In November 1951, Roland de Vaux and his team from the ASOR began a full excavation of Qumran.[17] By February 1952, the Bedouin people had discovered 30 fragments in what was to be designated Cave 2.[18] The discovery of a second cave eventually yielded 300 fragments from 33 manuscripts, including fragments of Jubilees, the Wisdom of Sirach, and Ben Sira written in Hebrew.[16][17] The following month, on 14 March 1952, the ASOR team discovered a third cave with fragments of Jubilees and the Copper Scroll.[19] Between September and December 1952 the fragments and scrolls of Caves 4, 5, and 6 were subsequently discovered by the ASOR teams.[17]

With the monetary value of the scrolls rising as their historical significance was made more public, the Bedouins and the

ASOR archaeologists accelerated their search for the scrolls separately in the same general area of Qumran, which was over 1 kilometer in length. Between 1953 and 1956, Roland de Vaux led four more archaeological expeditions in the area to uncover scrolls and artifacts.[16] The last cave, Cave 11, was discovered in 1956 and yielded the last fragments to be found in the vicinity of Qumran.[20]

Scrolls and fragments

See also: List of the Dead Sea Scrolls

The War Scroll, found in Qumran Cave 1.

The 972 manuscripts found at Qumran were found primarily in two separate formats: as scrolls and as fragments of previous scrolls and texts.

A portion of the second discovered copy of the Isaiah scroll, 1QIsa^b.

The original seven scrolls from Cave 1 at Qumran are: the Great Isaiah Scroll (1QIsa^a), a second copy of Isaiah (1QIsa^b), the Community Rule Scroll (4QS^a-j), the Pesher on Habakkuk (1QpHab), the War Scroll (1QM), the Thanksgiving Hymns (1QH), and the Genesis Apocryphon (1QapGen).[21]

Caves 4a and 4b

Cave 4 was discovered in August 1952, and was excavated from 22–29 September 1952 by Gerald Lankester Harding, Roland de Vaux, and Józef Milik.[22] Cave 4 is actually two hand-cut caves (4a and 4b), but since the fragments were mixed, they are labeled as 4Q. Cave 4 is the most famous of Qumran caves both because of its visibility from the Qumran plateau and its productivity. It is visible from the plateau to the south of the Qumran settlement. It is by far the most productive of all Qumran caves, producing ninety percent of the Dead Sea Scrolls and scroll fragments (approx. 15,000 fragments from 500 different texts), including 9–10 copies of Jubilees, along with 21 *tefillin* and 7 *mezuzot*.

Fragment/ Scroll #	Fragment/ Scroll Name	KJV Bible Association	Description
4QGen-Exod[a]		Genesis and the Exodus	= 4Q1
4QGen[b]		Genesis	= 4Q2
4QGen[c]		Genesis	= 4Q3
4QGen[d]		Genesis 1:18–27	= 4Q4
4QGen[e]		Genesis	= 4Q5
4QGen[f]		Genesis 48:1–11	= 4Q6
4QGen[g]		Genesis 48:1–11	= 4Q7
4QGen[h1]		Genesis 1:8–10	= 4Q8
4QGen[h2]		Genesis 2:17–18	= 4Q8a
4QGen[h-para]		A paraphrase of Genesis 12:4–5	= 4Q8b
4QGen[h-title]	The title of a Genesis manuscript		= 4Q8c

4QGen^j		Genesis	= 4Q9
4QGen^k		Genesis	= 4Q10
4Qpaleo-Gen-Exod^l		Genesis and the Exodus	Written in palaeo-Hebrew script = 4Q11
4QpaleoGen^m		Genesis	Written in palaeo-Hebrew script = 4Q12
4QExod^b		Exodus	= 4Q13
4QExod^c		Exodus	= 4Q14
4QExod^d		Exodus	= 4Q15
4QExod^e		Exodus 13:3–5	= 4Q16
4QExod^f		Exodus and Leviticus	= 4Q17
4QExod^g		Exodus 14:21–27	= 4Q18
4QExod^h		Exodus 6:3–6	= 4Q19
4QExod^j		Exodus	= 4Q20
4QExod^k		Exodus 36:9–10	= 4Q21
4QExod^m		Exodus	Written in palaeo-Hebrew script = 4Q22
4QLev-Num^a		Leviticus and Numbers	= 4Q23
4QLev-Num^b		Leviticus	= 4Q24
4QLev-Num^c		Leviticus	= 4Q25
4QLev-Num^d		Leviticus	= 4Q26
4QLev-Num^e		Leviticus	= 4Q26a
4QLev-Num^g		Leviticus	= 4Q26b
4QNum^b		Numbers	= 4Q27
4QDeut^n	"All Souls Deuteronomy"	Deuteronomy 8:5–10, 5:1–6:1	= 4Q41

4QCant[a]	Pesher on Canticles or Pesher on the Song of Songs	Song of Songs	Written in Hebrew = 4Q107
4QCant[b]	Pesher on Canticles or Pesher on the Song of Songs	Song of Songs	Written in Hebrew = 4Q107
4QCant[c]	Pesher on Canticles or Pesher on the Song of Songs	Song of Songs	= 4Q108
4Q112		Daniel	
4Q123	"Rewritten Joshua"		
4Q127	"Rewritten Exodus"		
4Q128-148	Various tefillin		
4Q156	Targum of Leviticus		
4QtgJob	Targum of Job		= 4Q157
4QRP[a]	Rewritten Pentateuch		= 4Q158
4Q161-164	Pesher on Isaiah		
4QpHos	The Hosea Commentary Scroll,[23] a Pesher on Hosea		= 4Q166
4Q167	Pesher on Hosea		
4Q169	Pesher on Nahum or Nahum Commentary		

179

4Q174	Florilegium or Midrash on the Last Days		
4Q175	Messianic Anthology or Testimonia	Contains Deuterono-my 5:28–29, 18:18–19, 33:8–11; Joshua 6:26	Written in Hasmonean script.
4Q179	Lamentations		cf. 4Q501
4Q196-200	Tobit		cf. 4Q501
4Q201ᵃ	The Enoch Scroll[23]		
4Q213-214	Aramaic Levi		
4Q4Q215	Testament of Naphtali		
4QCantᵃ	Pesher on Canticles or Pesher on the Song of Songs		= 4Q240
4Q246	Aramaic Apocalypse or The Son of God Text		
4Q252	Pesher on Genesis		
4Q258	Serekh ha-Yahad or Community Rule		cf. 1QSᵈ
4Q265-273	The Damas-cus Docu-ment		cf. 4QDᵃ/ᵍ = 4Q266/272, 4QDᵃ/ᵉ = 4Q266/270, 5Q12, 6Q15, 4Q265-73
4Q285	Rule of War		cf. 11Q14
4QRPᵇ	Rewritten Pentateuch		= 4Q364

4QRP^c	Rewritten Pentateuch		= 4Q365
4QRP^c	Rewritten Pentateuch		= 4Q365a (=4QTemple?)
4QRP^d	Rewritten Pentateuch		= 4Q366
4QRP^e	Rewritten Pentateuch		= 4Q367
4QInstruction	Sapiential Work A		= 4Q415-418
4QParaphrase	Paraphrase of Genesis and Exodus		4Q415-418
4Q434	Barkhi Napshi – Apocryphal Psalms		15 fragments: likely hymns of thanksgiving praising God for his power and expressing thanks
4QMMT	Miqsat Ma'ase Ha-Torah or Some Precepts of the Law or the Halakhic Letter		cf. 4Q394-399
4Q400-407	Songs of Sabbath Sacrifice or the Angelic Liturgy		cf. 11Q5-6
4Q448	Hymn to King Jonathan or The Prayer For King Jonathan Scroll	Psalm 154	In addition to parts of Psalm 154 it contains a prayer mentioning King Jonathan.
4Q510-511	Songs of the Sage		
4Q521	Messianic Apocalypse		Made up of two fragments

4Q523	MeKleine Fragmente, z.T. gesetzlichen Inhalts		Fragment is legal in content. PAM number, 41.944.[24]
4Q539	Testament of Joseph		
4Q541	Testament of Levi[d]		Aramaic frag. also called "4QApocryphon of Levi[b] ar"
4Q554-5	New Jerusalem		cf. 1Q32, 2Q24, 5Q15, 11Q18
Unnumbered			Nine unopened fragments recently rediscovered in storage[25]

Cave 5

Cave 5 was discovered alongside Cave 6 in 1952, shortly after the discovery of Cave 4. Cave 5 produced approximately 25 manuscripts.[22]

Fragment/Scroll #	Fragment/Scroll Name	KJV Bible Association	Description
5QDeut		Deuteronomy	=5Q1
5QKgs		1 Kings = 5Q2Joshua	=5Q9
5Q10	Apocryphon of Malachi		
5Q11	Rule of the Community		
5Q12	Damascus Document		
5Q13	Rule		
5Q14	Curses		
5Q15	New Jerusalem		
5Q16-25	Unclassified		
5QX1	Leather fragment		

Cave 6

Cave 6 was discovered alongside Cave 5 in 1952, shortly after the discovery of Cave 4. Cave 6 contained fragments of about 31 manuscripts.[22]

List of groups of fragments collected from Wadi Qumran Cave 6:[26][27]

Fragment/Scroll #	Fragment/Scroll Name	KJV Bible Association	Description
6QpaleoGen		Genesis 6:13–21	Written in palaeo-Hebrew script = 6Q1
6QpaleoLev		Leviticus 8:12–13	Written in palaeo-Hebrew script = 6Q2
6Q3		A few letters of Deuteronomy 26:19	
6QKings		1 Kings 3:12–14; 2 Kings 7:8–10; 1 Kings 12:28–31; 2 Kings 7:20–8:5; 1 Kings 22:28–31; 2 Kings 9:1–2; 2 Kings 5:26; 2 Kings 10:19–21; 2 Kings 6:32	Made up of 94 Fragments. = 6Q4
6Q5		Possibly Psalm 78:36–37	
6QCant		Song of Songs 1:1–7	Written in Hebrew = 6Q6
6QDaniel		Daniel 11:38; 10:8–16; 11:33–36	13 Fragments. =6Q7
6QGiants ar		Book of Giants from Enoch	= 6Q8

6QApocryphon on Samuel-Kings	Apocryphon on Samuel-Kings		Written on papyrus. = 6Q9
6QProphecy	Unidentified prophetic fragment		Written in Hebrew papyrus. = 6Q10
6QAllegory of the Vine	Allegory of the Vine		= 6Q11
6QapocProph	An apocryphal prophecy		= 6Q12
6QPriestProph	Priestly Prophecy		= 6Q13
6QD	Damascus Document		= 6Q15
6QBenediction	Benediction		= 6Q16
6QCalendrical Document	Calendrical Document		= 6Q17
6QHymn	Hymn		= 6Q18
6Q19		Possibly from Genesis	
6Q20		Possibly from Deuteronomy	
6Q21	Possibly prophetic text		Fragment containing 5 words.
6Q22	Unclassified fragments		
6Q23	Unclassified fragments		
6Q24-25	Unclassified fragments		
6Q26	Accounts or contracts		
6Q27-28	Unclassified fragments		
6QpapProv		Parts of Proverbs 11:4b-7a; 10b	Single six-line fragment. = 6Q30
6Q31	Unclassified fragments		

184

Cave 7

Cave 7 yielded fewer than 20 fragments of Greek documents, including 7Q2 (the "Letter of Jeremiah" = Baruch 6), 7Q5 (which became the subject of much speculation in later decades), and a Greek copy of a scroll of Enoch.[28][29][30] Cave 7 also produced several inscribed potsherds and jars.[31]

Fragment/Scroll #	Fragment/Scroll Name	KJV Bible Association	Description
7QLXXExod gr		Exodus 28:4–7	= 7Q1
7QLXXEpJer		Jeremiah 43–44	= 7Q2
7Q3-4	Unknown biblical text		
7Q5	Unknown biblical text		
7Q6-18	Unidentified fragments		Very tiny fragments written on papyrus.
7Q19	Unidentified papyrus imprint		Very tiny fragments written on papyrus

Cave 8

Cave 8, along with caves 7 and 9, was one of the only caves that is accessible by passing through the settlement at Qumran. Carved into the southern end of the Qumran plateau, archaeologists excavated cave 8 in 1957.

Cave 8 produced five fragments: Genesis (8QGen), Psalms (8QPs), a tefillin fragment (8QPhyl), a mezuzah (8QMez), and a hymn (8QHymn).[32] Cave 8 also produced several tefillin cases, a box of leather objects, tons of lamps, jars, and the sole of a leather shoe.[31]

List of groups of fragments collected from Wadi Qumran Cave 8:[26][27]

Fragment/Scroll #	Fragment/Scroll Name	KJV Bible Association	Description
8QGen		Genesis 17:12–19; 18:20–25	= 8Q1
8QPs		Psalm 17:5–9; 17:14; 18:6–9; 18:10–13	=8Q2
8QPhyl	Fragments from a "Phylactery"	Exodus 12:43–51 13:1–16; 20:11; Deuteronomy 5:1–14; 6:1–9; 11:13; 10:12–22; 11:1–12	=8Q3
8QMez		Deuteronomy 10:12–11:21 from a Mezuzah	=8Q4
8QHymn	Unidentified hymn		=8Q5

Cave 9

Cave 9, along with caves 7 and 8, was one of the only caves that is accessible by passing through the settlement at Qumran. Carved into the southern end of the Qumran plateau, archaeologists excavated cave 9 in 1957.

There was only one fragment found in Cave 9:

Fragment/Scroll #	Fragment/Scroll Name	KJV Bible Association	Description
9Qpap	Unidentified fragment		=9Q1 Written on papyrus.

Cave 10

In Cave 10 archaeologists found two ostraca with some writing on them, along with an unknown symbol on a grey stone slab:

Fragment/Scroll #	Fragment/Scroll Name	KJV Bible Association	Description
10QOstracon	Ostracon		=10Q1 Two letters written on a piece of pottery.

Cave 11

Cave 11 was discovered in 1956 and yielded 21 texts, some of which were quite lengthy. The Temple Scroll, so called because more than half of it pertains to the construction of the Temple of Jerusalem, was found in Cave 11, and is by far the longest scroll. It is now 26.7 feet (8.15 m) long. Its original length may have been over 28 feet (8.75 m). The Temple Scroll was regarded by Yigael Yadin as "The Torah According to the Essenes." On the other hand, Hartmut Stegemann, a contemporary and friend of Yadin, believed the scroll was not to be regarded as such, but was a document without exceptional significance. Stegemann notes that it is not mentioned or cited in any known Essene writing.[33]

Also in Cave 11, an eschatological fragment about the biblical figure Melchizedek (11Q13) was found. Cave 11 also produced a copy of Jubilees.

According to former chief editor of the DSS editorial team John Strugnell, there are at least four privately owned scrolls from Cave 11, that have not yet been made available for scholars. Among them is a complete Aramaic manuscript of the Book of Enoch.[34]

List of groups of fragments collected from Wadi Qumran Cave 11:

Fragment/Scroll #	Fragment/Scroll Name	KJV Bible Association	Description
11QpaleoLev^a		Leviticus 4:24–26; 10:4–7; 11:27–32; 13:3–9; 13:39–43; 14:16–21; 14:52-!5:5; 16:2–4; 16:34–17:5; 18:27–19:4; 20:1–6; 21:6–11; 22:21–27; 23:22–29; 24:9–14; 25:28–36; 26:17–26; 27:11–19	Written in palaeo-Hebrew script. = 11Q1
11QpaleoLev^b		Leviticus	Written in palaeo-Hebrew script. = 11Q2
11QDeut		Deuteronomy	= 11Q3
11QEz		Ezekiel	= 11Q4
11QPs^a		Psalms	= 11Q5
11QPs^b		Psalms 77:18–21; 78:1; 109:3–4; 118:1; 118:15–16; 119:163–165; 133:1–3; 141:10; 144:1–2	= 11Q6
11QPs^c		Psalms 2:1–8; 9:3–7; 12:5–9; 13:1–6; 14:1–6; 17:9–15; 18:1–12; 19:4–8; 25:2–7	= 11Q7

188

11QPsᵈ		Psalms 6:2–4; 9:3–6; 18:26–29; 18:39–42; 36:13; 37:1–4; 39:13–14; 40:1; 43:1–3; 45:6–8; 59:5–8; 68:1–5; 68:14–18; 78:5–12; 81:4–9; 86:11–14; 115:16–18; 116:1	= 11Q8
11QPsᵉ		Psalms 50:3–7	= 11Q9
11QtgJob		Targum of Job	= 11Q10
11QapocrPs		Apocryphal paraphrase of Psalms 91	= 11Q11
11QJub	Ethiopic text of Jubilees	Jubilees 4:6–11; 4:13–14; 4:16–17; 4:29–31; 5:1–2; 12:15–17; 12:28–29	= 11Q12
11QMelch	"Heavenly Prince Melchizedek"		= 11Q13
11QSM	"The Book of War"		= 11Q14
11QHymnsᵃ			= 11Q15
11QHymnsᵇ			= 11Q16
11QShirShabb	Songs of the Sabbath Sacrifice		= 11Q17
11QNJ ar	"New Jerusalem"		Written in Aramaic = 11Q18
11QTᵃ	"Temple Scroll"		= 11Q19
11QTᵇ	"Temple Scroll"		= 11Q20
11QTᶜ	"Temple Scroll"		= 11Q21
11Q22-28	Unidentified fragments		

11Q29			Serekh ha-Ya-had related
11Q30	Unidentified frag-ments		
11Q31	Unidentified wads		

Fragments with unknown provenance

Some fragments of scrolls do not have significant archaeological provenance nor records that reveal which designated Qumran cave area they were found in. They are believed to have come from Wadi Qumran caves, but are just as likely to have come from other archaeological sites in the Judaean Desert area.[35] These fragments have therefore been designated to the temporary "X" series.

Fragment/Scroll #	Fragment/Scroll Name	KJV Bible Association	Description
XQ1-3	"Tefillin from Qumran"	Deuteronomy 5:1 – 6:3; 10:12 – 11:12.[35]	First published in 1969; Phylacteries
XQ4	"Tefillin from Qumran"		Phylacteries
XQ5ᵃ		Jubilees 7:4–5	
XQ5ᵇ	Hymn		
XQ6	Offering		Small fragment with only one word in Aramaic.
XQ7	Unidentified fragment		Strong possibility that it is part of 4QInstruction.
XQpapEn		Book of Enoch 9:1	One small fragment written in Hebrew. = XQ8

EXHIBIT THREE

DEAD SEA SCROLLS[39]

Origin

There has been much debate about the origin of the Dead Sea Scrolls. The dominant theory remains that the scrolls were the product of a sect of Jews living at nearby Qumran called the Essenes, but this theory has come to be challenged by several modern scholars.

Qumran–Essene Theory

The view among scholars, almost universally held until the 1990s, is the "Qumran–Essene" hypothesis originally posited by Roland Guérin de Vaux[36] and Józef Tadeusz Milik,[37] though independently both Eliezer Sukenik and Butrus Sowmy of St Mark's Monastery connected scrolls with the Essenes well before any excavations at Qumran.[38] The Qumran–Essene theory holds that the scrolls were written by the Essenes, or by another Jewish sectarian group, residing at Khirbet Qumran. They composed the scrolls and ultimately hid them in the nearby caves during the Jewish Revolt sometime between 66 and 68 CE. The site of Qumran was destroyed and the scrolls never recovered. A number of arguments are used to support this theory.

- There are striking similarities between the description of an initiation ceremony of new members in the Community Rule and descriptions of the Essene initiation ceremony mentioned in the works of Flavius Josephus – a Jewish–Roman historian of the Second Temple Period.
- Josephus mentions the Essenes as sharing property among the members of the community, as does the Community Rule.

39   From Wikipedia, the free encyclopedia

- During the excavation of Khirbet Qumran, two ink-wells and plastered elements thought to be tables were found, offering evidence that some form of writing was done there. More inkwells were discovered nearby. De Vaux called this area the "scriptorium" based upon this discovery.
- Several Jewish ritual baths (Hebrew: *miqvah* = הוקמ) were discovered at Qumran, which offers evidence of an observant Jewish presence at the site.
- Pliny the Elder (a geographer writing after the fall of Jerusalem in 70 CE) describes a group of Essenes living in a desert community on the northwest shore of the Dead Sea near the ruined town of 'Ein Gedi.

The Qumran–Essene theory has been the dominant theory since its initial proposal by Roland de Vaux and J.T. Milik. Recently, however, several other scholars have proposed alternative origins of the scrolls.

Christian Origin Theory

Spanish Jesuit José O'Callaghan Martínez argued in the 1960s that one fragment (7Q5) preserves a portion of text from the New Testament Gospel of Mark 6:52–53.[39] This theory was falsified in the year 2000 by paleographic analysis of the particular fragment.[40]

In recent years, Robert Eisenman has advanced the theory that some scrolls describe the early Christian community. Eisenman also argued that the careers of James the Just and Paul the Apostle correspond to events recorded in some of these documents.[41]

Jerusalem Origin Theory

Some scholars have argued that the scrolls were the product of Jews living in Jerusalem, who hid the scrolls in the caves near Qumran while fleeing from the Romans during the destruction of Jerusalem in 70 CE. Karl Heinrich Rengstorf first proposed that the Dead Sea Scrolls originated at the library of the Jewish Temple in Jerusalem.[42] Later, Norman Golb suggested that the scrolls were the product of multiple libraries in Jerusalem, and not necessarily the Jerusalem Temple library.[8] [43] Proponents of the Jerusalem Origin theory point to the diversity of thought and handwriting among the scrolls as evidence against a Qumran origin of the scrolls. Several archaeologists have also accepted an origin of the scrolls other than Qumran, including Yizhar Hirschfeld[44] and most recently Yizhak Magen and Yuval Peleg,[45] who all understand the remains of Qumran to be those of a Hasmonean fort that was reused during later periods.

Qumran–Sectarian Theory

Qumran–Sectarian theories are variations on the Qumran–Essene theory. The main point of departure from the Qumran–Essene theory is hesitation to link the Dead Sea Scrolls specifically with the Essenes. Most proponents of the Qumran–Sectarian theory understand a group of Jews living in or near Qumran to be responsible for the Dead Sea Scrolls, but do not necessarily conclude that the sectarians are Essenes.

Qumran–Sadducean Theory

A specific variation on the Qumran–Sectarian theory that has gained much recent popularity is the work of Lawrence H. Schiffman, who proposes that the community was led by a group of Zadokite priests (Sadducees).[46] The most important document in support of this view is the "Miqsat Ma'ase Ha-Torah" (4QMMT), which cites purity laws (such as the transfer of impurities) identical to those attributed in rabbinic writings to the Sadducees. 4QMMT also reproduces a festival calendar that follows Sadducee principles for the dating of certain festival days.

Physical characteristics

Age

Radiocarbon dating

Main article: Carbon dating the Dead Sea Scrolls

Parchment from a number of the Dead Sea Scrolls have been carbon dated. The initial test performed in 1950 was on a piece of linen from one of the caves. This test gave an indicative dating of 33 CE plus or minus 200 years, eliminating early hypotheses relating the scrolls to the mediaeval period.[47] Since then two large series of tests have been performed on the scrolls themselves. The results were summarized by VanderKam and Flint, who said the tests give "strong reason for thinking that most of the Qumran manuscripts belong to the last two centuries BCE and the first century CE."[48]

Paleographic dating

Analysis of letter forms, or palaeography, was applied to the texts of the Dead Sea Scrolls by a variety of scholars in the field. Major linguistic analysis by Cross and Avigad dates fragments from 225 BCE to 50 CE.[49] These dates were determined by examining the size, variability, and style of the text.[50] The same fragments were later analyzed using radiocarbon dating and were dated to an estimated range of 385 BCE to 82 CE with a 68% accuracy rate.[49]

Ink and parchment

The scrolls were analyzed using a cyclotron at the University of California, Davis, where it was found that two types of black ink were used: iron-gall ink and carbon soot ink.[51] In addition, a third ink on the scrolls that was red in color was found to be made with cinnabar (HgS, mercury sulfide).[51] There are only four uses of this red ink in the entire collection of Dead Sea Scroll fragments.[52] The black inks found on the scrolls that are made up of carbon soot were found to be from olive oil lamps.[53] Gall nuts from oak trees, present in some, but not all of the black inks on the scrolls, was added to make the ink more resilient to smudging common with pure carbon inks.[51] Honey, oil, vinegar and water were often added to the mixture to thin the ink to a proper consistency for writing.[53] In order to apply the ink to the scrolls, its writers used reed pens.[54]

Shown here is a closeup of the ink and text of two of the fragments of the Dead Sea Scrolls. The two fragments, fragments 1 and 2 of 7Q6, are written on papyrus.

The Dead Sea scrolls were written on parchment made of processed animal hide known as vellum (approximately 85.5 – 90.5% of the scrolls), papyrus (estimated at 8.0 – 13.0% of the scrolls), and sheets of bronze composed of about 99.0% copper and 1.0% tin (approximately 1.5% of the scrolls).[54][55] For those scrolls written on animal hides, scholars with the Israeli Antiquities Authority, by use of DNA testing for assembly purposes, believe that there may be a hierarchy in the religious importance of the texts based on which type of animal was used to create the hide. Scrolls written on goat and calf hides are considered by scholars to be more significant in nature, while those written on gazelle or ibex are considered to be less religiously significant in nature.[56]

In addition, tests by the National Institute of Nuclear Physics in Sicily, Italy, have suggested that the origin of parchment of select Dead Sea Scroll fragments is from the Qumran area itself, by using X-ray and Particle Induced X-ray emission testing of the water used to make the parchment that were compared with the water from the area around the Qumran site.[57]

Deterioration, storage, and preservation

Two examples of the pottery that held some of the Dead Sea Scrolls documents found at Qumran.

The Dead Sea Scrolls that were found were originally preserved by the dry, arid, and low humidity conditions present within the Qumran area adjoining the Dead Sea.[58] In addition, the lack of the use of tanning materials on the parchment of the Dead Sea Scrolls and the very low airflow in the Qumran caves also contributed significantly to their preservation.[59] Some of the scrolls were found stored in clay jars within the Qumran caves, further helping to preserve them from deterioration. The original handling of the scrolls by archaeologists and scholars was done inappropriately, and, along with their storage in an uncontrolled environment, they began a process of more rapid deterioration than they had experienced at Qumran.[60] During the first few years in the late 1940s and early 1950s, adhesive tape used to join fragments and seal cracks caused significant damage to the documents.[60] The Government of Jordan had recognized the urgency of protecting the scrolls from deterioration and the presence of the deterioration among the scrolls.[61] However, the government did not have adequate funds to purchase all the scrolls for their protection and agreed to have foreign institutions purchase the scrolls and have them held at their museum in Jerusalem until they could be "adequately studied."[61]

In early 1953, they were moved to the Palestine Archaeological Museum (commonly called the Rockefeller Museum)[62] in East Jerusalem and through their transportation suffered more deterioration and damage.[63] The museum was underfunded and had limited resources with which to examine the scrolls, and, as a result, conditions of the "scrollery" and storage area were left relatively uncontrolled by modern standards.[63] The museum had left most of the fragments and scrolls lying between window glass, trapping the moisture in with them, causing an acceleration in the deterioration process. During a portion of the conflict during the 1956 Arab-Israeli War, the scrolls collection of the Palestine Archaeological Museum was stored in the vault of the Ottoman Bank in Amman, Jordan.[64] Damp conditions from temporary storage of the scrolls in the Ottoman Bank vault from 1956 to the Spring of 1957 led to a more rapid rate of deterioration of the scrolls. The conditions caused mildew to develop on the scrolls and fragments, and some of the fragments were partially destroyed or made illegible by the glue and paper of the manila envelopes in which they were stored while in the vault.[64] By 1958 it was noted that up to 5% of some of the scrolls had completely deteriorated.[61] Many of the texts had become illegible and many of the parchments had darkened considerably.[60][63]

Until the 1970s, the scrolls continued to deteriorate because of poor storage arrangements, exposure to different adhesives, and being trapped in moist environments.[60] Fragments written on parchment (rather than papyrus or bronze) in the hands of private collectors and scholars suffered an even worse fate than those in the hands of the museum, with large portions of fragments being reported to have disappeared by 1966.[65] In the late 1960s, the deterioration was becoming a major concern with scholars and museum officials alike. Scholars John Allegro and Sir Francis Frank were some of the first to strongly advocate for better preservation techniques.[63] Early attempts made by both the British and Israel Museums to remove the adhesive tape ended up exposing the parchment to an array of chemicals, including "British Leather Dressing," and darkening some of them significantly.[63] In the 1970s and 1980s, other preservation attempts were made that included removing the glass plates and replacing them with cardboard and removing pressure against the plates that held the scrolls in storage; however, the fragments and scrolls continued to rapidly deteriorate during this time.[60]

In 1991, the Israeli Antiquities Authority established a temperature controlled laboratory for the storage and preservation of the scrolls. The actions and preservation methods of Rockefeller Museum staff were concentrated on the removal of tape, oils, metals, salt, and other contaminants.[60] The fragments and scrolls are preserved using acid-free cardboard and stored in solander boxes in the climate-controlled storage area.[60]

Photography and assembly

Since the Dead Sea Scrolls were initially held by different parties during and after the excavation process, they were not all photographed by the same organization nor in their entirety.

First photographs by the American Schools of Oriental Research (1948)

The first individual to photograph a portion of the collection was John C. Trever (1916–2006), a biblical scholar and archaeologist, who was a resident for the American Schools of Oriental Research.[66] He photographed three of the scrolls discovered in Cave 1 on 21 February 1948, both on black-and-white and standard color film.[66][67][68] Although an amateur photographer, the quality of his photographs often exceeded the visibility of the scrolls themselves as, over the years, the ink of the texts quickly deteriorated after they were removed from their linen wrappings.

Infrared photography and plate assembly by the Palestine Archaeological Museum (1952–1967)

A majority of the collection from the Qumran caves was acquired by the Palestine Archeological Museum. The Museum had the scrolls photographed by Najib Albina, a local Arab photographer trained by Lewis Larsson of the American Colony in Jerusalem,[69] Between 1952 and 1967, Albina documented the five stage process of the sorting and assembly of the scrolls, done by the curator and staff of the Palestine Archeological Museum, using infrared photography. Using a process known today as broadband fluorescence infrared photography, or NIR photography, Najib and the team at the Museum produced over 1,750 photographic plates of the scrolls and fragments.[70][71][72][73] The photographs were taken with the scrolls laid out on animal skin, using large format film, which caused the text to stand out, making the plates especially useful for assembling fragments.[74] These are the earliest photographs of the museum's collection, which was the most complete in the world at the time, and they recorded the fragments and scrolls before their further decay in storage, so they are often considered the best recorded copies of the scrolls.[75]

Israel Antiquities Authority and NASA digital infrared imaging (1993–2012)

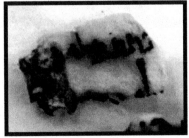

A previously unreadable fragment of the Dead Sea Scrolls photographed by the Jet Propulsion Laboratory at NASA in the early 1990s using digital infrared technology. The fragment, translated into English, reads "he wrote the words of Noah."

Beginning in 1993, the United States National Aeronautics and Space Administration used digital infrared imaging technology to produce photographs of Dead Sea Scrolls fragments. [76] In partnership with the Ancient Biblical Manuscript Center and West Semitic Research, NASA's Jet Propulsion Laboratory successfully worked to expand on the use of infrared photography previously used to evaluate ancient manuscripts by expanding the range of spectra at which images are photographed. [77] NASA used this multi-spectral imaging technique, adapted from its remote sensing and planetary probes, in order to reveal previously illegible text on fragments of the Dead Sea Scrolls. [77] The process uses a liquid crystal tunable filter in order to photograph the scrolls at specific wavelengths of light and, as a result, image distortion is significantly diminished. [78] This method was used with select fragments of the Dead Sea Scrolls to reveal text and details that cameras that take photographs using a larger light spectrum could not reveal. [78] The camera and digital imaging assembly was developed by Greg Berman, a scientist with NASA, specifically for the purpose of photographing illegible ancient texts. [79] On December–18-2012[80] the first output of this project was launched together with Google on a dedicated site http://www.deadseascrolls.org.il/. The site contains both digitizations of old images taken in the 1950s and about 1000 new images taken with the new NASA technology[81]

Israel Antiquities Authority and DNA scroll assembly (2006–2012)

Scientists with the Israeli Antiquities Authority have used DNA from the parchment on which the Dead Sea Scrolls fragments were written, in concert with infrared digital photography, to assist in the reassembly of the scrolls. For scrolls written on parchment made from animal hide and papyrus, scientists with the museum are using DNA code to associate fragments with different scrolls and to help scholars determine which scrolls may hold greater significance based on the type of material that was used. [82]

Israel Museum of Jerusalem and Google digitization project (2011–2016, Estimated)

In partnership with Google, the Museum of Jerusalem is working to photograph the Dead Sea Scrolls and make them available to the public digitally, although not placing the images in the public domain.[83] The lead photographer of the project, Ardon Bar-Hama, and his team are utilizing the Alpa 12 MAX camera accompanied with a Leaf Aptus-II back in order to produce ultra-high resolution digital images of the scrolls and fragments.[84] With photos taken at 1,200 megapixels, the results are digital images that can be used to distinguish details that are invisible to the naked eye. In order to minimize damage to the scrolls and fragments, photographers are using a 1/4000th of a second exposure time and UV-protected flash tubes.[83] The digital photography project, estimated in 2011 to cost approximately 3.5 million U.S. dollars, is expected to be completed by 2016.[84]

Scholarly examination

Scholar Eleazar Sukenik examining one of the Dead Sea Scrolls in 1951.

Early study by scholars

After most of the scrolls and fragments were moved to the Palestine Archaeological Museum in 1953, scholars began to assemble them and log them for translation and study in a room that became known as the "Scrollery."[85]

Language and script

The text of the Dead Sea Scrolls is written in four different languages: Hebrew, Aramaic, Greek, and Nabataean.

Language	Script	Percentage of Documents	Centuries of Known Use
Hebrew	Assyrian block script[86]	Estimated 76.0–79.0%	3rd century BC to present
Hebrew	Cryptic scripts "A" "B" and "C"[87][88][89]	Estimated 0.9%–1.0%[90]	Unknown
Biblical Hebrew	Paleo-Hebrew script[91]	Estimated 1.0–1.5%[89]	10th century BC to the 2nd century AD
Biblical Hebrew	Paleo-Hebrew scribal script[91]		
Aramaic	Aramaic square script	Estimated 16.0–17.0%[92]	8th century BC to present
Greek	Greek uncial script[91]	Estimated 3.0%[89]	3rd century AD to 8th centuries AD
Nabataean	Nabataean script[93]	Estimated 0.2%[93]	2nd century BC to the 4th century AD

Publication

Scholars assembling and examining the Dead Sea Scrolls fragments in what became known as the "Scrollery" room of the Palestine Archaeological Museum.

Physical publication and controversy

Some of the fragments and scrolls were published early. Most of the longer, more complete scrolls were published soon after their discovery. All the writings in Cave 1 appeared in print between 1950 and 1956; those from eight other caves were released in 1963; and 1965 saw the publication of the Psalms Scroll from Cave 11. Their translations into English soon followed.

Controversy

Publication of the scrolls has taken many decades, and delays have been a source of academic controversy. The scrolls were controlled by a small group of scholars headed by John Strugnell, while a majority of scholars had access neither to the scrolls nor even to photographs of the text. Scholars such as Hershel Shanks, Norman Golb and many others argued for decades for publishing the texts, so that they become available to researchers. This controversy only ended in 1991, when the Biblical Archaeology Society was able to publish the "Facsimile Edition of the Dead Sea Scrolls," after an intervention of the Israeli government and the Israeli Antiquities Authority (IAA). [94] In 1991 Emanuel Tov was appointed as the chairman of the Dead Sea Scrolls Foundation, and publication of the scrolls followed in the same year.

Physical description

The majority of the scrolls consist of tiny, brittle fragments, which were published at a pace considered by many to be excessively slow. During early assembly and translation work by scholars through the Rockefeller Museum from the 1950s through the 1960s, access to the unpublished documents was limited to the editorial committee.

Discoveries in the Judean Desert (1955–2009)

⎘ Emanuel Tov (1941–) who was Editor-in-Chief of the Dead Seas Scrolls Publication Project and, as a result, responsible for the publication of 32 volumes of the Discoveries in the Judean Desert series. He also worked to publish a six-volume printed edition with a majority of the non-Biblical Dead Sea Scrolls and make the same volumes available electronically on CD in a collection titled "The Dead Sea Scrolls Reader."

The content of the scrolls was published in a 40 volume series by Oxford University Press published between 1955 and 2009 known as *Discoveries in the Judean Desert.*[95] In 1952 the Jordanian Department of Antiquities assembled a team of scholars to begin examining, assembling, and translating the scrolls with the intent of publishing them.[96] The initial publication, assembled by Dominique Barthélemy and Józef Milik, was published as *Qumran Cave 1* in 1955.[95] After a series of other publications in the late 1980s and early 1990s and with the appointment of the respected Dutch-Israeli textual scholar Emanuel Tov as Editor-in-Chief of the Dead Sea Scrolls Publication Project in 1990 publication of the scrolls accelerated. Tov's team had published five volumes covering the Cave 4 documents by 1995. Between 1990 and 2009, Tov helped the team produce 32 volumes. The final volume, Volume XL, was published in 2009.

A Preliminary Edition of the Unpublished Dead Sea Scrolls (1991)

In 1991, researchers at Hebrew Union College in Cincinnati, Ohio, Ben Zion Wacholder and Martin Abegg, announced the creation of a computer program that used previously published scrolls to reconstruct the unpublished texts.[97] Officials at the Huntington Library in San Marino, California, led by Head Librarian William Andrew Moffett, announced that they would allow researchers unrestricted access to the library's complete set of photographs of the scrolls. In the fall of that year, Wacholder published 17 documents that had been reconstructed in 1988 from a concordance and had come into the hands of scholars outside of the International Team; in the same month, there occurred the discovery and publication of a complete set of facsimiles of the Cave 4 materials at the Huntington Library. Thereafter, the officials of the Israel Antiquities Authority agreed to lift their long-standing restrictions on the use of the scrolls.[98]

A Facsimile Edition of the Dead Sea Scrolls

(1991)

After further delays, attorney William John Cox undertook representation of an "undisclosed client," who had provided a complete set of the unpublished photographs, and contracted for their publication. Professors Robert Eisenman and James Robinson indexed the photographs and wrote an introduction to A Facsimile Edition of the Dead Sea Scrolls, which was published by the Biblical Archaeology Society in 1991.[99] Following the publication of the Facsimile Edition, Professor Elisha Qimron sued Hershel Shanks, Eisenman, Robinson and the Biblical Archaeology Society for copyright infringement of one of the scrolls, MMT, which he deciphered. The District Court of Jerusalem found in favor of Qimron in September 1993.[100] The Court issued a restraining order, which prohibited the publication of the deciphered text, and ordered defendants to pay Qimron NIS 100,000 for infringing his copyright and the right of attribution. Defendants appealed the Supreme Court of Israel, which approved the District Court's decision, in August 2000. The Supreme Court further ordered that the defendants hand over to Qimron all the infringing copies.

[101] The decision met Israeli and international criticism from copyright law scholars.[102]

The Facsimile Edition by Facsimile Editions Ltd, London, England (2007–2008)

In November 2007 the Dead Sea Scrolls Foundation commissioned the London publisher, Facsimile Editions Limited, to produce a facsimile edition of *The Great Isaiah Scroll* (1QIs^a), *The Order of the Community* (1QS), and *The Pesher to Habakkuk* (1QpHab).[103][104] The facsimile was produced from 1948 photographs, and so more faithfully represents the condition of the Isaiah scroll at the time of its discovery than does the current condition of the real Isaiah scroll.[103]

Of the first three facsimile sets, one was exhibited at the *Early Christianity and the Dead Sea Scrolls* exhibition in Seoul, South Korea, and a second set was purchased by the British Library in London. A further 46 sets including facsimiles of three fragments from Cave 4 (now in the collection of the National Archaeological Museum in Amman, Jordan) *Testimonia* (4Q175), *Pesher Isaiah^b* (4Q162) and *Qohelet* (4Q109) were announced in May 2009. The edition is strictly limited to 49 numbered sets of these reproductions on either specially prepared parchment paper or real parchment. The complete facsimile set (three scrolls including the Isaiah scroll and the three Jordanian fragments) can be purchased for $60,000.[103]

The facsimiles have since been exhibited in *Qumrân. Le secret des manuscrits de la mer Morte* at the Bibliothèque Nationale, Paris, France (2010) and *Verbum Domini* at the Vatican, Rome, Italy (2012) and Google.

Digital publication

Olive Tree Bible Software (2000–2011)

The text of nearly all of the non-biblical scrolls has been recorded and tagged for morphology by Dr. Martin Abegg, Jr., the Ben Zion Wacholder Professor of Dead Sea Scroll Studies at Trinity Western University located in Langley, British Columbia, Canada.[105] It is available on handheld devices through Olive Tree Bible Software - BibleReader, on Macs and Windows via emulator through Accordance with a comprehensive set of cross references, and on Windows through Logos Bible Software and BibleWorks.

The Dead Sea Scrolls Reader (2005)

The text of almost all of the non-Biblical texts from the Dead Sea Scrolls was released on CD-ROM by publisher E.J. Brill in 2005.[106] The 2400 page, 6 volume series, was assembled by an editorial team led by Donald W. Parry and Emanuel Tov.[107] Unlike the text translations in the physical publication, *Discoveries in the Judean Desert,* the texts are sorted by genres that include religious law, parabiblical texts, calendrical and sapiental texts, and poetic and liturgical works.[106]

Israel Antiquities Authority and Google digitization project (2010–2016)

High-resolution images, including infrared photographs, of some of the Dead Sea scrolls are now available online at the Israel Museum's website.[108]

On 19 October 2010, it was announced[109] that Israeli Antiquities Authority (IAA) would scan the documents using multi-spectral imaging technology developed by NASA to produce high-resolution images of the texts, and then, through a partnership with Google, make them available online free of charge, on a searchable database and complemented by translation and other scholarly tools. The first images, which according to the announcement could reveal new letters and words,[109] are expected to be posted online in the few months following the announcement, and the project is scheduled for completion within five years. According to IAA director Pnina Shor, "from the minute all of this will go online there will be no need to expose the scrolls anymore,"[109] referring to the dark, climate-controlled storeroom where the manuscripts are kept when not on display.[109]

On 25 September 2011 [110] the Israel Museum Digital Dead Sea Scrolls site went online. Google and the Israel Museum teamed up on this project,[111] allowing users to examine and explore these most ancient manuscripts from Second Temple times at a level of detail never before possible. The new website gives users access to searchable, high-resolution images of the scrolls, as well as short explanatory videos and background information on the texts and their history. As of May 2012, five complete scrolls from the Israel Museum have been digitized for the project and are now accessible online. These include the Great Isaiah Scroll, the Community Rule Scroll, the Commentary on Habakkuk Scroll, the Temple Scroll, and the War Scroll. All five scrolls can be magnified so that users may examine texts in detail.

Biblical significance

See also: Biblical canon

Before the discovery of the Dead Sea Scrolls, the oldest Hebrew language manuscripts of the Bible were Masoretic texts dating to the 10th century, such as the Aleppo Codex. (Today, the oldest known extant manuscripts of the Masoretic Text date from approximately the 9th century.[112]) The biblical manuscripts found among the Dead Sea Scrolls push that date back a millennium to the 2nd century BCE.[113] Before this discovery, the earliest extant manuscripts of the Old Testament were manuscripts such as Codex Vaticanus Graecus 1209 and Codex Sinaiticus (both dating from the 4th century) that were written in Greek.

According to *The Oxford Companion to Archaeology*:
The biblical manuscripts from Qumran, which include at least fragments from every book of the Old Testament, except

perhaps for the Book of Esther, provide a far older cross section of scriptural tradition than that available to scholars before. While some of the Qumran biblical manuscripts are nearly identical to the Masoretic, or traditional, Hebrew text of the Old Testament, some manuscripts of the books of Exodus and Samuel found in Cave Four exhibit dramatic differences in both language and content. In their astonishing range of textual variants, the Qumran biblical discoveries have prompted scholars to reconsider the once-accepted theories of the development of the modern biblical text from only three manuscript families: of the Masoretic text, of the Hebrew original of the Septuagint, and of the Samaritan Pentateuch. It is now becoming increasingly clear that the Old Testament scripture was extremely fluid until its canonization around A.D. 100.[114]

At the time of their writing the area was transitioning between the Greek Macedonian Empire and Roman dominance as Roman Judea. The Jewish *qahal* (society) had some measure of autonomy following the death of Alexander and the fracturing of the Greek Empire among his successors. The country was long called Ιουδαία or Judæa at that time, named for the Hebrews that returned to dwell there, following the well-documented diaspora.[115] The majority of Jews never actually returned to Israel from Babylon and Persia according to the Talmud, oral and archeological evidence.[116][117][*unreliable source?*]

Biblical books found

There are 225 Biblical texts included in the Dead Sea Scroll documents, or around 22% of the total, and with deuterocanonical books the number increases to 235.[118][119] The Dead Sea Scrolls contain parts of all but one of the books of the Tanakh of the Hebrew Bible and the Old Testament protocanon. They also include four of the deuterocanonical books included in Catholic and Eastern Orthodox Bibles: Tobit, Ben Sirach, Baruch 6, and Psalm 151.[118] The Book of Esther has not yet been found and scholars believe Esther is missing because, as a Jew, her marriage to a Persian king may have been looked down upon by the inhabitants of Qumran,[120] or because the book has the Purim festival which is not included in the Qumran calendar. [121] Listed below are the sixteen most represented books of the Bible found among the Dead Sea Scrolls in the 1970s, including the number of translatable Dead Sea texts that represent a copy of scripture from each Biblical book:[122]

Book	Number found
Psalms	39
Deuteronomy	33
1 Enoch	25
Genesis	24
Isaiah	22
Jubilees	21
Exodus	18
Leviticus	17
Numbers	11
Minor Prophets	10
Daniel	8
Jeremiah	6
Ezekiel	6
Job	6
1 & 2 Samuel	4
Sirach	1
Tobit	Fragments

Non-biblical books

The majority of the texts found among the Dead Sea Scrolls are non-biblical in nature and were thought to be insignificant for understanding the composition or canonization of the Biblical books, but a different consensus has emerged which sees many of these works as being collected by the Essene community instead of being composed by them.[123] Scholars now recognize that some of these works were composed earlier than the Essene period, when some of the Biblical books were still being written or redacted into their final form.[123]

Museum exhibitions and displays

Temporary public exhibitions

Small portions of the Dead Sea Scrolls collections have been put on temporary display in exhibitions at museums and public venues around the world. The majority of these exhibitions took place in 1965 in the United States and the United Kingdom and from 1993 to 2011 in locations around the world. Many of the exhibitions were co-sponsored by either the Jordanian government (pre-1967) or the Israeli government (post-1967). Exhibitions were discontinued after 1965 due to the Six-days War conflicts and have slowed down in post-2011 as the Israeli Antiquities Authority works to digitize the scrolls and place them in permanent cold storage.

Long-term museum exhibitions

Display at the Shrine of the Book at the Israel Museum, Jerusalem

Since its completion in April 1965,[141] the majority of the Dead Sea Scrolls collection has been moved to the Shrine of the Book, a part of the Israel Museum, located in Jerusalem. The museum falls under the auspices of the Israel Antiquities Authority, an official agency of the Israeli government. The permanent Dead Sea Scrolls exhibition at the museum features a reproduction of the Great Isaiah Scroll, surrounded by reproductions of other famous fragments that include Community Rule, the War Scroll, and the Thanksgiving Psalms Scroll.[142][143]

Display at the Jordan Museum, Amman, Jordan

Some of the Dead Sea Scrolls collection held by the Jordian government prior to 1967 was stored in Amman rather than at the Palestine Archaeological Museum in East Jerusalem. As a consequence, that part of the collection remained in Jordanian hands under their Department of Antiquities. Parts of this collection are anticipated to be on display at the Jordan Museum in Amman after the documents move. They were moved there in between June 2011 and August 2011 from the National Archaeological Museum of Jordan.[144] Among the display items are artifacts from the Qumran site and the Copper Scroll.

Ownership

Past ownership

🗗

Advertisement in the Wall Street Journal *dated 1 June 1954 for four of the "Dead Sea Scrolls."*

MISCELLANEOUS FOR SALE

"The Four Dead Sea Scrolls"

Biblical Manuscripts dating back to at least 200 BC, are for sale. This would be an ideal gift to an educational or religious institution by an individual or group.

Box F 206, The Wall Street Journal.

Arrangements with the Bedouin left the scrolls in the hands of a third party until a profitable sale of them could be negotiated. That third party, George Isha'ya, was a member of the Syrian Orthodox Church, who soon contacted St. Mark's Monastery in the hope of getting an appraisal of the nature of the texts. News of the find then reached Metropolitan Athanasius Yeshue Samuel, better known as Mar Samuel. After examining the scrolls and suspecting their antiquity, Mar Samuel expressed an interest in purchasing them. Four scrolls found their way into his hands: the now famous *Isaiah Scroll* (1QIsaª), the *Community Rule*, the *Habakkuk Pesher* (a commentary on the book of Habakkuk), and the *Genesis Apocryphon*. More scrolls soon surfaced in the antiquities market, and Professor Eleazer Sukenik and Professor Benjamin Mazar, Israeli archaeologists at Hebrew University, soon found themselves in possession of three, The *War Scroll*, *Thanksgiving Hymns*, and another, more fragmented, Isaiah scroll (1QIsaᵇ).

Four of the Dead Sea Scrolls went up for sale eventually, in an advertisement in the 1 June 1954, *Wall Street Journal*. On 1 July 1954, the scrolls, after delicate negotiations and accompanied by three people including the Metropolitan, arrived at the Waldorf-Astoria Hotel in New York. They were purchased by Professor Mazar and the son of Professor Sukenik, Yigael Yadin, for $250,000, approximately 2.14 million in 2012-equivalent dollars, and brought to Jerusalem.[145]

Current ownership

Most of the Dead Sea Scrolls collection is currently under the ownership of the Government of the state of Israel, and housed in the Shrine of the Book on the grounds of the Israel Museum. This ownership is contested by both Jordan and by the Palestinian Authority.

A list of known ownership of Dead Sea Scroll fragments:

Claimed Owner	Year Acquired	Number of Fragments/Scrolls Owned
Azusa Pacific University[146]	2009	5
Oriental Institute at the University of Chicago[147]	1956	1
Southwestern Baptist Theological Seminary[148]	2009; 2010; 2012	8

Rockefeller Museum – Government of Israel[149][150]	1967	> 15,000
The Schøyen Collection owned by Martin Schøyen[151]	1980; 1994; 1995	60
The Jordan Museum – Government of Jordan[152]	1947–1956	> 25

Ownership disputes

The official ownership of the Dead Sea Scrolls is disputed among the Hashemite Kingdom of Jordan, the State of Israel, and the Palestinian Authority. The debate over the Dead Sea Scrolls stems from a more general Israeli-Palestinian conflict over land and state recognition.

Parties Involved	Party Role	Explanation of Role
Jordan	Disputant; Minority Owner	Alleges that the Dead Sea Scrolls were stolen from the Palestine Archaeological Museum (now the Rockefeller Museum) operated by Jordan from 1966 until the Six-Day War when advancing Israeli forces took control of the Museum, and that therefore they fall under the rules of the 1954 Hague Convention for the Protection of Cultural Property in the Event of Armed Conflict.[153] Jordan regularly demands their return and petitions third-party countries that host the scrolls to return them to Jordan instead of to Israel, claiming they have legal documents that prove Jordanian ownership of the scrolls.[154]

Israel	Disputant; Current Majority Owner	After the Six-Day War Israel seized the scrolls and moved them to the Shrine of the Book in the Israel Museum. Israel refutes Jordan's claim and states that Jordan never lawfully possessed the scrolls since it was an unlawful occupier of the museum and region.[155][156][157]
Palestinian Authority	Disputant	The Palestinian Authority also holds a claim to the scrolls.[158]
Canada	Neutral Exhibition Host	In 2009, a part of the Dead Sea Scrolls collection held by the Israeli Antiquities Authority was moved and displayed at the Royal Ontario Museum in Toronto, Canada. Both Palestine and Jordan petitioned the international community, including the United Nations,[159] for the scrolls to be seized under disputed international law. Ottawa dismissed the demands and the exhibit continued, with the scrolls returning to Israel upon its conclusion.[160]
United Nations	Supranational Authority	Under Resolution 181 (II) adopted in 1947, East Jerusalem, which is home to the museum that held the scrolls until 1967, is part of a "Special International Regime for the City of Jerusalem" that is supposed to be administered by the United Nations, further complicating matters. East Jerusalem was under Jordanian occupation from 1948 to 1967 and has been under Israeli occupation since 1967.

Copyright disputes

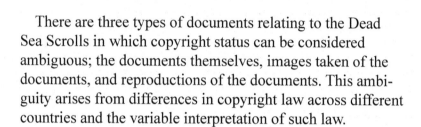

This section **needs attention from an expert in Law**. The specific problem is: **Complexity of copyright law surrounding historical documents in the United States and other nations.** WikiProject Law (or its Portal) may be able to help recruit an expert. *(June 2012)*

There are three types of documents relating to the Dead Sea Scrolls in which copyright status can be considered ambiguous; the documents themselves, images taken of the documents, and reproductions of the documents. This ambiguity arises from differences in copyright law across different countries and the variable interpretation of such law.

Copyright of the original scrolls and translations, Qimron v. Shanks (1992)

In 1992 a copyright case Qimron v. Shanks was brought before the Israeli District court by scholar Elisha Qimron against Hershel Shanks of the Biblical Archaeology Society for violations of United States copyright law regarding his publishing of reconstructions of Dead Sea Scroll texts done by Qimron in A Facsimile Edition of the Dead Sea Scrolls which were included without his permission. Qimron's suit against the Biblical Archaeology Society was done on the grounds that the research they had published was his intellectual property as he had reconstructed about 40% of the published text. In 1993, the district court Judge Dalia Dorner ruled for the plaintiff, Elisha Qimron, in context of both United States and Israeli copyright law and granted the highest compensation allowed by law for aggravation in compensation against Hershel Shanks and others.[161] In an appeal in 2000 in front of Judge Aharon Barak, the verdict was upheld in Israeli Supreme Court in Qimron's favor.[162] The court case established the two main principles from which facsimiles are examined under copyright law of the United States and Israel: authorship and originality.

The court's ruling not only affirms that the "deciphered text" of the scrolls can fall under copyright of individuals or groups, but makes it clear that the Dead Sea Scrolls themselves do not fall under this copyright law and scholars have a degree of, in the words of U.S. copyright law professor David Nimmer, "freedom" in access. Nimmer has shown how this freedom was in the theory of law applicable, but how it did not exist in reality as the Israeli Antiquities Authority tightly controlled access to the scrolls and photographs of the scrolls.[161]

References

Notes

1. ^ Down, David. "Unveiling the Kings of Israel." P.160. 2011.
2. ^ http://www.foxnews.com/science/2014/03/13/nine-un-opened-dead-sea-scrolls-found/
3. ^ "Nine manuscripts with biblical text unearthed in Qumran". ANSAmed. 27 February 2014. Retrieved 13 March 2014.
4. ^ From papyrus to cyberspace The Guardian 27 August 2008.
5. ^ Doudna, Greg, "Dating the Scrolls on the Basis of Radiocarbon Analysis," in The Dead Sea Scrolls after Fifty Years, edited by Flint Peter W., and VanderKam, James C., Vol.1 (Leiden: Brill, 1998) 430–471.
6. ^ ARC Leaney, Fom Judaean Caves, p.27,Religious Education Press, 1961.
7. ^ Ilani, Ofri, "Scholar: The Essenes, Dead Sea Scroll 'authors,' never existed," Ha'aretz, 13 March 2009.
8. ^ a b Golb, Norman, "On the Jerusalem Origin of the Dead Sea Scrolls," University of Chicago Oriental Institute, 5 June 2009.

9. ^ Abegg, Jr., Martin, Peter Flint, and Eugene Ulrich, The Dead Sea Scrolls Bible: The Oldest Known Bible Translated for the First Time into English, San Francisco: Harper, 2002.

10. ^ Retrieved 22 May 2012.

11. ^ Humphries, Mark. "Early Christianity." 2006.

12. ^ a b Evans, Craig. "Guide to the Dead Sea Scrolls." 2010.

13. ^ a b John C. Trever. The Dead Sea Scrolls. Gorgias Press LLC, 2003.

14. ^ "The Archaeological Site OF Qumran and the Personality Of Roland De Vaux." http://www.biblicaltheology.com/Research/TrstenskyF01.pdf. Retrieved 22 May 2012.

15. ^ VanderKam, James C., The Dead Sea Scrolls Today, Grand Rapids: Eerdmans, 1994. p. 9.

16. ^ a b c S.S.L. Frantisek Trstensky, "The Archaeological Site Of Qumran and the Personality Of Roland De Vaux." Retrieved 22 May 2012.

17. ^ a b c "Dead Sea Scrolls: Timetable," The Gnostic Society Library. Retrieved 23 May 2012.

18. ^ VanderKam, James C., The Dead Sea Scrolls Today, Grand Rapids: Eerdmans, 2009. p. 10.

19. ^ VanderKam, James C., The Dead Sea Scrolls Today, Grand Rapids: Eerdmans, 1994. p. 10.

20. ^ "The Digital Dead Sea Scrolls." "Discovery," The Israel Museum, Jerusalem. Retrieved 23 May 2012.

21. ^ Vermes, Geza, The Complete Dead Sea Scrolls in English, London: Penguin, 1998. ISBN 0-14-024501-4.

22. ^ a b c VanderKam, James C., The Dead Sea Scrolls Today, Grand Rapids: Eerdmans, 1994. pp. 10–11.

23. ^ a b http://www.loc.gov/exhibits/scrolls/scr3.html. Retrieved 21 May 2012.

24. ^ Buitenwerf, Rieuwerd, The Gog and Magog Tradition in Revelation 20:8, in, H. J. de Jonge, Johannes Tromp, eds., The book of Ezekiel and its influence, Ashgate Publishing, Ltd., 2007, p.172; scheduled to be published in

Charlesworth's edition, volume 9

25. ^ (Jerusalem: Israel Antiquities Authority, 2014) http:// www.timesofisrael.com/nine-tiny-new-dead-sea-scrolls-come-to-light/

26. ^ a b c Garcia Martinez, Florentino and Tigchelaar, Eibert. "The Dead Sea Scrolls Study Edition." Vol. 1. 1999.

27. ^ a b c Fritzmyer, Joseph. "A Guide to the Dead Sea Scrolls and Related Literature." 2008.

28. ^ Baillet, Maurice ed. Les 'Petites Grottes' de Qumrân (ed., vol. 3 of Discoveries in the Judean Desert; Oxford: Oxford University Press, 1962), 144–45, pl. XXX.

29. ^ Muro, Ernest A., "The Greek Fragments of Enoch from Qumran Cave 7 (7Q4, 7Q8, &7Q12 = 7QEn gr = Enoch 103:3–4, 7–8)," Revue de Qumran 18 no. 70 (1997).

30. ^ Puech, Émile, "Sept fragments grecs de la Lettre d'Hénoch (1 Hén 100, 103, 105) dans la grotte 7 de Qumrân (= 7QHén gr)," Revue de Qumran 18 no. 70 (1997).

31. ^ a b Humbert and Chambon, Excavations of Khirbet Qumran and Ain Feshkha, 67.

32. ^ Baillet ed. Les 'Petites Grottes' de Qumrân (ed.), 147–62, pl. XXXIXXXV.

33. ^ Stegemann, Hartmut. "The Qumran Essenes: Local Members of the Main Jewish Union in Late Second Temple Times." Pages 83–166 in The Madrid Qumran Congress: Proceedings of the International Congress on the Dead Sea Scrolls, Madrid, 18–21 March 1991, Edited by J. Trebolle Barrera and L. Vegas Montaner. Vol. 11 of Studies on the Texts of the Desert of Judah. Leiden: Brill, 1992.

34. ^ Shanks, Hershel. "An Interview with John Strugnell," Biblical Archaeology Review, July/August 1994". Bib-arch.org. Retrieved 21 October 2010.

35. ^ a b Grossman, Maxine. "Rediscovering the Dead Sea Scrolls." Pgs. 66–67. 2010.

36. ^ de Vaux, Roland, Archaeology and the Dead Sea Scrolls (Schweich Lectures of the British Academy, 1959). Ox-

ford: Oxford University Press, 1973.

37. ^ Milik, Józef Tadeusz, Ten Years of Discovery in the Wilderness of Judea, London: SCM, 1959.

38. ^ For Sowmy, see: Trever, John C., The Untold Story of Qumran, (Westwood: Fleming H. Revell Company, 1965), p. 25.

39. ^ O'Callaghan–Martínez, Josep, Cartas Cristianas Griegas del Siglo V, Barcelona: E. Balmes, 1963.

40. ^ Enste, Stefan. (2000). Kein Markustext in Qumran: Eine Untersuchung der These; Qumran-Fragment 7Q5 = Mk 6, 52–53 (No Mark text: an enquiry of the thesis; Qumran fragment 7Q5 = Gospel of Mark 6: 52–53). Göttingen: Vandenhoeck & Ruprecht. ISBN 9783525539453

41. ^ Eisenman, Robert H. James, the Brother of Jesus: The Key to Unlocking the Secrets of Early Christianity and the Dead Sea Scrolls. 1st American ed. New York: Viking, 1997.

42. ^ Rengstorf, Karl Heinrich. Hirbet Qumran und die Bibliothek vom Toten Meer. Translated by J. R. Wilkie. Stuttgart: W. Kohlhammer, 1960.

43. ^ Golb, Norman, Who Wrote the Dead Sea Scrolls? The Search for the Secret of Qumran, New York: Scribner, 1995.

44. ^ Hirschfeld, Yizhar, Qumran in Context: Reassessing the Archaeological Evidence, Peabody: Hendrickson Publishers, 2004.

45. ^ Magen, Yizhak, and Yuval Peleg, The Qumran Excavations 1993–2004: Preliminary Report, JSP 6 (Jerusalem: Israel Antiquities Authority, 2007) Download.

46. ^ Schiffman, Lawrence H., Reclaiming the Dead Sea Scrolls: their True Meaning for Judaism and Christianity, Anchor Bible Reference Library (Doubleday) 1995.

47. ^ Doudna, G. "Carbon-14 Dating," in Encyclopedia of the Dead Sea Scrolls, Schiffman, Lawrence, Tov, Emanuel, & VanderKam, James, eds., Vol.1 (Oxford: 2000)

48. ^ VanderKam, James C. & Flint, Peter (2002). The Mean-

ing of the Dead Sea Scrolls. New York: HarperSanFrancisco. p. 32.

49. ^ a b Grossman, Maxine. "Rediscovering the Dead Sea Scrolls." Pgs. 48–51. 2010.

50. ^ Schofield, Alison. "From Qumran to the Yahad." P. 81. 2009.

51. ^ a b c http://realscience.breckschool.org/upper/fruen/ files/Enrichmentarticles/files/IronGallInk/IronGallInk. html. Retrieved 31 May 2012.

52. ^ Nirel and Broshi. "The Red Ink of the Dead Sea Scrolls." 2007.

53. ^ a b http://www.itsgila.com/headlinerscrolls.htm. Retrieved 31 May 2012.

54. ^ a b Magness, Jodi. "The Archaeology of Qumran and the Dead Sea Scrolls." P.33. 2002.

55. ^ McFarlane, Callie. "A Clear Destiny." P.126. 2011.

56. ^ Access 9 June 2012.

57. ^ Retrieved 1 June 2012.

58. ^ Library of Congress. "Scrolls from the Dead Sea." http://www.loc.gov/exhibits/scrolls/dead.html. 2010. Retrieved 13 June 2012.

59. ^ Retrieved 13 June 2012.

60. ^ a b c d e f g Pnina Shor, "Conservation of the Dead Sea Scrolls," Israel Antiquities Authority. Retrieved 13 June 2012.

61. ^ a b c Burrows, Millar. "More Light on the Dead Sea Scrolls." 1958.

62. ^ "West meets East - The Story of the Rockefeller Museum". imj.org.il. The Israel Museum, Jerusalem. Retrieved 18 February 2014.

63. ^ a b c d e Vanderkam, James and Flint, Peter. "The Meaning of the Dead Sea Scrolls." Pgs. 63–65. 2005.

64. ^ a b Fitzmyer, Joseph A. "Responses to 101 Questions on the Dead Sea Scrolls." 1992.

65. ^ Trever, John. "The Dead Sea Scrolls: A Personal Account." 2003.

66. ^ a b VanderKam,James, and Flint, Peter. "The Meaning of the Dead Sea Scrolls." 2005. P.26.
67. ^ Evans, Craig. "Guide to the Dead Sea Scrolls." P.396. 2010.
68. ^ Retrieved 31 May 2012.
69. ^ Israel Antiquities Authority Personnel Records. Dated 1952 and 1960
70. ^ Verhoeven, G. "Imaging the invisible using modified digital still cameras for straightforward and low-cost archaeological near-infrared photography." Journal of Archaeological Science. 2008
71. ^ VanderKam, James, and Flint, Peter. "The Meaning of the Dead Sea Scrolls." 2005.
72. ^ Dorrell, Peter G. Photography in Archaeology and Conservation 2nd Edition. 1994
73. ^ American Schools of Oriental Research. The Biblical Archaeologist. Volumes 55–56. 1992.
74. ^ VanderKam, James, and Flint, Peter. The Meaning of the Dead Sea Scrolls. 2005.
75. ^ Shanks, Hershel. Freeing the Dead Sea Scrolls: And Other Adventures of an Archaeology Outsider (2010)
76. ^ Retrieved 31 May 2012
77. ^ a b "Multi-Spectral Digital Imaging of Dead Sea Scrolls and Other Ancient Documents." trs-new.jpl.nasa.gov/dspace/bitstream/2014/35946/1/93-1675.pdf. Retrieved 31 May 2012.
78. ^ a b "Seeing Into the Past." http://www.nasa.gov/vision/earth/technologies/scrolls.html. Retrieved 31 May 2012.
79. ^ Retrieved 9 June 2012.
80. ^ Miller, Eyal (2012-12-18). "Official Blog: "In the beginning"... bringing the scrolls of Genesis and the Ten Commandments online". Googleblog.blogspot.co.il. Retrieved 2013-03-26.
81. ^ "The Digital Library". The Dead Sea Scrolls. Retrieved 2013-03-26.
82. ^ Retrieved 9 June 2012.

83. ^ a b http://dss.collections.imj.org.il/project. Retrieved 27 May 2012.
84. ^ a b http://idealab.talkingpointsmemo.com/2011/09/how-one-photographer-helped-google-digitize-the-dead-sea-scrolls.php. Retrieved 27 May 2012.
85. ^ Retrieved 14 June 2012
86. ^ The Orion Center for the Study of the Dead Sea Scrolls and Associated Literature. http://orion.mscc.huji.ac.il/resources/FAQ.shtml. Retrieved 18 June 2012.
87. ^ Wise, Michael et al. "A New Translation: The Dead Sea Scrolls." P.375. 1996.
88. ^ Day, Charles. "Those who are persecuted because of righteousness, are those who pursue righteousness: an examination of the origin and meaning Matthew 5:10." Retrieved 18 June 2012.
89. ^ a b c Elledge, C.D. "The Bible and the Dead Sea Scrolls." P.88. 2005.
90. ^ Reeves, John C. and Kampen, John. "Pursuing the Text." P. 111–112. 1994.
91. ^ a b c Glob, Norman. "Who Wrote the Dead Sea Scrolls." 2012.
92. ^ Wise, Michael et al. "A New Translation: The Dead Sea Scrolls." P.9. 1996.
93. ^ a b Schiffman, Lawrence H. et al. "The Dead Sea scrolls: fifty years after their discovery : proceedings of the Jerusalem Congress, July 20–25, 1997." 1997.
94. ^ 'Copies Of Dead Sea Scrolls To Go Public – Release Would End Scholars' Dispute' – The Seattle Times 22 September 1991
95. ^ a b http://orion.mscc.huji.ac.il/resources/djd.shtml. Retrieved 12 June 2012.
96. ^ Retrieved 12 June 2012[dead link]
97. ^ Retrieved 12 June 2012.
98. ^ Encyclopædia Britannica article: Dead Sea Scrolls.
99. ^ Eisenman, Robert H. and James Robinson, A Facsimile Edition of the Dead Sea Scrolls' in two volumes (Biblical

Archaeology Society of Washington, DC, Washington, DC, 1991).

100. ^ Civil Case (Jer) 41/92 Qimron v. Shanks et al (30 March 1993) [Hebrew].

101. ^ Unofficial translation of CA 2709/93, 2811/93 Eisenman et al v. Qimron (30 August 2000).

102. ^ Michael D. Birnhack, The Dead Sea Scrolls Case: Who Is an Author? 23 (3) EIPR 128 (2001); Roberta Rosenthal Kwall, Inspiration and Innovation: The Intrinsic Dimension of the Artistic Soul 81 NOTRE DAME L. REV. 1945 (2006); David Nimmer, Authorship and Originality, 38 HOUSTON L. REV. 1, 159 (2001); Urszula Tempska, Originality" after the Dead Sea Scrolls Decision: Implications for the American Law of Copyright, 6 MARQ. INTELL. PROP. L. REV. 119 (2002); Timothy H. Lim, Intellectual Property and the Dead Sea Scrolls, Dead Sea Discoveries Vol 9, No. 2 (2002) p. 187.

103. ^ a b c Georgson, Seth (2012). Book Digitization: a Practical and Urgent Necessity for the Wisconsin Evangelical Lutheran Synod (M.Divinity). Wisconsin Lutheran Seminary. p. 26. Retrieved 15 December 2012.

104. ^ Retrieved 16 November 2007.

105. ^ Retrieved 13 June 2012.

106. ^ a b "From Other Publishers: Dead Sea Scrolls Reader Released." http://maxwellinstitute.byu.edu/publications/insights/?vol=25&num=2&id=423. Retrieved 13 June 2012.

107. ^ Retrieved 13 June 2012.

108. ^ The Digital Dead Sea Scrolls

109. ^ a b c d Joseph Krauss (19 October 2010). "Israel to put Dead Sea scrolls online". Yahoo! News/AFP. Retrieved 20 October 2010.

110. ^ Miller, Eyal (2011-09-26). "Official Blog: From the desert to the web: bringing the Dead Sea Scrolls online". Googleblog.blogspot.co.il. Retrieved 2013-03-26.

111. ^ http://dss.collections.imj.org.il/ Dead Sea Scrolls

Digital Project at the Israel Museum, Jerusalem

112. ∧ Retrieved 12 June 2012.[dead link]

113. ∧ Retrieved 12 June 2012.[dead link]

114. ∧ Fagan, Brian M., and Charlotte Beck, The Oxford Companion to Archeology, entry on the "Dead sea scrolls," Oxford University Press, 1996.

115. ∧ Antiquities of the Jews, Josephus first part of the sentence, Book of Lamentations later half of the sentence

116. ∧ References in the Talmud to entirely Jewish cities in what is today Iraq, such as Sura and Pumpudethea where the Babylonian Talmud was later writ, archeologists found evidence of Babylonian recognition of the unified Jewish societies of ancient Babylon, exiled from smoldering Jerusalem.

117. ∧ Cardinal O'Connor stated in an Easter and repeated in a Good Friday address before Saint Patrick's Cathedral, "many Jews were not even close enough to make the pilgrimage to Judea, by the time of the Savior.."

118. ∧ a b Martin G. Abegg; Peter Flint; Eugene Ulrich (7 August 2012). The Dead Sea Scrolls Bible. HarperCollins. pp. 16–. ISBN 978-0-06-203112-9. Retrieved 3 April 2013.

119. ∧ Abegg et al. "The Dead Sea Scrolls Bible: The Oldest Known Bible Translated for the First Time into English." 1999.

120. ∧ Retrieved 13 June 2012.

121. ∧ James VanderKam; Peter Flint (10 July 2005). The Meaning of the Dead Sea Scrolls: Their Significance For Understanding the Bible, Judaism, Jesus, and Christianity. Continuum International Publishing Group. pp. 180–. ISBN 978-0-567-08468-2. Retrieved 15 March 2013.

122. ∧ Gaster, Theodor H., The Dead Sea Scriptures, Peter Smith Pub Inc., 1976. ISBN=0-8446-6702-1.

123. ∧ a b Nóra Dávid; Armin Lange; Kristin De Troyer; Shani Tzoref (2012). The Hebrew Bible in Light of the Dead Sea Scrolls. Vandenhoeck & Ruprecht. pp. 9–.

ISBN 978-3-525-53555-4. Retrieved 16 March 2013.
124. ^ Retrieved 22 May 2012.
125. ^ a b http://siris-sihistory.si.edu/ipac20/ipac. jsp?&profile=all&source=~!sichronology&uri=-full=3100001~!1131~!0#focus. Retrieved 1 June 2012.
126. ^ Ulrich, Eugene. "The Dead Sea Scrolls and the Origins of the Bible." P.132. 1999.
127. ^ Retrieved 22 May 2012.
128. ^ Retrieved 22 May 2012.
129. ^ Retrieved 22 May 2012.
130. ^ Retrieved 22 May 2012.
131. ^ Retrieved 22 May 2012.
132. ^ 22 May 2012.
133. ^ Retrieved 1 June 2012.
134. ^ Retrieved 1 June 2012.
135. ^ Retrieved 1 June 2012.
136. ^ a b http://www.rom.on.ca/exhibitions/special/deadseascrolls.php. Retrieved 22 May 2012
137. ^ Retrieved 22 May 2012.
138. ^ Retrieved 1 June 2012.
139. ^ Retrieved 13 July 2012.
140. ^ http://www.seethescrolls.com. Retrieved 13 October 2012.
141. ^ Retrieved 10 June 2012.
142. ^ Retrieved 10 June 2012.
143. ^ Retrieved 10 June 2012.
144. ^ Retrieved 11 June 2012.
145. ^ Retrieved 13 June 2012.
146. ^ Retrieved 1 June 2012.
147. ^ https://oi.uchicago.edu/OI/MUS/HIGH/OIM_A30303_72dpi.html. Retrieved 13 June 2012.
148. ^ Retrieved 13 June 2012.
149. ^ Retrieved 13 June 2012.
150. ^ Retrieved 13 June 2012.
151. ^ Retrieved 13 June 2012.
152. ^ Retrieved 13 June 2012.

153. ^ Retrieved 14 June 2012

154. ^ Retrieved 14 June 2012.

155. ^ Nisreen El-Shamayleh, "Anger over Dead Sea Scrolls" (video), Al Jazeera, 3 November 2010.

156. ^ Simon McGregor-Wood, "Who Owns the Dead Sea Scrolls?", ABC News, 14 January 2010.

157. ^ Ahmad Khatib, "Jordan wants the Dead Sea Scrolls back from Israel", Agence France-Presse, 11 January 2010.

158. ^ Retrieved 14 June 2012.

159. ^ Jordan demands return of Dead Sea Scrolls 'seized' by Israel, Haaretz, 13 January 2010.

160. ^ Retrieved 14 June 2012.

161. ^ a b Nimmer, David. Houston Law Review. "Copyright in the Dead Sea Scrolls." http://www.houstonlaw-review.org/archive/downloads/38-1_pdf/HLR38P1.pdf. Retrieved 15 June 2012.

162. ^ Retrieved 15 June 2012.

Bibliography

- Abegg, Jr., Martin, Peter Flint, and Eugene Ulrich, The Dead Sea Scrolls Bible: The Oldest Known Bible Translated for the First Time into English, San Francisco: Harper, 2002. ISBN 0-06-060064-0, (contains the biblical portion of the scrolls)
- Abegg, Jr. Martin, James E. Bowley, Edward M. Cook, Emanuel Tov. The Dead Sea Scrolls Concordance, Vol 1."The Dead Sea Scrolls Concordance, Volume 1 – BRILL". Brill.nl. 1 January 2007. Retrieved 21 October 2010. Brill Publishing 2003. ISBN 90-04-12521-3.
- Allegro, John Marco, The Dead Sea Scrolls and the Christian Myth (ISBN 0-7153-7680-2), Westbridge Books, U.K., 1979.*Edward M. Cook, Solving the Mysteries of the Dead Sea Scrolls: New Light on the Bible, Grand Rapids, MI: Zondervan, 1994.
- Berg, Simon. Insights into the Dead Sea Scrolls: A Beginner's Guide, BookSurge Publishing, 2009.
- Boccaccini, Gabriele. Beyond the Essene Hypothesis: The Parting of Ways between Qumran and Enochic Judaism, Grand Rapids: Eerdmans, 1998.
- Burrows, Millar. The Dead Sea Scrolls. New York: Viking, 1955. ISBN 0-5176-2535-0
- Burrows, Millar. More Light on the Dead Sea Scrolls; New Scrolls and New Interpretations, with Translations of Important Recent Discoveries. New York: Viking, 1958.
- Charlesworth, James H. "The Theologies of the Dead Sea Scrolls." Pages xv–xxi in The Faith of Qumran: Theology of the Dead Sea Scrolls. Edited by H. Ringgren. New York: Crossroad, 1995.
- Collins, John J., Apocalypticism in the Dead Sea Scrolls, New York: Routledge, 1997.
- Collins, John J., and Craig A. Evans. Christian Beginnings and the Dead Sea Scrolls, Grand Rapids: Baker,

2006.
- Cross, Frank Moore, The Ancient Library of Qumran, 3rd ed., Minneapolis: Fortress Press, 1995. ISBN 0-8006-2807-1
- Davies, A. Powell, The Meaning of the Dead Sea Scrolls. (Signet, 1956.)
- Davies, Philip R., George J. Brooke, and Phillip R. Callaway, The Complete World of the Dead Sea Scrolls, London: Thames & Hudson, 2002. ISBN 0-500-05111-9
- de Vaux, Roland, Archaeology and the Dead Sea Scrolls (Schweich Lectures of the British Academy, 1959). Oxford: Oxford University Press, 1973.
- Dimant, Devorah, and Uriel Rappaport (eds.), The Dead Sea Scrolls: Forty Years of Research, Leiden and Jerusalem: E. J. Brill, Magnes Press, Yad Izhak Ben-Zvi, 1992.
- Eisenman, Robert H., The Dead Sea Scrolls and the First Christians, Shaftesbury: Element, 1996.
- Eisenman, Robert H., and Michael O. Wise. The Dead Sea Scrolls Uncovered: The First Complete Translation and Interpretation of 50 Key Documents Withheld for Over 35 Years, Shaftesbury: Element, 1992.
- Eisenman, Robert H. and James Robinson, A Facsimile Edition of the Dead Sea Scrolls 2 vol., Washington, D.C.: Biblical Archaeology Society, 1991.
- Fitzmyer, Joseph A., Responses to 101 Questions on the Dead Sea Scrolls, Paulist Press 1992, ISBN 0-8091-3348-2
- Galor, Katharina, Jean-Baptiste Humbert, and Jürgen Zangenberg. Qumran: The Site of the Dead Sea Scrolls: Archaeological Interpretations and Debates: Proceedings of a Conference held at Brown University, 17–19 November 2002, Edited by Florentino García Martínez, Studies on the Texts of the Desert of Judah 57. Leiden: Brill, 2006.

- García-Martinez, Florentino, The Dead Sea Scrolls Translated: The Qumran Texts in English, (Translated from Spanish into English by Wilfred G. E. Watson) (Leiden: E.J.Brill, 1994).
- Gaster, Theodor H., The Dead Sea Scriptures, Peter Smith Pub Inc., 1976. ISBN=0-8446-6702-1
- Golb, Norman, Who Wrote the Dead Sea Scrolls? The Search for the Secret of Qumran, New York: Scribner, 1995.
- Golb, Norman, On the Jerusalem Origin of the Dead Sea Scrolls, University of Chicago Oriental Institute, 5 June 2009.
- Heline, Theodore, Dead Sea Scrolls, New Age Bible & Philosophy Center, 1957, Reprint edition March 1987, ISBN 0-933963-16-5
- Hirschfeld, Yizhar, Qumran in Context: Reassessing the Archaeological Evidence, Peabody: Hendrickson Publishers, 2004.
- Israeli, Raphael, Piracy in Qumran: The Battle over the Scrolls of the Pre-Christ Era, Transaction Publishers: 2008 ISBN 978-1-4128-0703-6
- Khabbaz, C., "Les manuscrits de la mer Morte et le secret de leurs auteurs," Beirut, 2006. (Ce livre identifie les auteurs des fameux manuscrits de la mer Morte et dévoile leur secret).
- Magen, Yizhak, and Yuval Peleg, The Qumran Excavations 1993–2004: Preliminary Report, JSP 6 (Jerusalem: Israel Antiquities Authority, 2007)Download
- Magen, Yizhak, and Yuval Peleg, "Back to Qumran: Ten years of Excavations and Research, 1993–2004," in The Site of the Dead Sea Scrolls: Archaeological Interpretations and Debates (Studies on the Texts of the Desert of Judah 57), Brill, 2006 (pp. 55–116).
- Magness, Jodi, The Archaeology of Qumran and the Dead Sea Scrolls, Grand Rapids: Eerdmans, 2002.
- Maier, Johann, The Temple Scroll, [German edition

was 1978], (Sheffield:JSOT Press [Supplement 34], 1985).

- Milik, Józef Tadeusz, Ten Years of Discovery in the Wilderness of Judea, London: SCM, 1959.
- Muro, E. A., "The Greek Fragments of Enoch from Qumran Cave 7 (7Q4, 7Q8, &7Q12 = 7QEn gr = Enoch 103:3–4, 7–8)." Revue de Qumran 18, no. 70 (1997): 307, 12, pl. 1.
- O'Callaghan-Martínez, Josep, Cartas Cristianas Griegas del Siglo V, Barcelona: E. Balmes, 1963.
- Qimron, Elisha, The Hebrew of the Dead Sea Scrolls, Harvard Semitic Studies, 1986. (This is a serious discussion of the Hebrew language of the scrolls.)
- Rengstorf, Karl Heinrich, Hirbet Qumran und die Bibliothek vom Toten Meer, Translated by J. R. Wilkie. Stuttgart: W. Kohlhammer, 1960.
- Roitman, Adolfo, ed. A Day at Qumran: The Dead Sea Sect and Its Scrolls. Jerusalem: The Israel Museum, 1998.
- Sanders, James A., ed. Dead Sea scrolls: The Psalms scroll of Qumrân Cave 11 (11QPsa), (1965) Oxford, Clarendon Press.
- Schiffman,Lawrence H., Reclaiming the Dead Sea Scrolls: their True Meaning for Judaism and Christianity, Anchor Bible Reference Library (Doubleday) 1995, ISBN 0-385-48121-7, (Schiffman has suggested two plausible theories of origin and identity – a Sadducean splinter group, or perhaps an Essene group with Sadducean roots.) Excerpts of this book can be read at COJS: Dead Sea Scrolls.
- Schiffman, Lawrence H., and James C. VanderKam, eds. Encyclopedia of the Dead Sea Scrolls. 2 vols. New York: Oxford University Press, 1999.
- Shanks, Hershel, The Mystery and Meaning of the Dead Sea Scrolls, Vintage Press 1999, ISBN 0-679-78089-0 (recommended introduction to their discovery

and history of their scholarship)
- Stegemann, Hartmut. "The Qumran Essenes: Local Members of the Main Jewish Union in Late Second Temple Times." Pages 83–166 in The Madrid Qumran Congress: Proceedings of the International Congress on the Dead Sea Scrolls, Madrid, 18–21 March 1991, Edited by J. Trebolle Barrera and L. Vegas Mountainer. Vol. 11 of Studies on the Texts of the Desert of Judah. Leiden: Brill, 1992.
- Thiede, Carsten Peter, The Dead Sea Scrolls and the Jewish Origins of Christianity, PALGRAVE 2000, ISBN 0-312-29361-5
- Thiering, Barbara, Jesus the Man, New York: Atria, 2006.
- Thiering, Barbara, Jesus and the Riddle of the Dead Sea Scrolls (ISBN 0-06-067782-1), New York: Harper Collins, 1992
- VanderKam, James C., The Dead Sea Scrolls Today, Grand Rapids: Eerdmans, 1994.
- Vermes, Geza, The Complete Dead Sea Scrolls in English, London: Penguin, 1998. ISBN 0-14-024501-4 (good translation, but complete only in the sense that he includes translations of complete texts, but neglects fragmentary scrolls and more especially does not include biblical texts.) (7th ed. 2011 ISBN 978-0-14-119731-9)
- Wise, Michael O., Martin Abegg, Jr., and Edward Cook, The Dead Sea Scrolls: A New Translation, (1996), HarperSanFrancisco paperback 1999, ISBN 0-06-069201-4, (contains the non-biblical portion of the scrolls, including fragments)
- Yadin, Yigael. The Temple Scroll: The Hidden Law of the Dead Sea Sect, New York: Random House, 1985.

Other sources

- Dead Sea Scrolls Study Vol 1: 1Q1-4Q273, Vol. 2: 4Q274-11Q31, (compact disc), Logos Research Systems, Inc., (contains the non-biblical portion of the scrolls with Hebrew and Aramaic transcriptions in parallel with English translations)
- Comprehensive Cross Reference interactive module for Dead Sea Scrolls, Josephus, Philo, Nag Hammadi Library, Pseudepigrapha, Old Testament Apocrypha, New Testament Apocrypha, Plato, Pythagoras, Dhammapada, Egyptian Book of the Dead, Tacitus, Talmud, New and Old Testaments, Apostolic and Early Church Fathers [1]

Further reading

- Harrison, R.K., The Dead Sea Scrolls: an Introduction, in series, The Cloister Library, New York: Harper Torchbooks, 1961.

External links

- The Leon Levy Dead Sea Scrolls Digital Library hosted by the Israel Antiquities Authority Jerusalem
- The Digital Dead Sea Scrolls hosted by the Israel Museum, Jerusalem
- Shrine of the Book, home of the physical scrolls at the Israel Museum, Jerusalem

Exhibits and academic projects

- The Dead Sea Scrolls: Mysteries of the Ancient World (2009) at The Jewish Museum (New York)
- Dead Sea Scrolls facsimile of 1QIsa 1Qs and 1QpHab, Facsimile-editions.com

- Qumran Visualization Project, UCLA
- Timetable of the Discovery and Debate about the Dead Sea Scrolls, VirtualReligion.net
- The Dead Sea Scrolls Collection at the Gnostic Society Library
- The Dead Sea Scrolls (FARMS), Brigham Young University
- Dead Sea Scroll Exhibit at Azusa Pacific University displays five Dead Sea Scrolls fragments in Azusa, California
- Scrolls From the Dead Sea: The Ancient Library of Qumran and Modern Scholarship at the Library of Congress
- Library of Congress On-line Exhibit, ibiblio.org
- The Dead Sea Scrolls Project at the Oriental Institute of the University of Chicago features several articles by Norman Golb, some of which take issue with statements made in popular museum exhibits of the Dead Sea Scrolls
  - The Qumran Essene Theory and recent strategies employed in its defense Norman Golb (2007)
- The Orion Center for the Study of the Dead Sea Scrolls and Associated Literature, Hebrew University of Jerusalem, includes bibliography
- Ancient Treasures and the Dead Sea Scrolls at the Canadian Museum of Civilization
- Dead Sea Scrolls at the Royal Ontario Museum Media coverage and academic articles
- Dead Sea Scrolls collected news and commentary at The New York Times
- The Importance of the Discoveries in the Judean Desert Israel Antiquities Authority
- What Are the Dead Sea Scrolls?. Chabad.org interview with Dr. Lawrence Schiffman, reviewed by him.
- Pesher Technique: Dr. Barbara Thiering's Writings Barbara Thiering's (unconventional) theories connect-

ing the scrolls with the Bible

- The Dead Sea Scrolls as a source on Palestine History of 1st century AD. Sergey E. Rysev.
- "Jannaeus, His Brother Absalom, and Judah the Essene," Stephen Goranson, on Teacher of Righteousness and Wicked Priest identities.
- "Others and Intra-Jewish Polemic as Reflected in Qumran Texts," Stephen Goranson, evidence that English "Essenes" comes from Greek spellings that come from Hebrew 'osey hatorah, a self-designation in some Qumran texts.
- Introduction to the Dead Sea Scrolls, Biblical Archaeology Review
- Searching for the Better Text: How errors crept into the Bible and what can be done to correct them, Biblical Archaeology Review
- The Dead Sea Scrolls and Why They Matter, Biblical Archaeology Review

EXHIBIT FOUR[39]

SAMARITAN PENTATEUCH

The Samaritan Pentateuch, sometimes called Samaritan Torah, (Hebrew: תינורמוש הרות torah shomroniyt), is a version of the Hebrew language Pentateuch, the first five books of the Bible, traditionally written in the Samaritan alphabet and used by the Samaritans. It constitutes their entire biblical canon.

Samaritan practices are based on their version of the Five Books of Moses, which is slightly different from the Masoretic text or the Greek Septuagint texts. Some six thousand differences exist between the Samaritan and the Masoretic text. Most are minor variations in the spelling of words or grammatical constructions, but others involve significant semantic changes such as the uniquely Samaritan commandment to construct an altar on Mount Gerizim. Nearly two thousand textual variations from the Masoretic text agree with the Septuagint and some are shared with the Latin Vulgate. Throughout their history, Samaritans have made use of translations of the Samaritan Pentateuch into Aramaic, Greek and Arabic as well as liturgical and exegetical works based upon it.

Its value for determining the original text of the Pentateuch has been a subject of contentious debate especially after the publication of a manuscript of the Samaritan Pentateuch in Europe in the 17th century. Some Pentateuchal manuscripts discovered among the Dead Sea Scrolls have been identified as bearing a "pre-Samaritan" text type.[1] Wide agreement now exists among textual critics that the Samaritan Pentateuch represents an authentic ancient textual tradition despite the presence of some unique variants introduced by the Samaritans.[2]

Wikipedia p.p. 236-257

Contents

Origin and canonical significance
Samaritan traditions

Samaritan and the Samaritan Torah

Samaritans believe that God authored their Pentateuch and gave Moses the first copy along with the two tablets containing the Ten Commandments.[3] They believe their copies preserve this divinely composed text uncorrupted to the present day. Samaritans commonly refer to their Pentateuch as הטשוק ("The Truth").[3] They trace their descent via the northern Kingdom of Israel, which had parted ways with the southern Kingdom of Judah after the death of King Solomon (see 1 Kings 12). (Jews have traditionally connected their origin with the later events described in 2 Kings 17:24–41).[4]

Samaritans receive only the Pentateuch into their biblical canon.[5] They do not recognize divine authorship or inspiration in any other book in the Jewish Tanakh.[6] A Samaritan Book of Joshua partly based upon the Tanakh's Book of Joshua exists, but Samaritans regard it as a noncanonical secular historical chronicle.[7]

Scholarly perspective

Modern scholarship connects the formation of the Samaritan community and their Pentateuch as a distinctive sectarian textual tradition with events which followed the Babylonian Captivity. [8] According to The Interpreter's Bible (Volume 1),

The usual assumption had been that it was made somewhere around 432 B.C., when Manasseh, the son-in-law of Sanballat, went off to found a community in Samaria, as related in Neh. 13:28 and Josephus Antiquities XI.7.2; 8.2. Josephus himself, however, dates this event in the days of Alexander the Great, and though there is a notorious confusion in Josephus at this point, he may be right about the Gerizim temple dating from 332, and that may have been the date of the copying of their Pentateuch. Recent scholarship, however, is inclined to think that the real schism between the peoples did not take place until Hasmonean times when the Gerizim temple was destroyed in 128 B.C. The script of the Samaritan Pentateuch, its close connections at many points with the Septuagint, and its even closer agreements with our present Hebrew text, all suggest a date about 122 B.C.[9]

The adoption of the Pentateuch as the sacred text of the Samaritans before their final schism with the Palestinian Jewish community provides evidence that it was already widely accepted as a canonical authority in that region.[9]

Comparison with other versions

Comparison with the Masoretic

Detail of Samaritan Pentateuch

Manuscripts of the Samaritan Pentateuch are written in a different Hebrew script than is used in other Hebrew Pentateuchs. Samaritans employ the Samaritan alphabet which is derived from the paleo-Hebrew alphabet used by the Israelite community prior to the Babylonian captivity. Afterwards Jews adopted a script based on the Aramaic alphabet that developed into the Hebrew alphabet. Originally all manuscripts of the Samaritan Pentateuch consisted of unvocalized text written using only the letters of the Samaritan alphabet. Beginning in the 12th century, some manuscripts show a partial vocalization resembling the Jewish Tiberian vocalization used in Masoretic manuscripts.[10] More recently a few manuscripts have been produced with full vocalization.[11] However, many extant manuscripts show no tendency towards vocalization. The Pentateuchal text is divided into 904 paragraphs. Divisions between sections of text are marked with various combinations of lines, dots or an asterisk; a dot is used to indicate the separation between words.[12]

The critical apparatus accompanying the London Polyglot's publication of the Samaritan Pentateuch lists six thousand instances where the Samaritan differs from the Masoretic text.

[13] However, as different printed editions of the Samaritan Pentateuch are based upon different sets of manuscripts, the precise number varies significantly from one edition to another. [2] Only a minority are significant; most can be categorized as one of the following types:

- More matres lectionis in the Samaritan Pentateuch to indicate vowels compared with the Masoretic.[2]
- Loss of the gutturals in spoken Samaritan Hebrew influenced how Samaritan scribes transcribed words containing these letters.[14]
- Scribal errors caused by the mistaking of one Hebrew letter for another with a similar appearance.[15]
- Scribal errors resulting in the transposition of letters in a word, or words in a sentence.[16]
- Replacement of archaic Hebrew grammatical constructions with more modern ones.[17]
- Textual adjustments to resolve grammatical difficulties and replace rare grammatical forms with more common ones.[17]
- A variety of minor grammatical variations such as the Samaritan's preference for the Hebrew preposition 'al where the Masoretic has 'el.[2]

Among the most notable semantic variations reflecting deliberate scribal intention are those related to the Samaritan place of worship on Mount Gerizim. The Samaritan version of the Ten Commandments commands that an altar be built on Mount Gerizim on which all sacrifices should be offered.[18][19] The Samaritan version contains the additional text at Exodus 20:17:

"And when it so happens that LORD God brings you to the land of Canaan, which you are coming to possess, you shall set up there for you great stones and plaster them with plaster and you write on the stones all words of this law. And it becomes for you that across the Jordan you shall raise these stones, which I command you today, in mountain Gerizim. And you build there the altar to the LORD God of you. Altar of stones. Not you shall wave on them iron. With whole stones you shall build the altar to LORD God of you. And you bring on it ascend offerings to LORD God of you, and you sacrifice peace offerings, and you eat there and you rejoice before the face of the LORD God of you. The mountain this is across the Jordan behind the way of the rising of the sun, in the land of Canaan who is dwelling in the desert before the Galgal, beside Alvin-Mara, before Sechem."[20]

This commandment is absent from the corresponding text of the Ten Commandments in the Masoretic. The Samaritan Pentateuch's inclusion of the Gerizim variation within the Ten Commandments places additional emphasis on the divine sanction given to that community's place of worship.[2] This variation has similarities to Deuteronomy 27:2-8 and is supported by changes to the verbal tense within the Samaritan text of Deuteronomy indicating that God has already chosen this place. The future tense ("will choose") is used in the Masoretic.[2] And whereas Deuteronomy 27:4 in the Masoretic commands an altar to be constructed on Mount Ebal, the Samaritan texts has Mount Gerizim.

Several other types of theologically motivated variants are found in the Samaritan Pentateuch. It shows a tendency to remove anthropomorphic language describing God and introduce intermediaries to perform actions the Masoretic attributes directly to God. Where the Masoretic describes Yahweh as a "man of war" (Exodus 15:3), the Samaritan has "hero of war," a phrase applied to spiritual beings, and in Numbers 23:4, the Samaritan reading "The Angel of God found Balaam" replaces the Masoretic "And God met Balaam."[21] A few variations reflect Samaritan notions of propriety, such as the alteration in Genesis 50:23 of the Masoretic "upon the knees of Joseph" to "in the days of Joseph." Samaritan scribes, who interpreted this verse literally, found it improper that the mother of Joseph's grandchildren would give birth on his knees.[22] Distinctive variants in the Samaritan are also found in certain legal texts where Samaritan practice varies from that prescribed within rabbinical halachic texts.[2]

In about thirty-four instances, the Samaritan Pentateuch imports text from parallel or synoptic passages in other parts of the Pentateuch.[2] These textual expansions record conversations and events that are implied or presupposed by other parts of the narrative, but not explicitly recorded in the Masoretic text. For example, the Samaritan text in the Book of Exodus on multiple occasions records Moses repeating to Pharaoh exactly what both the Samaritan and Masoretic record God instructing Moses to tell him. The result is repetitious, but the Samaritan makes it clear that Moses spoke exactly as God commanded him.[2] In addition to these substantial textual expansions, the Samaritan Pentateuch on numerous occasions adds subjects, prepositions, particles, appositives, and the repetition of words and phrases within a single passage to clarify the meaning of the text.[2]

Comparison with the Septuagint and Latin Vulgate

The Septuagint (LXX) agrees with the Samaritan in approximately 1900 of the six thousand variations from the Masoretic. [13] Many of these agreements reflect inconsequential grammatical details, but some are significant. For example, Exodus 12:40 in the Samaritan and the LXX reads:[23]

"Now the sojourning of the children of Israel and of their fathers which they had dwelt in the land of Canaan and in Egypt was four hundred and thirty years."

In the Masoretic text, the passage reads:

"Now the sojourning of the children of Israel, who dwelt in Egypt, was four hundred and thirty years."

Some passages in the Latin Vulgate show agreements with the Samaritan against the Masoretic. For example, Genesis 22:2 in the Samaritan has "land of Moreh" (Hebrew: הארומ) while the Masoretic has "land of Moriah" (Hebrew: הירמ). "Land of Moreh" is considered to be a Samaritan variant because "Moreh" describes the region around Shechem,[24] where Mount Gerizim is situated. The Vulgate translates this phrase as in terram visionis ("in the land of vision") which implies that Jerome was familiar with the reading "Moreh," a Hebrew word whose consonants suggest "vision."[25]

Evaluations of its relevance for textual criticism

The earliest recorded assessments of the Samaritan Pentateuch are found in rabbinical literature and Christian patristic writings of the first millennium CE. The Talmud records Rabbi Eleazar b. Simeon condemning the Samaritan scribes: "You have falsified your Pentateuch...and you have not profited aught by it."[12] Some early Christian writers found the Samaritan Pentateuch useful for textual criticism. Cyril of Alexandria, Procopius of Gaza and others spoke of certain words missing from the Jewish Bible, but present in the Samaritan Pentateuch. [12][26] Eusebius of Caesarea wrote that the "Greek translation [of the Bible] also differs from the Hebrew, though not so much from the Samaritan" and noted that the Septuagint agrees with the Samaritan Pentateuch in the number of years elapsed from Noah's Flood to Abraham.[27] Christian interest in the Samaritan Pentateuch fell into neglect during the Middle Ages.[28]

The publication of a manuscript of the Samaritan Pentateuch in 17th-century Europe reawakened interest in the text and fueled a controversy between Protestants and Roman Catholics over which Old Testament textual traditions are authoritative. Roman Catholics showed a particular interest in the study of the Samaritan Pentateuch on account of the antiquity of the text and its frequent agreements with the Septuagint and the Latin

Vulgate, two Bible translations to which Catholics have traditionally ascribed considerable authority.[17] Some Catholics including Jean Morin, a Jesuit-convert from Calvinism to Catholicism, argued that the Samaritan Pentateuch's correspondences with the Latin Vulgate and Septuagint indicated that it represents a more authentic Hebrew text than the Masoretic. [29] Several Protestants replied with a defense of the Masoretic text's authority and argued that the Samaritan text is a late and unreliable derivation from the Masoretic.[30]

The 18th century Protestant Hebrew scholar Benjamin Kennicott's analysis of the Samaritan Pentateuch stands as a notable exception to the general trend of early Protestant research on the text.[31] He questioned the underlying assumption that the Masoretic text must be more authentic simply because it has been more widely accepted as the authoritative Hebrew version of the Pentateuch:

"We see then that as the evidence of one text destroys the evidence of the other and as there is in fact the authority of versions to oppose to the authority of versions no certain argument or rather no argument at all can be drawn from hence to fix the corruption on either side."[32]

Kennicott also states[33] that the reading Gerizim may actually be the original reading, since that is the mountain for proclaiming blessings, and that it is very green and rich of vegetation (as opposed to Mt. Ebal, which is barren and the mountain for proclaiming curses) amongst other arguments.

German scholar Wilhelm Gesenius published a study[34] of the Samaritan Pentateuch in 1815 which biblical scholars widely embraced for the next century. He argued that the Septuagint and the Samaritan Pentateuch share a common source in a family of Hebrew manuscripts which he named the "Alexandrino-Samaritanus." In contrast to the proto-Masoretic "Judean" manuscripts carefully preserved and copied in Jerusalem, he regarded the Alexandrino-Samaritanus as having been carelessly handled by scribal copyists who popularized, simplified, and expanded the text.[35] Gesenius concluded that the Masoretic text is almost invariably superior to the Samaritan.[36]

In 1915 Paul Kahle published a paper[37] which compared passages from the Samaritan text to Pentateuchal quotations in the New Testament and pseudepigraphal texts including the Book of Jubilees, the First Book of Enoch and the Assumption of Moses. He concluded that the Samaritan Pentateuch preserves "many genuine old readings and an ancient form of the Pentateuch."[17] Support for Kahle's thesis was bolstered by the discovery of biblical manuscripts among the Dead Sea Scrolls, approximately five percent[1] of which contain a text similar to the Samaritan Pentateuch.[38] Apart from the sectarian variants unique to the Samaritan Pentateuch such as the reference to the worship of God on Mount Gerizim, the Dead Sea Scroll texts have demonstrated that a Pentateuchal text type resembling the Samaritan Pentateuch goes back to the second century BCE and perhaps even earlier.[39][40] Other Dead Sea Scroll Pentateuchal manuscripts show a close affinity to the later Masoretic text. These discoveries have demonstrated that manuscripts bearing a "pre-Samaritan" text of at least some portions of the Pentateuch such as Exodus[41] and Numbers[42] circulated alongside other manuscripts with a "pre-Masoretic" text. One Dead Sea Scroll copy of the Book of Exodus, conventionally named 4QpaleoExodm, shows a particularly close relation to the Samaritan Pentateuch:

> The scroll shares all the major typological features with the SP, including all the major expansions of that tradition where it is extant (twelve), with the single exception of the new tenth commandment inserted in Exodus 20 from Deuteronomy 11 and 27 regarding the altar on Mount Gerizim.[43]

Frank Moore Cross has described the origin of the Samaritan Pentateuch within the context of his local texts hypothesis. He views the Samaritan Pentateuch as having emerged from a manuscript tradition local to Palestine. The Hebrew texts that form the underlying basis for the Septuagint branched from the Palestinian tradition as Jews emigrated to Egypt and took copies of the Pentateuch with them. Cross states that the Samaritan and the Septuagint share a nearer common ancestor than either does with the Masoretic, which he suggested developed from local texts used by the Babylonian Jewish community. His explanation accounts for the Samaritan and the Septuagint sharing variants not found in the Masoretic and their differences reflecting the period of their independent development as distinct Egyptian and Palestinian local text traditions.[2] On the basis of archaizing and pseudo-archaic forms, Cross dates the emergence of the Samaritan Pentateuch as a uniquely Samaritan textual tradition to the post-Maccabaean age.[44]

Scholars have tended to presuppose that the Samaritan Pentateuch consists of two "layers," one composed of the sectarian variants introduced by Samaritan scribes and a second layer reflecting the text's earlier transmission history as a "pre-Samaritan" Palestinian local text. In light of recent research "it is now clear that the Samaritan layer is very thin."[45] Although the majority of scholars continue to favor the Masoretic as a superior text, many other scholars have now adopted Kahle's thesis.[17] Scholars now widely agree though that many textual variants previously classified as "Samaritan" actually derive from even earlier phases of the Pentateuch's textual history.

Kennicott's claim that Gerizim is the original reading continues to be a subject of discussion. Dead Sea Scroll fragment 4Q41(981) contains a text of Deuteronomy 5:1–25 which makes no reference to Mount Gerizim, but matches the Masoretic Text. The New Testament also agrees with the Masoretic version designating Jerusalem as the "chosen place."[46] However, some scholars hold that Deuteronomy 27:4–7 constitutes one occasion where the Samaritan's "Gerizim" may be the original reading."[19][47]

Derivative works

Translations

The Samaritan Targum, composed in the Samaritan dialect of Aramaic, is the earliest translation of the Samaritan Pentateuch. Its creation was motivated by the same need to translate the Pentateuch into the Aramaic language spoken by the community which led to the creation of Jewish Targums such as Targum Onkelos. Samaritans have traditionally ascribed the Targum to Nathanael, a Samaritan priest who died circa 20 BCE.[48] The Samaritan Targum has a complex textual tradition represented by manuscripts belonging to one of three fundamental text types exhibiting substantial divergences from one another. Affinities that the oldest of these textual traditions share with the Dead Sea Scrolls and Onkelos suggest that the Targum may originate from the same school which finalized the Samaritan Pentateuch itself.[49] Others have placed the origin of the Targum around the beginning of the third century[48] or even later.[50] Extant manuscripts of the Targum are "extremely difficult to use"[51] on account of scribal errors caused by a faulty understanding of Hebrew on the part of the Targum's translators and a faulty understanding of Aramaic on the part of later copyists.

Scholia of Origen's Hexapla and the writings of some church fathers contain references to "the Samariticon" (Greek: το Σαμαρειτικον).,[48] a work that is no longer extant. Despite earlier suggestions that it was merely a series of Greek scholia translated from the Samaritan Pentateuch,[12] scholars now concur that it was a complete Greek translation of the Samaritan Pentateuch either directly translated from it or via the Samaritan Targum.[52] It may have been composed for the use of a Greek-speaking Samaritan community residing in Egypt.[48]

With the displacement of Samaritan Aramaic by Arabic as the language of the Samaritan community in the centuries following the Muslim conquest of Syria, they employed several Arabic translations of the Pentateuch. The oldest was an adaptation of Saadia Gaon's Arabic translation of the Jewish Torah. Although the text was modified to suit the Samaritan community, it still retained many unaltered Jewish readings. [53] By the 11th or 12th centuries, a new Arabic translation directly based upon the Samaritan Pentateuch had appeared in Nablus. Manuscripts containing this translation are notable for their bilingual or trilingual character; the Arabic text is accompanied by the original Samaritan Hebrew in a parallel column and sometimes the Aramaic text of the Samaritan Targum in a third.[54] Later Arabic translations also appeared; one featured a further Samaritan revision of Saadia Gaon's translation to bring it into greater conformity with the Samaritan Pentateuch and others were based upon Arabic Pentateuchal translations used by Christians.[55]

In April 2013, a complete English translation of the Samaritan Pentateuch comparing it to the Masoretic version was published. [56] One of the co-authors, Benyamim Tsedaka, is himself a member of the Samaritan community and lectures widely on Samaritan history, beliefs and traditions.

Exegetical and liturgical texts

Several biblical commentaries and other theological texts based upon the Samaritan Pentateuch have been composed by members of the Samaritan community from the fourth century CE onwards.[57] Samaritans also employ liturgical texts containing catenae extracted from their Pentateuch.[58]

Manuscripts and printed editions

Manuscripts

Samaritans attach special importance to the Abisha Scroll used in the Samaritan synagogue of Nablus. It consists of a continuous length of parchment sewn together from the skins of rams that, according to a Samaritan tradition, were ritually sacrificed.[59] The text is written in gold letters.[12] Rollers tipped with ornamental knobs are attached to both ends of the parchment and the whole is kept in a cylindrical silver case when not in use.[60] Samaritans claim it was penned by Abishua, great-grandson of Aaron (1 Chronicles 6:50), thirteen years after the entry into the land of Israel under the leadership of Joshua, son of Nun,[61] although contemporary scholars describe it as a composite of several fragmentary scrolls each penned between the 12th and 14th centuries CE.[62] Other manuscripts of the Samaritan Pentateuch consist of vellum or cotton paper written upon with black ink.[12] Numerous manuscripts of the text exist, but none written in the original Hebrew or in translation predates the Middle Ages.[17]

Printed editions

Wider interest in the Samaritan Pentateuch was awakened in 1616 when the traveler Pietro della Valle purchased a copy of the text in Damascus. This manuscript, now known as Codex B, was deposited in a Parisian library. In 1645, an edited copy of Codex B was published in Le Jay's (Paris) Polyglot by Jean Morin. It was republished in Walton's Polyglot in 1657. Subsequently, Archbishop Ussher and others procured additional copies which were brought to Europe and later, America.[63]

Until the latter half of the 20th century, critical editions of the Samaritan Pentateuch were largely based upon Codex B. The most notable of these is Der Hebräische Pentateuch der Samaritaner (The Hebrew Pentateuch of the Samaritans) compiled by August von Gall and published in 1918. An extensive critical apparatus is included listing variant readings found in previously published manuscripts of the Samaritan Pentateuch. His work is still regarded as being generally accurate despite the presence of some errors, but it neglects important manuscripts including the Abisha Scroll which had not yet been published at the time.[17][64] Textual variants found in the Abisha scroll were published in 1959 by Federico Pérez Castro[51] and between 1961 and 1965 by A. and R. Sadaqa in Jewish and Samaritan Versions of the Pentateuch – With Particular Stress on the Differences Between Both Texts.[17] In 1976 L.F. Giron-Blanc published a Samaritan Pentateuch codex dating to 1100 CE in a critical edition supplemented with variants found in fifteen previously unpublished manuscripts.[51] Certain recently published critical editions of Pentateuchal books take Samaritan variants into account, including D.L. Phillips' edition of Exodus.[65]

Several publications containing the text of the Samaritan Targum have appeared. In 1875 the German scholar Adolf Brüll published his Das samaritanische Targum zum Pentateuch (The Samaritan Targum to the Pentateuch). More recently a two volume set edited by Abraham Tal appeared featuring the first critical edition based upon all extant manuscripts containing the Targumic text.[66]

Notes

1. ^ a b The Canon Debate, McDonald & Sanders editors, 2002, chapter 6: Questions of Canon through the Dead Sea Scrolls by James C. VanderKam, page 94, citing private communication with Emanuel Tov on biblical manuscripts: Qumran scribe type c.25%, proto-Masoretic Text c. 40%, pre-Samaritan texts c.5%, texts close to the Hebrew model for the Septuagint c.5% and nonaligned c.25%.
2. ^ a b c d e f g h i j k Purvis, J.D. "Samaritan Pentateuch," pp. 772–775 in Interpreter's Dictionary of the Bible, Supplementary Volume. Keith Crim, gen. ed. Nashville: Abingdon, 1976. ISBN 9780687192694
3. ^ a b Gaster, T.H. "Samaritans," pp. 190–197 in Interpreter's Dictionary of the Bible, Volume 4. George Arthur Buttrick, gen. ed. Nashville: Abingdon, 1962.
4. ^ Tov 2001, pp. 82–83.

5. ^ Vanderkam 2002, p. 91.
6. ^ Although a paucity of extant source material makes it impossible to be certain that the earliest Samaritans also rejected the other books of the Tanakh, the third-century church father Origen confirms that the Samaritans in his day "receive[d] the books of Moses alone." (Commentary on John 13:26)
7. ^ Gaster, M. (1908). "A Samaritan Book of Joshua". The Living Age 258: 166.
8. ^ Tov 2001, p. 83.
9. ^ a b Buttrick 1952, p. 35.
10. ^ Brotzman 1994, pp. 64–65.
11. ^ Tov 2001, p. 81. "Only in recent generations have the Samaritans written a few manuscripts – only for use outside their community – with full vocalization."
12. ^ a b c d e f Fallows, Samuel; Andrew Constantinides Zenos, Herbert Lockwood Willett (1911). The Popular and Critical Bible Encyclopædia and Scriptural Dictionary, Volume 3. Howard-Severance. p. 1701.
13. ^ a b Hjelm 2000, p. 77.
14. ^ Thomson 1919, pp. 286–289.
15. ^ Thomson 1919, pp. 289–296.
16. ^ Thomson 1919, pp. 296–301.
17. ^ a b c d e f g h Vanderkam 2002, p. 93.
18. ^ "Overview of the Differences Between the Jewish and Samaritan Versions of the Pentateuch". Web.meson.org. Retrieved 2011-12-05.
19. ^ a b Soggin, J. Alberto (1989). Introduction to the Old Testament: From Its Origins to the Closing of the Alexandrian Canon. Westminster John Knox Press. p. 26. ISBN 9780664221560. "But there is at least one case, Deut.27.4–7, in which the reading 'Gerizim' in the Samaritan Pentateuch, confirmed by Σ and by the Old Latin, seems to be preferable to that of the Massoretic text, which has Ebal, the other mountain standing above Nablus."

20. ^ "Exodus - Interlinear Pentateuch". Google. Retrieved 2014-01-05.
21. ^ Thomson 1919, p. 312.
22. ^ Vanderkam 2002, p. 94.
23. ^ Easton, Matthew George (1897). "Samaritan Pentateuch." Easton's Bible Dictionary (New and revised ed.). T. Nelson and Sons.
24. ^ Barton 1903, p. 31.
25. ^ Thomson 1919, pp. 312–313.
26. ^ Du Pin, Louis Ellies (1699). A compleat history of the canon and writers of the books of the Old and New Testament, Volume 1. H. Rhodes. p. 167.
27. ^ Pamphili, Eusebius (translator: Robert Bedrosian). "Eusebius' Chronicle: The Hebrew Chronicle". History Workshop. Retrieved 10 July 2012.
28. ^ Montgomery 1907, p. 286.
29. ^ Montgomery 1907, p. 288.
30. ^ Thomson 1919, pp. 275–276.
31. ^ Saebo, Magne (2008). Hebrew Bible / Old Testament: The History of Its Interpretation. Vandenhoeck & Ruprecht. ISBN 9783525539828.
32. ^ Kennicott 1759, p. 32.
33. ^ Kennicott 1759, p. 20.
34. ^ Gesenius, Wilhelm (1815). De Pentateuchi Samaritani origine, indole et auctoritate commentatio philologico-critica. Halae.
35. ^ Vanderkam 2002, pp. 92–93.
36. ^ Gesenius believed that the Samaritan Pentateuch contained only four valid variants as compared to the Masoretic text. (Montgomery 1907, p. 288.)
37. ^ Kahle, Paul. Theologische Studien und Kritiken 88 (1915): 399–429.
38. ^ Some examples include the Dead Sea Scroll manuscripts conventionally designated as 4QpaleoExodm, 4QExod-Levf and 4QNumb. See Vanderkam 2002, p. 95.
39. ^ Tov 2001, p. 80.

40. ^ Vanderkam 2002, p. 95.

41. ^ Vanderkam 2002, p. 106.

42. ^ Vanderkam 2002, p. 110.

43. ^ Skehan, Patrick, Eugene Ulrich and Judith Sanderson (1992). Discoveries in the Judean Desert, Volume IX. Quoted in Hendel, Ronald S. "Assessing the Text-Critical Theories of the Hebrew Bible After Qumran," p. 284 in Lim, Timothy and John Collins (2010). The Oxford Handbook of the Dead Sea Scrolls. Oxford: Oxford University Press. ISBN 9780199207237.

44. ^ Frank Moore Cross Harvard Theological Review July 1966 "The language of the Samaritan Pentateuch also includes archaizing forms and pseudo-archaic forms which surely point to the post-Maccabaean age for its date"

45. ^ Crown 2001, p. 401.

46. ^ John 4:21, 22, Luke 9:53

47. ^ Charlesworth, James H. "The Discovery of an Unknown Dead Sea Scroll: The Original Text of Deuteronomy 27?". Ohio Wesleyan Magazine. Retrieved 29 July 2012. A newly published Dead Sea Scroll fragment of Deuteronomy has "Gerizim" instead of "Ebal" in Deuteronomy 27:4.

48. ^ a b c d Herbermann, Charles, ed. (1913). "Samaritan Language and Literature." Catholic Encyclopedia. Robert Appleton Company.

49. ^ Crown 2001, p. 18.

50. ^ Buttrick 1952, p. 57.

51. ^ a b c Brotzman 1994, p. 66.

52. ^ Marcos, Natalio (2000). The Septuagint in Context: Introduction to the Greek Version of the Bible. Brill. p. 168. ISBN 9789004115743.

53. ^ Crown 2001, p. 23.

54. ^ Crown 2001, p. 24.

55. ^ Crown 2001, pp. 24–25.

56. ^ Tsedaka, Benyamim; Sharon Sullivan (2012). The Israelite Samaritan Version of the Torah: First English

Translation Compared with the Masoretic Version. Grand Rapids, Michigan, USA: Wm. B. Eerdmans Publishing Company. ISBN 9780802865199.

57. ^ Montgomery 1907, pp. 293–297.
58. ^ Montgomery 1907, pp. 297–298.
59. ^ Barton 1903, p. 9.
60. ^ Barton 1903, pp. 9–10.
61. ^ The Abisha scroll makes this claim for itself in a note inserted between columns of text at Deuteronomy 5. (Montgomery 1907, p. 287)
62. ^ Eshel 2003, p. 215.
63. ^ Cowper, B. Harris (1863). Journal of Sacred Literature and Biblical Record. Williams and Norgate. p. 131.
64. ^ Brotzman notes that Gall's edition "because of the principles used to prepare it, must be used with caution." (Brotzman 1994, p. 66.)
65. ^ Phillips, D.L. Hebrew-English: Paleo Exodus: Scripture at the End of the Iron II Period. Edwin Mellen, 2004.
66. ^ Tal, Abraham F. (1981). The Samaritan Targum of the Pentateuch: a critical edition (2 vols.)(Texts and Studies in the Hebrew Language and Related Subjects, 5.). Tel-Aviv: Tel-Aviv University.

References

• Barton, William E. (1903). The Samaritan Pentateuch: The Story of a Survival among the Sects. Oberlin, Ohio: The Bibliotheca Sacra Company.
• Brotzman, Ellis R. (1994). Old Testament Textual Criticism: A Practical Introduction. Baker Academic. ISBN 9780801010651.
• Buttrick, George Arthur and board, eds. (1952). The Interpreter's Bible, Vol. 1. Nashville, Tennessee: Abingdon Press.
• Crown, Alan David (2001). Samaritan Scribes and Manuscripts. Mohr Siebeck. ISBN 9783161474903.

- Eshel, Esther and Hanan Eshel (2003). "Dating the Samaritan Pentateuch's Compilation in Light of the Qumran Biblical Scrolls." In Tov, Emmanuel; Eva Ben-David and Weston W. Fields. Emanuel: Studies in Hebrew Bible, Septuagint, and Dead Sea Scrolls in Honor of Emanuel Tov. Brill. ISBN 9789004126794.
- von Gall, August (ed.): Der hebräische Pentateuch der Samaritaner; Berlin 1966 (photomechanical reprint of Gießen 1914–1918); reprint Walther de Gruyter, 1993, ISBN 3110092581
- Hjelm, Ingrid (2000). The Samaritans and Early Judaism: A Literary Analysis. Continuum International Publishing Group. ISBN 9781841270722.
- Kennicott, Benjamin (1759). The State of the Printed Hebrew text of the Old Testament. Oxford.
- Metzger, Bruce Manning; Michael David Coogan (1993). The Oxford Companion to the Bible. Oxford University Press. ISBN 9780195046458.
- Montgomery, James Alan (1907). The Samaritans, the earliest Jewish sect: their history, theology and literature. The J.C. Winston Co.
- Thomson, J.E.H. (1919). The Samaritans: Their Testimony to the Religion of Israel. Edinburgh and London: Oliver and Boyd.
- Tov, Emanuel (2001). Textual Criticism of the Hebrew Bible. Uitgeverij Van Gorcum. ISBN 9789023237150.
- Vanderkam, James; Peter Flint (2002). The Meaning of the Dead Sea Scrolls. Harper San Francisco. ISBN 9780060684655.

Bibliography

- The Torah: Jewish and Samaritan versions compared (Hebrew Edition, December 2008). Compiler Mark E. Shoulson. Evertype. ISBN 1-904808-18-2 / ISBN 978-1-904808-18-3.

- Die Vokale Des Gesetzes: Die Samaritanische Lesetradition Als Textzeugin Der Tora (Beihefte Zur Zeitschrift Fur Die Alttestamentliche Wissenschaft) (German Edition) by Stefan Schorch. Pub. Walter de Gruyter (June 3, 2004). ISBN 3-11-018101-0 / ISBN 978-3-11-018101-2

External links

Online texts

- Blayney, Benjamin (1790). Pentateuchus Hebreao-Samaritanus. Oxford: Clarendon.
- Brüll, Adolf (1875). Das samaritanische Targum zum Pentateuch (Targum Shomroni 'al hatorah). Frankfurt a.M.
- von Gall, August (1918). Der Hebräische Pentateuch der Samaritaner. Verlag von Alfred Töpelmann.
- Heidenheim, Marqah (1884). Bibliotheca Samaritana (Volume 1, Volume 2, Volume 3). Leipzig: Otto Schulze.
- Samaritan Pentateuch in English and Hebrew (with Idiomatic Translation, Morphology and DSS variants)
- Samaritan Pentateuch – online edition with select verses from the Samaritan Targum, English translation and critical apparatus.

Other links

- Jewish Encyclopedia: Samaritans: Samaritan Version of the Pentateuch
- James H. Charlesworth. Announcing a Dead Sea Scrolls Fragment of Deuteronomy

BIBLIOGRAPHY

Geisler, Norman L. & Wix, William E., A General Introduction to
the Bible, Moody Press, Chicago, IL 1975

Goodspeed, Edgar J., The Apostolic Fathers, Harper & Brothers,
New York 1950

Guthrie, Donald, New Testament Introduction, Inter-Varsity Press,
Downers Grove, IL 1974

Halley's Bible Handbook

Harrison, Roland Kenneth, Introduction to the Old Testament,
Wiliam B Eerdmans Pub. Co., Grand Rapids, Michigan 1975

Kittel, Rudolf, Biblia Hebraica, Wurttemberische Bibelanstalf
Stuttgart, 1973

Lightfoot, J.B., The Apostolic Fathers, Baker Book House, Grand
Rapids, Michigan 1974

Matthiae, Paolo, Ebla, an Empire Rediscovered, Doubleday &
Company, Garden City, New York 1980

Miller, H.S., General Biblical Introduction, The Word-Bearer
Press, Houghto, N.Y. 1956

New American Standard Bible, The Lockman Foundation,
LaHara, CA 1976

Pinnock, Clarkk, Biblical Revelation, Moody Press, Chicago IL
1970

Richards, Lawrence O., The Word Bible Handbook, Word Books,
Waco, TX 1983

Scholer, David M., A Basic Bibliographic Guide for New Testament
Exegesis, William B. Eerdmans Publishing Company,
Grand Rapids, Michigan, 1974

The Greek New Testament, Second Edition, United Bible
Societies, Warttemberg, Stuttgart, West Germany, 1968

Trever, John C., The Untold Story of Qumron 1965. The Dead Sea
Scrolls: A Personal Account, 2003. Dead Sea Scrolls in
Perspective, D & F Scott Pub 2004

Word, Archie, How, When and Where We Got Our Bible, The
Church Speaks Publishing, Portland Oregon

Yamauchi, Edwin, The Stones & the Scriptures, Baker Book House,
Grand Rapids, Michigan 1972

EXHIBITS

1. The Dead Sea Scrolls, Bibliography
2. The Dead Sea Scrolls, Description
3. The Dead Sea Scrolls, Origin
4. The Samaritan Pentateuch
5. The King James Versions
6. New American Standard Version
7. New International Version
8. The Living Bible
9. The English Standard Version

Other Books by Dr. Charles A. Crane

Ashamed of Joseph, Mormon Foundations Crumble.
180 Pages, $16.95. A Biography of the Mormon Prophet
Joseph Smith from a Christian view point.

Christianity and Mormonism, From Bondage to Liberty.
197 Pages, $16.95. How the Latter Day Saints religion leads
people to bondage and how they are liberated when they
come to Christ.

Mastering Your Money,
83 large pages, $8.95. Learning to live by biblical principles
for financial success.

A Practical Guide For Soul Winning.
166 Large pages, $19.95. Applying biblical discipleship prin-
ciples to grow the local church

These books can be ordered from

Charles Crane
Eagle Christian Church
100 Short Lane
Eagle, Idaho 83616.

Add $3.00 for mailing in the USA.

Larger quantities discounts apply.

CPSIA information can be obtained
at www.ICGtesting.com
Printed in the USA
FSOW04n0812070815
9557FS

9 780996 014656